More Praise for Felice Dunas's
PASSION PLAY . . .

"*Passion Play* is the best book on sexuality I've ever read. It shows how sex can be transformative, not just pleasurable, and makes specific what other books only allude to. It should be required reading for every lover."

—HAROLD BLOOMFIELD, M.D.,
author of *Healing Anxiety with Herbs*

PASSION PLAY

Ancient Secrets for

a Lifetime of Health and Happiness

Through Sensational Sex

FELICE DUNAS, PH.D.,
with PHILIP GOLDBERG

Riverhead Books, New York

RIVERHEAD BOOKS
Published by The Berkley Publishing Group
A member of Penguin Putnam Inc.
375 Hudson Street
New York, New York 10014

The practices, techniques and exercises included in this book should be used in conjunction with, and not as a replacement for, the reader's physician or other health professional, who should be consulted about persistent physical and/or emotional conditions. The publisher and authors are not responsible for any adverse effects or unforeseen consequences resulting from the use of the information contained in this book.

Copyright © 1997 by Felice Dunas, Ph.D., and Philip Goldberg
Book design by Judith Stagnitto Abbate
Cover design copyright © 1997 by Jack Ribik
Frontispiece: Gustav Klimt, *The Kiss*, 1907–1908 (detail). Oil on canvas, 180 x 180 cm.
Österreichische Galerie, Vienna.
Photograph by Erich Lessing/Art Resource, NY
Illustrations on pages 24, 62, 63, 93, 95, 161, 162 by Jackie Aher
Illustrations on pages 52, 133–139, 172 by Peggy Jackson

First Riverhead hardcover edition: September 1997
First Riverhead trade paperback edition: November 1998
Riverhead trade paperback ISBN: 1-57322-698-X

The Penguin Putnam Inc. World Wide Web site address is
http://www.penguinputnam.com

The Library of Congress has catalogued the Riverhead hardcover edition as follows:

Dunas, Felice.
Passion play : ancient secrets for a lifetime of health and happiness through
sensational sex / by Felice Dunas, Ph.D., with Philip Goldberg.
p.   cm.
ISBN 1-57322-076-0 (alk. paper)
1. Sex customs—China.   2. Sex therapy.   3. Medicine, Chinese.
I. Goldberg, Philip, date.   II. Title
HQ18.C6D86   1997   97-8420 CIP
306.7'0951—dc21

Printed in the United States of America

10   9   8   7   6   5   4   3

ACKNOWLEDGMENTS

The only true commodity is human effort. The following people have invested their effort in this book. I consider their gifts priceless. My heartfelt gratitude goes out to:

Phil Goldberg, for going above and beyond, for continually staying true to my concerns and for finding the language to make traditional Chinese medicine layperson-friendly.

My agent, Lynn Franklin, who nurtured this book through its long gestation. Thank you for your commitment to the quality of this work and of our relationship.

Amy Hertz, my editor. Thank you for your unwavering support and astute editing, from the minute you read the proposal through the long process of writing, rewriting and beyond.

All my patients who were willing to change their views of what erotic love has to offer and move beyond their personal inhibitions. Your efforts validate the importance of healing through pleasure and the magnificent wisdom of traditional Chinese medicine.

My teachers, past and present, who opened the door to my destiny and continue to guide me.

Deepak Chopra, who listened to my book idea over a cup of tea and scribbled Lynn Franklin's phone number on a napkin. Thank you for extending your friendship despite your hectic schedule.

My brother, Jedd, for his two cents and ongoing optimism and support.

Dan Pine, for helping me with the beginning and the end.

Jennie Belise-Bienenfeld and Erika Shickle, for their comments and clerical assistance.

Lori Deutsch, whose invaluable editorial assistance helped clarify the finer points of this text.

And above all, my daughter, Elannah, for having more patience than any parent of a teenager has the right to expect. This book came of age as she did, and no one has been more affected by the challenges it brought to my life. When asked by members of an audience what it was like having a mother who traveled the world teaching people about making love, she replied, "I know more about the subject than most adults, but even though I'm not naive, I still choose to be innocent." Thank you, honey, for being a moral person and a loving, supportive daughter. I hope you always choose to be innocent, at least until you're thirty.

To the memory of my father, Edwin C. Dunas, whose excruciating illness, treatment and untimely death during my childhood taught me the value of healing through pleasure.

To the memory of my stepfather, Raymond Marcus, M.D., whose personal frustration with the limits of his profession inspired me to venture into other worlds of medicine.

And to my mother, Avis Dunas, who supported me in pursuing my unconventional profession and from whom I inherited my sense of adventure and curiosity.

CONTENTS

Sex contains all, bodies, souls,
Meanings, proofs, purities, delicacies, results,
promulgations,
Songs, commands, health, pride, the maternal
mystery, the seminal milk,
All hopes, benefactions, bestowals, all the
passions, loves, beauties, delights of
the earth.

WALT WHITMAN

PREFACE

My studies in traditional Chinese medicine began when I was fourteen years old. My stepfather had been an M.D. specializing in internal medicine at a major Los Angeles hospital. As a young child I would see the pain on his face when he could not make a patient well. At the wise old age of eight, I decided to find a way to help him heal everybody. By the time I was eighteen I had apprenticed with skilled practitioners and was treating patients with acupuncture and Chinese herbal medicines. In subsequent years, as I attained my credentials and began seeing patients on an extended basis, I observed a fascinating phenomenon: People who came to me for purely medical reasons would report unexpected side effects of treatment. As their physical conditions improved, they noticed that their relationships grew stronger and more harmonious; their emotions were more stable, conflicts diminished, familiar problems were seen in a fresh light. And their sex lives perked up.

Many of these patients had struggled with their sexuality and relationships for years but were unable to maintain long-term changes in behavior or improve their sex lives in a lasting way. Now some of their goals had been achieved as a byproduct of overall health improvements brought about by acupuncture, herbs and lifestyle adjustments. This led me to research the ancient teachings on sexuality, which had been passed down through the centuries as a part of traditional Chinese medicine.

A LEGACY
OF LUSCIOUS LOVING

The boudoirs of ancient China were laboratories of sorts, where scholars, physicians, philosophers, royalty and nobility performed a vast amount of research on sex. Out of that endeavor grew a profound body of knowledge and a repertoire of practices whose value has been confirmed repeatedly over two thousand years of continuous use.

The earliest Chinese writings on sex are credited to Huang Ti, the Yellow Emperor, who reigned from 2697 to 2598 B.C. A legendary ruler, the Yellow Emperor merged myriad separate communities into the Chinese nation, and created the foundation for the Chinese medical tradition. In the ancient texts that bear his name, the ruler engages in dialogue with several mentors. For his inquiry into sex, he had three female teachers, the most celebrated of whom was Su Nu, or Plain Girl ("plain" being an inadequate translation of a term that implied a combination of innocence and divine wisdom). The text that grew out of her discourse—*The Plain Girl's Classic,* or *Counsels of the Simple Girl*—is thought to be the first treatise on sex in the history of human civilization.

Although the culture she lived in was, by contemporary standards, highly sexist and patriarchal, this forerunner of Dr. Ruth asserted the fundamental equality of the sexes while at the same time acknowledging the profound differences between them. Viewing men and women in the context of nature's universal masculine and feminine principles, Su Nu taught that sexuality was an expression of the divine. Achieving sexual harmony with one's mate, she stated, allows both sexes to blossom in their own identities and to create fruitful lives in properly run families and communities.

The ancients fully appreciated the joy of sex. Their poetry and art were as erotic, romantic and bawdy as anything Hollywood turns out, and their techniques produced states of ecstasy that make what we call "good sex" seem like scratching an itch by comparison. They also realized that sexuality has curative and transformational power. According to traditional Chinese medicine, there are three forms of healing: healing through pain, as with surgery; healing through suffering, as with chemotherapy (or, in psychological terms, through grief); and healing through pleasure, as with making love when done in an appropriate manner.

ANCIENT SKILLS
FOR MODERN LOVERS

I began to share these teachings with selected patients, such as the couples you'll meet in this book (whose names and identifying characteristics have been changed to protect their privacy). I found their wisdom to be just as relevant to modern lovers as it was to the emperors of old. Here was the flip side of what I had earlier discovered: Not only does a healthy body lead to better sex, but better sex produces healthier bodies and souls. Since then I have imparted relevant portions of this legacy to patients and participants at my seminars, always with rewarding results. Physical symptoms ranging from high blood pressure to back pain to gynecological and prostate problems would improve; chronic tension would dissolve; energy and vitality would increase; sexual skill and satisfaction would skyrocket; and intimacy, harmony and love would blossom.

Sex in America: A Definitive Survey found that about 60 percent of married couples had sex "a few times per month" or less. Surprisingly, most of them are content with this situation. I'm glad they're not unhappy, but I have to say: They don't know what they're missing. Some would argue that if those marriages were happier, the spouses would have sex more often. That may be true, but the Chinese sages would say that the opposite is also true: The couples surveyed would be happier together if they had satisfying, high-quality sex more often. In ancient China, marriage was considered a stairway to holiness, and sexual intimacy a vehicle for couples to achieve health, harmony, longevity and unity with the divine.

While the ideas in this book can be effective in a casual relationship or one-night stand, their power is greater within a committed monogamous union. In that context, couples can explore the practices with love, respect, mutual support and the patience to look forward to long-term results. I urge you and your beloved to approach this book in that spirit. If you are single and experiment with these ideas outside of a monogamous relationship, I urge you to observe all safe-sex precautions.

In the last decade, respect for Chinese and other non-Western medical traditions has blossomed in America (see Appendix). I'm proud to have played a role in that increased acceptance and to have helped thousands of people benefit from these profound practices. (At no time should any recommendation in this book be considered license to avoid proper medical care. Please consult a physician should you require medical attention.) Now, with this book, I hope to bring the sexual aspect of Chinese medical wisdom to the forefront so that its rich rewards can be widely experienced. Five thousand years of history illuminate every page of this book. Among the features you can look forward to are:

- insight into the basic differences between men and women
- practical ways to use sexuality to improve the emotional dynamics of your relationship
- techniques and exercises that enhance sexual fulfillment, deepen intimacy and turn ordinary pleasure into ecstasy
- ways to use lovemaking to improve health and ensure a vigorous sex life well into old age
- lifestyle practices that promote healthier sex and relationships

By following the advice in the chapters to come, you can turn your bedroom into a sacred, magical place. You will learn to transform sex from a pastime to an art form. In turn, sex will transform you.

Chapter 1

MEDICINE IN OUR LOINS
The Therapeutic Power of Sex

*Ignorance of the necessity for sexual intercourse
to the health and virtue of both man and woman is
the most fundamental error in medical
and moral philosophy.*

—GEORGE DRYSDALE,
The Elements of Social Science (1854)

*Those who understand the nature of sex will nurture
their vigor and prolong their life. Those who
treat its principle with contempt will injure their
spirit and shorten their life.*

—TUNG HSUAN TZU,
c. fifth–seventh centuries

Cursed by a wicked fairy, the princess falls into a deep, dark sleep. Trees, vines and thorny bushes grow around her castle, enveloping everything but its high towers. One hundred years later, while hunting, a prince notices the castle spires. He is told that witches live within the walls, that ghosts haunt the place, that terrible ogres will eat anyone who dares to approach. But one withered old man tells him that a beautiful princess is asleep in the castle and only a noble prince can awaken her. That's enough for a hero. Pushing aside all fear, the prince fights his way through the thicket. As he nears the castle, the tangles magically unfold. He enters and finds his way to a golden room where he sees the fairest sight he's ever beheld. He kneels and kisses the sleeping princess. With bated breath he waits to see the effect of his kiss. Slowly she awakens. "Is that you, my prince?" she whispers. When he hears her voice, the prince's heart melts and he declares his eternal love.

The tale of Sleeping Beauty might sound old-fashioned in an age of gender equity, but it still strikes a chord in our souls. In its simplicity it captures something basic about men and women. Essential feminine and masculine principles, termed yin and yang by ancient Chinese philosophers, are reflected in the storybook couple. Of course, the tale says nothing about their sex life, but I do know this: If Beauty and her prince used the techniques in this book in the royal bedroom, they would indeed have lived happily ever after—and healthier and longer as well.

In my practice I meet couples whose fairy tales are *not* coming true. I help them get back on track, physically, emotionally and sexually. Jenny and Jack had been married thirteen years when they came to me for acupuncture treatments. Jack had injured his shoulder falling off a ladder, and had chronic tension in his neck and occasional tinnitus (ringing in the ears); Jenny suffered from migraines, severe menstrual cramps and chronic yeast infections. They had come to me for relief from their physical symptoms, but they ended up with more than they bargained for.

I witnessed their marital discord in our first meeting, when Jenny criticized her husband for making them late and continued to insert barbs throughout our conversation. Jack held his tongue. Later, I learned that when they first met, Jenny had been attracted to Jack's easygoing nature and composure under stress. Jack admired Jenny for being outgoing and assertive. At first it was a good match: Jack calmed Jenny down when she needed it, and she invigorated and inspired him to accomplish his goals. As the years passed, however, their strengths became weaknesses. Jenny grew to resent feeling she had to be in charge all the time, but she feared that if she were to give up control, the structure of their life together would collapse. Feeling let down and abandoned, she belittled

Jack's masculinity. Though Jack felt angry and exasperated, he swallowed his frustration and withdrew into a shell of indifference.

He pulled away from sex as well. Jenny approached him frequently, only to be rebuffed. When they did make love, she worked hard to have an orgasm, but failed more often than not. She felt deserted and sexually frustrated, which only made her more edgy. What she didn't know was that Jack had not lost his sexual desire: he was masturbating daily, having found himself easier to please than his wife.

When they reached my office, the couple was at an impasse. Jenny needed desperately to access her softer, more feminine side and to be more genuinely receptive sexually. To do so, she needed Jack to assert his strength. In turn, Jack needed to have his masculine power emerge, but for this he had to have Jenny's respect, trust and encouragement. After years of consistent stress, their inherent differences, complementary at first, had exacerbated and were poisoning their marriage.

I treated them with acupuncture, herbs and diet. After about four months, Jenny's migraines were less frequent and Jack's shoulder pain was gone. To their surprise, there were other changes as well. The seemingly intractable conflicts that had threatened their marriage began to appear solvable. Jenny became less of a shrew, so Jack was less wimpy; he was less of a wimp, so she became less shrewish. I knew things had changed when Jenny told me that they'd had their best sex since their honeymoon. Jack had felt comfortable enough to initiate lovemaking again, and the next day in my office Jenny was cooing like a dove. I then proposed teaching them some of the sexual techniques in this book, explaining that they would not only heighten their pleasure but could perhaps help heal their remaining symptoms and further the process of emotional healing as well. I thought Jenny's cramps and vaginal infections might be, in part, the result of sexual frustration. As for Jack's tinnitus, in Chinese medicine it is sometimes caused by a weakness in the system that generates the body's sexual energy. I thought Jack's twice-daily masturbation habit could be depleting that system.

I taught Jenny to relax in bed and allow herself to be more sexually receptive. I recommended that the couple slow down and allow much more time for foreplay, showing them ways to add variety and spice to that phase of lovemaking. This would solidify their fragile intimacy and give Jenny more time to warm up and open up. Before long, she became more at ease with her natural sexuality and was experiencing regular orgasms without great effort. Her cramps lessened and her infections occurred less frequently. Seeing that he was able to please his wife, Jack's confidence grew. He stopped masturbating; even though he now had fewer orgasms, his satisfaction was more complete. The ringing in his ears subsided gradually, and the tightness in his neck disappeared as the tension between him and Jenny dissolved.

Ellen and Bob presented a different challenge. Ellen came to me for help with a chronically running nose, a slight cough and difficulty sleeping. Bob had a severe case of psoriasis and a tendency to strain muscles and tendons.

The couple was engaged, but Ellen was having second thoughts. "When we first met, Bob was sensitive, patient and kind," she said. "But he's hardened. He doesn't even listen anymore." Ellen felt lonely within her relationship. And scared. "Lately, Bob gets mad a lot," she added. "He's never hit me or anything, but he's a bully in other ways, and I'm afraid he might lose control."

Predictably, Bob was unhappy too. "I don't know what happened to her," he complained. "I used to love her spontaneity and sense of adventure. But now she's always tired. She wants me to take care of everything."

A sculptor whose career was skyrocketing, Ellen worked long hours that taxed her mental and physical stamina. Bob, too, was leaving his spirit and strength at work. A personnel director, he spent his days listening and empathizing. When they were together, Ellen had difficulty expressing herself and Bob did not have the patience to try to comprehend. She felt rejected; he felt abandoned. She withdrew into secrecy; he expressed his pain as anger.

Sexually, Ellen's desire had gone into hiding, while Bob teemed with aggressive lust. He wanted it often and he wanted it new and adventurous. When he was able to get Ellen into bed, she would be undemonstrative and quiet, greeting anything creative or unfamiliar as if it were toxic. She took much longer to become aroused than she had when her body was stronger, and she needed an exceptional amount of caressing. This was in stark contrast to her lover. He was in high gear the minute he entered the bedroom and ejaculated quickly—sometimes so quickly that it embarrassed him, which only made him more volatile. Frustrated by what he saw as a lack of sexual interest from Ellen, he would scream at her and stomp out of the room. That, of course, only made her more reluctant to get close to him.

While treating their physical symptoms, I suggested that they might benefit from certain sexual practices that had, for centuries, created harmony between spouses. Bob was using sex to release tension. Ellen's reluctance only made him more tense, even though he had the release of orgasm. Plus, the stress between them exacerbated his psoriasis. Going along for the sexual ride further weakened Ellen's physical condition: just as she would finally start to get aroused, Bob would climax and she'd be left feeling agitated and sad—and sadness, in Chinese Medicine, can cause respiratory disorders, the condition for which she'd sought treatment.

I explained to Bob the importance of delaying orgasm, not just for his fiancée's pleasure but for his own well-being, and coached him in ways to accomplish that goal (you will find these principles in chapter 6). The new approach enabled him to relax while making love and gave him greater control over his impulse to ejaculate. It made intercourse something for Ellen to look forward to rather than dread. Bob's excess aggression dissipated along with his physical symptoms—and so did the sadness and anxiety that had weakened Ellen's lungs and kept her awake nights.

HEAVENLY PLEASURE MEDICINE

Henry Miller once wrote, "For some, sex leads to sainthood; for others it is the road to hell." Like all powerful forces, the energy that drives sexuality can be used for good or ill. Many cultures, including our own, have emphasized the potential dangers of unleashing the sex drive—disease, exploitation, unwanted pregnancy, broken families, crimes such as rape, incest and pedophilia. To protect ourselves from the dark side of sex, we have evolved safeguards, just as we have for nuclear power and other energy sources with the potential to either help or harm. These precautions have taken the form of laws and customs geared to suppressing sexual expression.

The ancient Chinese also recognized the dual nature of sexuality. In their view, unhappy bedrooms resulted in poor health, marriage and family problems and even a breakdown of social order. But the sexual sages whose ideas form the basis of this book recognized an important truth: Sexuality can bring joy and blessings to the same extent that it can cause suffering. They held that by maximizing our potential as sexual beings we could strengthen ourselves as individuals and at the same time create greater harmony in the family and society as a whole.

We in the West still have a long way to go in that regard. Despite the sexual revolution, an explosion of sex research and unprecedented candor about sexuality, the sex act itself remains underrated, undervalued and underutilized. Certainly, we've come a long way from the days when erotic pleasure was a dark secret and sex was approved of only as a means of procreation. But we still do not appreciate the potential of this powerful aspect of our nature.

Look at your own experience. Isn't life easier when you're having great sex? Don't mountains turn into molehills? Isn't your step lighter and your mind clearer? Don't everyday annoyances bother you less? Aren't you more at peace with yourself, more optimistic, more content with your lot in life? You no doubt feel healthier, too—more vital and vigorous, with greater physical stamina and emotional strength. Your relationships—with everyone, but especially your lover—are more harmonious. You feel grateful, appreciative, more closely connected to the natural forces that give direction to your life. If you don't think these statements are true, you have probably never had great sex on a regular basis.

Think of sex as analogous to physical exercise. If you fail to exercise, you miss the opportunity to enhance your health, and over the long run can do yourself harm. If you work out improperly, you can injure or exhaust yourself. But appropriate exercise makes you feel good, improves your health and well-being, and retards aging. Should you choose to, you can attain the extraordinary fitness of an athlete. It's that way with sex as well. Those who go without it lose out on a source of revitalization, and possibly open the door to health disorders. For those who squander or misuse their sexual resources, sex can lead to physical and emotional pain. But for those who nourish and protect their sexuality, who use it properly with a loving and supportive partner, sex can bring profound benefits to body and soul. And if you take it to the level of superior sex, with the energy-generating techniques in this book, those benefits become truly magnificent.

Think of the various aspects of sex as continuums:

On a continuum of pleasure, sex can produce pain, turnoff and regret at the negative extreme; moderate enjoyment, satisfaction and exuberant sensuality in the middle; ecstatic bliss at the positive extreme.

On a continuum of emotional closeness, sex can alienate partners from each other or produce varying degrees of closeness, culminating in the consummate intimacy of spiritual oneness.

On a health continuum, sex can be traumatic, exhausting and depleting; it can be a means of releasing tension and reducing stress; it can put a bounce in your step, a twinkle in your eye and vital energy in your muscles and veins; and at the positive extreme, it can be a tool for preventing and healing illness and extending one's life span.

The superior sex techniques you are about to learn can move you in a positive direction on each of these continuums, regardless of where you start out. The same is true of proficiency. If you are having problems in bed, these tools can help you solve them. If you are sexually competent, they will make you more creative and skillful. If you are highly skilled, they will make you an expert. If you are an expert, you can achieve the mastery of an artist.

THE MANY REASONS
TO MAKE WHOOPEE

Let's look more closely at some of the vastly unappreciated benefits of a great sex life.

Healthy Sex, Healthy Body

The human body is a profoundly sophisticated machine that must be used—and used appropriately—in order to function in an optimal manner. Numerous medical studies have shown that the proper use of individual organs and systems reduces the risk of disease. For instance, aerobic exercise strengthens the cardiovascular system. Lifting weights improves muscle tone and bone integrity. Women who breast-feed their infants are less likely to get breast cancer than those who bottle-feed.

As with any body part, the more we properly use our sexual organs the healthier they will be. Chinese medicine holds that the best way to avoid sexual and reproductive disorders is to make love frequently, using techniques that make the act invigorating, not exhausting. Western medicine seems to support this thesis. For example, urologists advise men with erection problems to be *more* sexually active, not less so, because sexual arousal increases the flow of oxygen into the penile tissue, allowing for firmer erections. Men with certain prostate and bladder problems are sometimes advised to step up their sexual activity as well. An active sex life also contributes to higher testosterone levels, which results in a stronger sex drive. For women, studies indicate that regular sex can help stabilize irregular menstrual periods. Also, for women going through menopause, sexual activity has been shown to reduce the frequency and intensity of hot flashes and decrease the likelihood of tissue atrophy in the vagina.

The health rewards of an active sex life go beyond the areas of the body we associate with sex. For example, research indicates that regular sex helps women maintain proper estrogen levels, and higher estrogen correlates with cardiovascular fitness, emotional health, reduced risk of osteoporosis and other benefits. Scientists also say that vigorous sex can bestow some of the value associated with aerobic exercise, such as improving circulation, strengthening the heart and lungs, reducing stress and boosting the immune system. We also know that sex stimulates the release of endorphins, the opiatelike brain chemicals that diminish pain and generate feelings of well-being. And, as most of us have noticed, sex can be a powerful tension-reducer.

If all this is true of ordinary sex, imagine what having superior sex with someone you love can do.

Traditional Chinese medicine expands the vision of the health benefits of sex. As we will see in chapter 3, sexual energy is viewed as synonymous with the vital life force called *chi*. When released through proper sexual practices, this energy moves through the entire body like a tonic, bringing with it the power to strengthen organs and heal illness wherever it resides in the system. Disorders related to tension or fatigue, muscle pain, sexual dysfunction, problems associated with blood flow (particularly in the pelvic region)—these are most readily relieved through superior sex. The more one masters the techniques presented in later chapters, the more the healing capacity of sex increases. Curing specific ailments with sexual energy, as if it were a prescription medicine, would take a higher degree of expertise than anyone could reasonably expect to achieve with a book. However, the value of chi as a balm or elixir for the entire body is often noticed right from the start. And it is not uncommon for novices like the patients described earlier to notice improvements in particular ailments.

Perhaps more important, according to traditional Chinese medicine, superior sex is the most effective and sophisticated form of preventive medicine. As a long-term strategy, for those who practice it diligently, it can be even more powerful than good diet, exercise and other beneficial lifestyle habits. A natural antiaging tonic, superior sex keeps the body young and immunity strong.

Having too little sex or engaging in improper sex can contribute to disease. What do I mean by improper sex? Obviously, sex that is abusive, exploitative, coercive or violent, but also sex whose sole purpose is tension relief (using sex merely to reduce tension is like eating just to fill your belly); sex that is emotionally void, depressing or saddening; sex that is physically unsatisfying or frustrating; sex that is too quick or exclusively orgasm oriented; sex that is boring or monotonous; sex that is physically draining or exhausting; sex with an inappropriate partner or at an inappropriate time (for example, when one is fatigued or digesting a large meal). Even the experiences most people would call "good sex" can be a mixed bag, producing negative side effects along with pleasure and release if the conditions are not right. Over the long haul, these side effects can contribute to physical and psychological problems we might never realize are linked to sex.

According to traditional Chinese medicine, superior sex, along with the healthy lifestyle practices in chapter 9, can help prevent health problems. These include disorders of the reproductive system: for women, infertility, PMS, lack of orgasm, vaginal infections, vaginal dryness, polyps, tumors (both benign and malignant) and endometriosis; for men, erectile problems, low sperm count, hypersexuality, premature ejaculation and inability to ejaculate, prostate swelling and infections and tumors. For both sexes, disorders that can possibly be prevented or delayed with proper sexual behavior and lifestyle include fatigue, cold hands and feet, insomnia, kidney diseases, lower back pain and knee pain, migraines, vision problems, hearing loss, panic attacks, bloating, heartburn, memory loss and ringing in the ears.

Sex as an Antiaging Tonic

In a recent memoir, Mao Zedong's personal physician wrote that the chairman frequently had sex with young girls. It was, he said, an attempt by Mao to prolong his life, just as Chinese men of privilege have always done.

In the West we have assumed that sexuality wanes with age. We know that when men reach their twenties their production of testosterone begins a long, steady decline, and when women reach menopause, estrogen production plummets. For the most part, we accept declining sexual interest and performance as a normal result of biological changes. Attempts at countering the tendency center on hormone replacement therapy, in which synthetic or animal-based substances are used to replenish the body's supply. By contrast, the Chinese developed natural ways to maintain youthfulness and sexual vigor. These include the exercises and lifestyle suggestions in this book, plus superior sex on a regular basis. Western researchers on aging have also discovered that it helps to remain sexually active: studies show that sexual arousal—even if produced by watching an erotic film—increases the production of sex hormones in older people.

One of the side effects of ordinary sex, even when it's satisfying, is the gradual loss of sexual stamina. By contrast, the techniques in this book *generate* energy. Think of superior sex as a sexual investment strategy. Just as we plan ahead and arrange our finances to ensure that we'll have ample resources for our retirement years, we can invest our sexual energy so as to have plenty available for satisfying passion as we age. Unlike long-term financial investments, these practices enable you to enjoy your resources in the present and at the same time preserve them for the future. They yield a high rate of interest along with regular dividends of pleasure, marital harmony and sexual vigor. They will give you more energy for sex in the present and enable you to love your honey like a bunny when you're ninety.

Making Love Makes More Love

Sexual passion enhances the emotional bond between lovers. In any long-term relationship, each partner has personality traits that the other would like to see go away. They seldom do. So, it helps a great deal if, when irritants arise, you can focus on everything that is lovable about your spouse. Sexual activity makes this easier. It alters blood chemistry, causing subtle effects on perception that elevate one's judgment and sense of reality. One's vision turns from what is annoying to what is magnificent and blessed. Lovemaking reduces fear and anger, coating the rough edges of life with a warm afterglow and softening the harsh reality of conflicts and disagreements. Rather than seeing only his stubbornness or her selfish streak, you are inclined to pay attention to the uniquely wonderful qualities that brought you together and keep you together.

Erotic love also serves as a soothing tonic when things get tough, strengthening your emotional bond and restoring intimacy when circumstances threaten to pull you apart. If a relationship is a safety net, making love well adds stitches and strengthens its fiber. Now, I know that having sex doesn't *always* make you feel more loving. Sometimes it makes you feel angry or hurt or humiliated. But if you approach sex the way it is detailed in the coming chapters, you will find that it does indeed make more love for you and your sweetheart.

Making love makes more love in another way as well. A leading cause of marital problems is sexual malaise. We simply get bored with each other over time. Horny husbands complain about their wives' "headaches." Sexy wives complain about husbands whose noses are buried in the sports page or a business report. Is it inevitable? Does passion have to wane over time? Was novelist Peter De Vries right when he joked that sex in marriage was like medicine: "Three times a day for the first week, then once a day for another week, then once every three or four days until the condition clears"? Not at all. Sexual malaise can be prevented and cured with liberal doses of skill and imagination.

As the Chinese noted centuries ago, the engine of love is fueled by variety, creativity and surprise. There is enough information in the coming chapters to keep an imaginative couple busy for years, plus sexual practices that keep the feeling between them humming with delicious yearning.

Sex Elevates the Soul

We are designed to enjoy sex and be soothed by it. When approached with love and zest, lovemaking dissolves anxiety, depression, loneliness and despair. It elevates the spirit and opens us to joy, enriching our capacity to feel and making life more whole. A passionate couple who learns the skills of superior sex will find that the experience can evolve from mere enjoyment to euphoria to ecstasy. The connection with each other intensifies, dissolving individual boundaries and creating an experience of profound oneness. With that comes a heightened awareness of, appreciation for, and connection to the rest of creation.

When practiced with artistry, sex allows us to use our bodies to rise above our animal nature and draw closer to that which is divine in us. That is why the ancients viewed superior sex as essentially a form of prayer or meditation, a spiritual practice that can unite the individual with the universal life force. This may be more than you bargained for when you picked up this book, but if you are spiritually inclined, the practices in this book can help you turn lovemaking into a sacred, holy ritual.

HOLISTIC SEX

In recent years, scientific advances have brought Western medicine closer and closer to a basic principle of traditional Chinese medicine: that body, mind and emotions are inseparable. Traditional Chinese medicine holds that improving physical health also improves mental and emotional well-being. In that regard, the Chinese anticipated by thousands of years the current revolution in biopsychology, in which biochemical agents such as Prozac are used to treat mental conditions, and also the growing field of psychoneuroimmunology, which studies how the mind affects the immune system.

Because of this essential unity of all aspects of our lives, our sexuality is affected by our physical health, our thoughts and our emotions. In turn, sexuality has a profound and powerful impact on our bodies, minds, emotions and relationships.

By analogy, imagine a table with four legs. One leg represents sexuality, the others represent mind, body and feelings. Pushing any of the legs moves the table as a whole, since no single leg can change positions without altering the position of the others. Hence, every sexual experience affects all other aspects of the individual. Now imagine that a second table is attached to the first. This represents a partner or mate. A change in any one leg will now affect the position of *both* tables. In other words, what happens to one partner will affect the mind, body, emotions and sexuality of the other partner as well. If you are married or in a love relationship, you probably know this to be true.

The Chinese sexual arts were developed with these holistic principles in mind. This book is designed to help you apply them.

TEN SECONDS CAN MAKE YOUR DAY

Are you ready to take a small first step toward a great sex life? Are ten seconds a day too much to devote to this glorious end? Here is a simple suggestion: From now on, when you see your mate after a day's work or any extended absence, make the first act between you a kiss that lasts at least ten seconds.

Does this seem trivial? Silly? Unnecessary? Ask yourself this: When was the last time you shared a kiss that lasted a full ten seconds while vertical? If you can't remember one, you've been missing out on something special. If you *can* remember, I'll bet you feel warm inside. That kiss probably made your knees go weak and your face flush. It probably brightened your whole day.

When I ask my patients whom they give their first hug or kiss to when they come home at the end of the day, the answer is usually their son or daughter. Unless they have a dog, in which case the animal gets the first sign of affection. Of course, the last person on the list is the spouse, assuming he or she makes the cut at all. And what does the spouse get? A big hug and smooch like the kids? Some playful caresses like the pet? No. He or she gets a quick peck and maybe a little squeeze. If that's true for you, make yesterday the last day that will ever happen.

I guarantee that if you bring home a big, sloppy ten-second kiss for your beloved every day, you'll be astonished at the results. A wonderful way to tap into the river of love that flows beneath the trivial concerns of everyday life, it's an instant reminder of why you are together, and it gets the rest of the evening off to a good start. Make it a wet, juicy kiss; the ancient Chinese considered the saliva of one's lover an elixir. While you're at it, add a warm, full-body hug. It not only feels great, but it's good for your children: watching you embrace is a healthy reminder that romantic love is an important part of your life, as it will someday be in theirs.

One word of caution: Don't overdo it. Once, a few months after I made this suggestion at a seminar, I ran into one of the participants. He said he and his wife had started to practice the exercise but had gotten burned out after only four days. It seems he thought I said to kiss for ten minutes!

When I corrected him, he exclaimed, "No wonder!" and dashed home to his wife with lips puckered.

Chapter 2

THE FIRST AND OLDEST DANCE
The Coupling of Masculine and Feminine

*They that know the Tao of yin and yang can blend
the five pleasures. But they that know not may
die an untimely death. How could they ever
enjoy the sexual pleasures?*

—SU NU CHING, first century

*Pursuit and seduction are the essence of sexuality.
It's part of the sizzle.*

—CAMILLE PAGLIA

To understand the mating dance of men and women, let's turn to one of the world's oldest philosophies, the Yin-Yang Theory of China. According to this 5,000-year-old wisdom, everything in the universe can be placed on a continuum whose central point, like a seesaw, is perfect balance. On one side of that point is yin, on the other is yang. Every object and phenomenon contains both of these aspects, but in different and constantly shifting proportions. The two principles are complementary, interdependent and mutually supporting. Neither can exist in isolation; each is a necessary condition for the existence of the other.

Through the interplay of yin and yang (literally, the shady and sunny sides of the mountain) life in its infinite expressions unfolds. Naturally, that includes human behavior. Yin-Yang Theory explains how our bodies and minds work as clearly as it does the rhythms of a forest. As we will see in detail, women are predominantly yin, and men predominantly yang, but each gender contains both yin and yang. First, here is a brief list of qualities that differentiate yin and yang throughout nature:

YIN	YANG
feminine	masculine
below	above
cold	hot
receptive	creative
enduring	fleeting
transformation	initiation
wet	dry
hidden	apparent
dark	light
night	day
inclusive	exclusive
slow	fast
rest	activity
water	fire
moon	sun
earth	heaven

Yin is mysterious and secretive, cool, comforting, calming and patient. It moves slowly and takes a long time to evolve. It draws things to it and quietly changes them. Like water, it moves in a downward direction and affects what it contacts slowly and subtlely, but with lasting power.

By contrast, yang is quick, aggressive, direct and focused. Like fire, it is hot, moves upward and out, and affects things quickly and dramatically.

Human Nature

Human behavior can also be placed on a yin-yang continuum. Here are some examples that will be referred to throughout the book (while they represent feminine and masculine, yin and yang do not mean simply woman and man; both sexes contain yin and yang qualities, although in different proportions):

YIN BEHAVIOR	YANG BEHAVIOR
nurtures what already exists	creates that which is new
introverted	extroverted
withholds thoughts, feelings, and information	openly expressive
domestic	adventurous
refrains from action	takes action
holistic or nondiscriminating	analytic or discerning
disorganized	organized
listens	speaks
reactive	proactive
dying	being born
calming	motivating
conciliatory	combative
inner-directed	outer-directed

Sleeping Beauty is the ultimate expression of yin. The epitome of feminine allure, she spends a century completely inactive, hidden from the light. She needs only to exist in her state of natural magnetism to draw the prince to her. He is quintessential yang. Drawn irresistibly to the feminine, he acts without hesitation to penetrate the darkness, risking defeat (rejection, in today's terms) to win his heart's desire. It's safe to say that if Beauty did not respond to him at first, the prince would have persevered, dedicating himself to waking her up, just as men have always done to win a woman's love.

PRIMARY AND
SECONDARY TRAITS

From the list of yin and yang attributes, it is probably apparent that you have some of each. Men often exhibit yin traits such as receptivity and nurturance, and women have yang traits such as creativity and aggressiveness. Women are often proactive and men reactive; women can express themselves vehemently and men can respond passively and patiently; women can be adventurous and bold and men can prefer to sit quietly at home. This is because women contain yang and men contain yin, as illustrated in the familiar *T'ai-chi T'u* symbol, in which the dark areas represent yin and the light sections yang. The small dots on each side indicate the yin within yang and the yang within yin.

In a male body, yang energy is the primary force while yin is secondary; in a female body, yin energy is primary and yang is secondary. This has a precise parallel in physiology: testosterone (the primary male sex hormone) is a secondary hormone for women, while estrogen (the primary female sex hormone) is secondary for men.

The yin-yang symbol

The preponderance of yin in women and yang in men explains many commonly observed gender differences. For example, women are innately better listeners than men, as yin's initial inclination is to receive, while yang's is to contribute, as in putting his two cents in to try to solve someone else's problem. Sexually, because yang initiates action, men have historically been the pursuers in the mating game. Since receiving is a yin trait, women have generally waited to receive proposals and overtures—or, as with Sleeping Beauty, the first kiss. Because yang is fast and yin is slow, men are quick to get sexually aroused, while women need time to warm up. In fact, the influence of yin and yang on sexual behavior is roughly analogous to that of estrogen and testosterone: whether male or female, individuals with a high level of testosterone are more sexually aggressive, whereas estrogen makes one more sexually receptive. When female animals are injected with testosterone, they become as sexually bold as the males of their species.

THE PROPAGATION MODEL OF MALE–FEMALE BEHAVIOR

Nature's design for making babies reveals an ideal pattern of interaction for men and women. Making babies is the bottom-line purpose of sexual expression, and thus the best way to understand the natural male-female dynamic. In the act of propagation, he gives, then he waits, then he receives. The female pattern is: She receives, then transforms what she has received, then she gives. Let's look at this basic pattern more closely:

- Yang energy (from either partner) initiates lovemaking.
- Yin energy (from the other partner) receives the initiation and transforms it into a mutual act.
- He contributes his erection (yang).
- She receives his erection, merges it with her body and converts his offering into the act of intercourse (yin).
- He contributes his semen (yang).
- She receives his semen, merges it with her egg and *transforms* it into new life (yin). (Transformation is a creative act and creating is a yang activity; in this case it represents the yang within yin.)
- He waits (yin).
- She births the child and brings it into the world (yang).
- He receives the child, and their life together is transformed (yin).

In "Sleeping Beauty" the prince initiates by entering the castle where Beauty waits to receive him. He contributes his kiss. She receives it. While he waits, she is affected deeply and powerfully, then awakens. She gives back his expression of affection, transformed by her love. The prince receives her gesture. Their love brings new life to both of them. Not only are the prince and princess altered irrevocably but so, too, the entire kingdom. The lovers get to live happily ever after and everyone in the castle awakens.

According to traditional Chinese medicine, progress in a relationship, and in society as a whole, is made possible by the masculine ability to initiate combined with the feminine capacity to receive and then convert what is received—sperm, conversations, habits, conflicts, children, money, etc.—into something new. When evaluating patients, I have found that those whose patterns of giving and receiving accord with these gender principles have healthier bodies and more harmonious relationships. Patients with serious illnesses and dysfunctional relationships are typically out of sync with those patterns. As one ancient sage put it, "The debility of men is caused by faulty ways in the mating of yin and yang." As we will see, these basic patterns can be applied to all areas of life where men and women interact, from the office to the boudoir.

BEING TRUE
TO YIN AND YANG

It is vital for men and women to be adept at the skills associated with their primary energetic qualities. A woman who is true to her yin energy allows her man to give to her, sexually, emotionally and materially. Having received, she processes what she has taken in and lets her man know what she thinks and feels. In this way she can transform not only what the man has given to her, but the man himself. Yin's impact is deep and enduring, like the contours of a canyon etched by water.

By contrast, if she does not access her yin capacities, a woman becomes less receptive and does not give adequate feedback. This cuts her off from deeper intimacy with others and weakens not only the woman but her relationship as well. The strength of a love affair depends more on yin qualities than yang. Yang ignites passion, pulling couples together like moths to a flame; yin provides comfort and sustenance, the calm quiet platform on which long-term growth can occur. This subtle strength of yin gives women more power than is generally recognized. Without receptivity nothing can be shared—not thoughts, feelings, love or anything else meaningful. The pioneering psychologist Abraham Maslow observed that psychologically healthy people are less needy and therefore better able to receive love. As a result, they are capable of true giving.

Being true to yang energy requires the ability to create and contribute *in an appropriate manner.* That means giving what the other person needs, wants and is capable of receiving. It also means being available for feedback and using it as fuel for more effective giving in the future. According to Yin-Yang Theory, a man who steps out of selfishness and into altruism is being masculine in the truest sense. By giving appropriately, he helps his woman fulfill her desires and in turn derives tremendous power from her loving and generous responses.

By contrast, a man whose behavior is *deficient* in yang qualities might be seen as a weakling or coward. He will lack vision, fail to pursue his goals vigorously and perhaps let others—including his lover—take advantage of him. If a man gives *inappropriately,* offering what he wants to give, not what his woman needs, he cuts himself off from his primary strength and neither partner is fulfilled.

The delicate interplay of yin and yang has a circular effect: A woman who is skilled at receiving and transforming will enhance her man's ability to give; a man who knows that his woman has been powerfully and happily affected by him becomes motivated to give even more. And when a man gives skillfully, his woman feels safer, which allows her to be more open and vulnerable.

Utilize Your Secondary Trait

While behaving in accord with one's primary quality is vital, the importance of one's secondary trait should not be underestimated. A woman who uses her secondary trait (yang) effectively can help her man fulfill his desires without becoming subservient or suppressing her own needs. If she is *not* capable of utilizing her yang, she will not be assertive enough to get what she wants, from life or from her man. She might be easily dominated and controlled.

A man who is in harmony with his yin can be easygoing and flexible and yet remain strong. He bends in the direction he is pushed and turns what he is given to his advantage. Such a man contributes to his relationship by listening well, empathizing, and quietly steering himself and his partner in a direction that fulfills both their goals. A man who *cannot* access his secondary trait will not be good at listening or feeling compassion. He might be brutish and domineering. Indeed, we see in the social ills that plague us what happens when yang energy is unleashed without the balancing influence of yin: violence, abuse, narrow-mindedness and the like.

WHEN YIN AND YANG
ARE OUT OF BALANCE

Like the relative proportions of darkness and light, the ratio between yin and yang shifts constantly throughout nature. Where balance exists, bodies are strong and durable, personalities are harmonious, and male-female coupling mirrors the cosmic interplay of yin and yang: it creates and sustains life—in the sense not just of procreation, but of a greater and more profound life for both partners.

But the ever-shifting nature of yin and yang assures that disharmony will occur. Throughout the book you will find reference to excesses and deficiencies of yin and yang. These imbalances, caused by the myriad factors that affect our bodies—diet, stress, emotional and environmental conditions, etc.—have an impact on everything from our sense of well-being to the health of our organs, to our behavior, our sexuality and our relationships. Where couples are concerned, individual imbalances compound each other (remember the metaphor of the two tables tied together).

For example, one of the most common patterns I see in my practice is what I call the Bitch-Wimp Syndrome. According to Chinese medicine, our primary aspect is the one most readily dissipated by stress and aging: over time, women tend to become yin deficient and men become yang deficient. When that happens to romantic partners, the ratio of yin to yang changes. The man operates less from his masculine strength, and the woman feels less safe expressing her feminine attributes. (Jenny and Jack in chapter 1 are excellent examples of this syndrome.)

The twin deficiencies create a vicious cycle. Having lost some of her yin ability to be receptive and flexible, a woman becomes either overly controlling or excessively giving. This causes her man to feel overpowered, rejected and inferior. Having lost some of his ability to create, take charge and give altruistically, he focuses on his own needs. This makes the woman feel let down, disappointed and alone. In a desperate attempt to recover his yang power, the man might focus his entire attention on his career or become a weekend warrior. In extreme cases, he might lash out at his wife or children. The woman might try to restore her yin by placing inordinate importance on her children or needy friends. She might even become ill as a way to force herself to be totally receptive.

Eventually, the imbalance will cause both partners to lose their desire for each other. Either or both may be tempted to have an affair. In traditional Chinese medicine, the urge that drives people to cheat on their mates is not just psychological; sometimes, the *body* hungers for someone new in an effort to regain its yin-yang balance. A woman whose yang-deficient man does not give adequately might yearn for a connection with masculine energy; a man whose yin-deficient spouse is unreceptive may find himself drawn to a soft, feminine stranger.

Another common pattern of imbalance, the Brute-Victim Syndrome, occurs when both partners are deficient in their *secondary* aspects. This magnifies their primary traits—yin for her, yang for him—to an unhealthy extreme. (Ellen and Bob in chapter 1 are prime examples.) He becomes impatient, insensitive and callous, perhaps to the point of volatility. She, unable to express her needs or take steps to satisfy them, withdraws into yin secrecy. Sexually, they are likely to be at loggerheads. Without sufficient yang, the woman's libido will be as hidden as buried treasure, while her partner, lacking the calming benefit of yin, can rage like a sexual hurricane. He wants it often and he wants it now. She seldom wants sex, and when she does consent, she's docile and slow to respond. If attracted to other men, she will be drawn to one who's secure enough in his yin to offer comfort, understanding and gentle loving. He will crave a woman who projects enough yang to promise a lusty alternative.

Whether or not someone attempts to heal an imbalance by having an affair also depends on the yin-yang equation. Yin's way of improving a situation is to make subtle changes in what already exists. Restless yang responds to problems by looking for an entirely new solution. Therefore, a frustrated man is more likely than his female counterpart to seek a fresh new object of passion. Men who honor their commitments despite the urge to wander are being influenced by their yin. One of yin's jobs is to contain yang and curb its excesses. If an opportunity to fool around comes along, yang will shout, "Go for it!" Yin will argue, "Stay where you are and make it better."

The same dynamic applies to women. When a woman seeks out an affair, that's her secondary trait at work. Initially, her yin will move her to strengthen her relationship, but if her man does not respond, she may activate her yang to solve her problem. When a woman sees a chance to fulfill her yin desires, she can exhibit very yang behavior to make it happen.

Fortunately, traditional Chinese medicine has ways to restore yin and yang to their proper balance, and sexual formulas to satisfy both yang's craving for newness and yin's need for a secure nest.

HARNESSING THE POWER OF SEDUCTION

In the early days, Julie and her husband, Dan, had a whiz-bang sex life. But a few years into the marriage, Julie started to lose interest. This made her feel confused and guilty: with her consistent orgasms, she was so far ahead of her frustrated friends that she felt she had no right to complain.

At one point in our discussion, Julie joked, "Dan's idea of seduction is to poke me on the arm and say 'How about now?' He actually thinks that turns me on." It seemed that her husband was skillful enough to satisfy her physical needs, but not her desire for imagination and romance. He'd prepare for a fishing trip as if it were a holy pilgrimage, but he approached lovemaking as if it were no more special than a drive to the mall. Julie felt taken for granted. Their intimacy was sacred to her, and it appeared to mean very little to her husband.

I asked Julie if Dan had a favorite meal. She said he adored her lasagna. "Suppose you made it every time you ate dinner at home?" I asked. "Do you think he'd get bored?" Of course, she acknowledged. Then I asked, "Suppose every time you served that special dish, you took it out of the freezer, heated it up, slammed it on the table and said, 'Here, eat!'? No wine, no candles, no appetizer, no side dish." Julie understood the analogy immediately: Her husband was unintentionally cheapening something she valued, eliminating the preparation and atmosphere that would make it special.

I encouraged Julie to express her concerns to Dan. At first he was perplexed. As far as he was concerned, his blueprint for sex got the job done. Why risk embarrassment or failure by trying anything new? Fortunately, he listened anyway. Later, he told me, "I always thought, 'If it ain't broke, don't fix it.' I guess that makes sense when it comes to engines, but not making love."

I've been quoting Dan for over a decade. I tell men that if they keep using the same stale seduction formulas, they should not be surprised if their wives have a lot of headaches. I also tell women not to leave seduction entirely in the hands of their man. A man's yin likes to be lured into the realm of erotic mystery by his woman's yang. In fact, many of my male patients complain that their women don't actively and imaginatively seduce them. Oddly enough, even women who are assertive and creative at work can be as passive as their grandmothers when it comes to sex.

Laboratory research on animals provides a clue to solving the seduction blahs. When a male mammal is placed in a cage with a female in heat, the pair quickly mates. After he ejaculates, the male rests for a certain amount of time before mounting again. That phase, known as the refractory period, varies from one species to another. But, whether it's a rooster, a rat or a ram, after the next ejaculation the refractory period is longer than the first. The one after that is even longer, and the next one longer still, and so on: each time he ejaculates, the male needs more time to recover. Eventually he loses interest altogether, ignoring the come-hither signals of the female with whom he's been sharing a cage.

But look what happens if at any point the female is replaced with a new cage mate: that male perks right back up. This is known as the Coolidge Effect. Why Coolidge? When he was president of the United States, Calvin Coolidge visited a farm with his wife. On noticing a large number of chicks and thousands of eggs, Mrs. Coolidge asked how many roosters it took to do all that fertilizing. Not many, said the proud farmer. Each rooster does his duty many times a day. "You might point that out to Mr. Coolidge," said the First Lady. The president countered by asking the farmer if the roosters had to limit themselves to only one hen. No, replied the farmer, they have virtual harems. "You might point that out to Mrs. Coolidge," said Silent Cal.

Obviously, among humans, replacing one's lover is not usually an ac-ceptable solution to sexual monotony. But here is the loophole: The vigor of the male animal can also be restored by changing the appearance or scent of the original mate. Needless to say, human females do not need scientists to tell them the value of perfumes, revealing outfits and new hairstyles. The more significant implication of that finding is the importance of change itself.

The ancient Chinese did research on humans, not animals, and learned the same thing. Members of the palace staff were instructed to watch what went on in the royal bed chambers between emperors or no-blemen and their wives or concubines. These astute observers would record the responses of both participants to see which techniques worked and which did not. The result was a body of wisdom on the arts of seduction and sex play that still holds up today. One of the key tenets is the importance of freshness and variety.

Think of it: The sexiest garments in the Victoria's Secret catalog and Chanel's most intoxicating scents would lose their appeal if you wore them every night. Love letters and roses would get tiresome if you re-ceived them all the time. But even flossing, brushing and getting under the covers in your pajamas can be exciting the first time you do it together. The first rule of seduction, therefore, is to make creative use of surprise.

The Yin and Yang of Seduction Strategy

It is the yang aspect of either the man or woman that initiates the action. But let the propagation model (see page 25) guide you: Yang has to give appropriately, i.e., something the other person is able to receive and work with. Once the initial move has been made, the receiver processes what he or she has taken in (yin), then gives a response in return (yang). If the gesture is well chosen, well presented and well timed, the initiator will get what he or she had hoped for: a hot roll in the hay.

Ironically, men are more guilty of predictability than women. I say ironic because yang is the force that initiates change. However, it is also orderly, structured and focused. When men hit upon a method that appears to work, they cling to it like loyal puppies. They can even become complacent, like Julie's well-meaning husband, Dan.

Seduction strategies that are attuned to yin-yang principles not only are more likely to be successful, they also set the stage for inspired, harmonious lovemaking—which leads to powerful health benefits for the bodies, minds and spirits of the lovers. Most of us approach sex primarily through our dominant traits. Therefore, as a rule, to seduce a woman you have to inspire the yin in her; to seduce a man you have to inspire his yang. Once again, these are generalizations; it's normal for any individual to sometimes behave in accord with his or her secondary trait.

Let's look at three contrasting tendencies of yin and yang and what they tell us about how to seduce the majority of women and men.

The Ups and the Downs

Whoever said that the way to a man's heart is through his stomach was setting her sights too high. In the male body, sexual energy moves primarily in the yang direction, upward from the bottom of the torso to the top, because male sexuality is predominantly yang. Hence, most men (and the yang aspect of women) can be seduced with direct appeals to the genitals. From there, the energy rises up and hits him where it counts, opening his heart and mind.

Basically, if you want to get a man into bed, you can let him know in no uncertain terms. A woman can say or do things to turn on a man that she might consider crude or vulgar if the roles were reversed. "I want you"—communicated either directly or with subtle body language—works wonders. And if you add "Now!" so much the better.

Like water, yin moves downward, trickling from above to below. That's why women usually need to be inspired from the top down before they can open up sexually. They need to enjoy a man's company, to think well of him and to feel that he and the situation are right for them. Therefore, to excite a woman's sexuality (and the yin aspect of a man), engage her mind and heart and let the energy work down to her genitals. If her heart opens, so will her legs.

In some circumstances, a direct appeal to a woman's genitals does work, but her total sexuality will get involved only with assistance from her mind and heart. You have a far better chance of scoring with "I adore you" than with "I want your body." Also, yin-driven women need to resolve emotional tension and conflict before they feel comfortable enough to make love.

The opposite is true of yang-driven men: with them, getting turned on sexually makes everything right with the universe. Therefore, ladies, when your man wants to make love right after an argument, understand that he's actually paying you a compliment. Clumsy and ill-timed as it may seem, he's attempting to open his heart and get close to you again. Since yang energy moves from the genitals up to the heart and mind, it's easier for a man to open up emotionally after he's been stimulated sexually.

Again, these are gender generalities. Women who are yang-oriented can have lusty spontaneous sex with anonymous studs; yin-driven men can make love only with women they respect and care for. But for the most part the old clichés hold true: women need a reason, men need a place; women need love to get to sex, men use sex to get to love. All because yin moves gradually to where yang begins.

The Fast and the Slow

Like lighting a fire, yang is quick to be ignited. Like bringing water to a boil, yin takes time to heat up. Thus, it doesn't take long to get a yes out of most men. Women generally need a longer seduction process. Candlelight dinners, slow dancing, moonlit strolls, flowers—all the staples of romance contribute to the gradual buildup of yin sexuality. This might seem like a nuisance to an impatient, yang-driven man. But the slow buildup is balanced by another yin trait: once a woman is hot, her heat lasts a long time. Think of the difference between dousing a fire and waiting for boiling water to cool off.

Of course, in keeping with their secondary traits, the yang aspect of a woman's sexuality can be ignited quickly and the yin aspect of a man's needs more time. Women often notice that when they get sexually aggressive their men respond with surprising reluctance. That's because being put in the receptive position activates his yin, and yin takes longer to warm up. This also explains another common phenomenon: why older men require more stimulation to get turned on. As they age, men burn up their yang chi, so their bodies become proportionately more yin.

Bottom line: If you want to seduce a typical man, you can jump his bones the minute he walks in the door; if you want to seduce a typical woman, you'd be wise to plan ahead and start the process well in advance.

The Ins and the Outs

Yang is stimulated by outer qualities and yin by inner qualities. Men tend to respond to that which is right in front of them, like beautiful faces and curvaceous figures. They care about the shape of a rear end and the size of a bust because yang is stimulated by things that protrude. Sure, women like to gaze at good-looking hunks, and some get wobbly at the sight of muscular arms and well-sculpted pecs. That's their yang aspect reacting. But men have a lot more yang in them, which is why *Playboy* and *Penthouse* sell millions of copies while *Cosmopolitan* and *Vogue* do the same without pictures of naked men.

Because their primary trait is yin, women are drawn to that which is hidden or within. How a man thinks and feels is of great importance to them. Their turn-ons are qualities that endure, such as stability, loyalty and integrity. One might argue that women are attracted to superficial things like fancy cars and other trappings of wealth. But those are symbols of long-term security, a principal yin concern.

Girls are taught how to catch a boy's eye; boys are taught to behave like gentlemen. Girls buy makeup and tight skirts; boys memorize pickup lines. Women buy sexy lingerie; men buy flowers. These are not arbitrary cultural patterns; they're reflections of inner-directed yin and outer-directed yang.

THE LANGUAGE OF LOVE

Can you imagine Shakespeare's famous balcony scene with Juliet declaring her love to Romeo? Would we weep over the yearning of Cyrano de Bergerac if he were a woman writing love letters to a man? Would the line "Come up and see me sometime" be as memorable if it had been uttered by Cary Grant instead of Mae West?

In the arsenal of seduction, words have tremendous firepower. But to use them successfully you have to aim in the right direction. The best target is your beloved's primary energetic trait. Romantic language—whether in love letters, songs, sonnets, or greeting cards—appeals to yin, while bawdy tales and suggestive come-ons appeal to yang.

Yin and yang are also attracted to different types of fantasy, a key element in seduction. Exciting the imagination with words can stimulate desire in both sexes. But superficial, action-oriented yang responds to visual images, such as gorgeous bodies, and adventurous scenarios, like quickies in exotic settings. Yin favors romantic fantasies, especially love stories with happily-ever-after endings. Think about who watches porno and who reads romance novels.

Speak to Her Heart

In general, words are more important in seducing women because the impact of language begins in the head and is carried downward by yin to the heart and genitals. So use words that relieve her anxiety—about you, the circumstances and the future. Make her feel happy, joyful and excited—about herself and her romantic prospects. Joy opens the heart.

Stimulate her yin with fantasies that create a sense of anticipation. It could be as simple as telling her how much you're looking forward to seeing her in her new dress. Or something more elaborate, like describing the romantic trip you're going to take together. You can also evoke explicitly sexual images; tell her you can't wait to make love to her and add a hint of what you intend to do. But remember, "I want to screw your brains out" is not likely to work on a woman unless she is already hot. Yin would rather hear that you're going to slowly kiss her all over. Start the fantasy process hours or even days ahead of time. If you let her simmer slowly in the sauce of anticipation, you'll be richly rewarded.

Because yin represents being, women want to be appreciated for who they are and have their natural gifts acknowledged. Tell her things like, "I love how good and decent you are," "My life is so much brighter with you," "Just thinking about you makes me happy." And be sure to give specific examples.

Words to the Wise

Men respond well to *sexual* words. Once aroused, yang moves up to the heart and brain, at which point even strong silent types are moved to spout poetry and declarations of love.

Tell him how much you love what he does in bed. Whisper that you get wet just thinking about the last time you made love and can't wait to do it again. If you like, add explicit details to stimulate his imagination. Fantasies that evoke the senses stimulate yang energy, so tell him what you'll smell like and what you'll be wearing, if anything.

Because yang is action oriented, men want to hear that you like what they *do.* Let him know that you see him as masterful. Pay tribute to his competence and let him know how much it means to you. "I can't believe all that you accomplished this morning," "Wow that was amazing!"—bright-eyed statements like those work wonders on yang. If appropriate, praise his bravery too. Tell him that you admire how he stood up to his boss or responded in a crisis. "My hero!" inspires the knight in shining armor in every man and helps bring out his masculine sexual strength.

Once again, don't forget the secondary traits. For maximum balance in a long-term relationship make sure to inspire a woman's yang by appreciating the things she does, and inspire a man's yin by acknowledging who he is.

Here are some seduction principles based on the tendencies of yin and yang. Following them will open the door to a powerful, intimate, durable, life-enhancing sexual relationship.

HOW TO SEDUCE
A WOMAN

1. Use your imagination. You don't give her the same birthday gift every year, so why invite her to make love the same way, at the same time, in the same place? Make the gift of seduction as varied as her birthday presents—but a lot more frequent.

2. Begin well ahead of time. If you want her to be ready to make love that night, call her at lunchtime and tell her you can't wait to see her. Have flowers delivered. Send an E-mail love letter or recite a romantic poem on her phone machine.

3. Plan romantic adventures. Let her interests guide your choice of activities. If she likes art, take her to an exhibit. If she enjoys walking, take a moonlight stroll to an unexplored area. If she loves good food, try a restaurant she's always wanted to go to.

4. Start from the top. Remember, yin moves downward. Stimulate her mind with romantic fantasy. Satisfy her intellect that you're sincere and trustworthy. Excite her heart by letting her know how you

feel about her. Making her feel happy and secure will lead to a gushing of the yin fountain.

5. Use words. Find novel ways to let her know you appreciate who she is and what she brings to your life.

6. Take your time. Women don't like to feel that sex is demanded or expected of them before they're ready. If you make your move too quickly, her yin–oriented body may not be able to keep pace.

7. Make her wait. Don't come on to her when she expects you to. Tension and curiosity create a delicious yearning. For variety, start out strong and then pull back. Make her wonder if you'll ever get back to business.

8. Give her gifts that she wants to receive, not things that you want her to have.

9. Be her hero. Ask yourself what you can bring to her life that would make her feel safe, protected and enchanted. What is she missing that a romantic prince could bring to her? If you don't feel particularly heroic, act as if you were. At the very least, be gallant. Is chivalry dead in your romance? Resurrect it!

10. Show appreciation. Pay attention to details—the effort she makes to look good or improve her parenting skills, her acts of kindness and consideration, the ways she makes your life more comfortable or interesting. But don't just shower her with compliments when you want to get her into bed. She'll see through that in a second. Praise her when it's clear that you have no immediate agenda.

11. Use humor. Laughter inspires comfort and dissipates fear—and fear inhibits sexuality.

12. Do some research. Glance through romantic novels and women's magazines, and watch movies that are popular with women—or at least with your partner and her friends. See how the male characters get women into bed.

13. Ask her how she likes to be seduced. Women are complex and often hard to figure out. Sometimes a direct question works best.

HOW TO SEDUCE A MAN

1. Get right to the point. Remember, with men you start low and work your way up. Stimulate his sexuality and yang will rise up to enliven his heart and mind.

2. Show your sexual interest when you are out in the world together. You don't have to have sex between cocktails and entrees, but if you let him know you're thinking of it he will not only be delighted, he will start to plan ways to satisfy you when you get home.

3. Surprise him with sexual overtures. Put your hand on his thigh or rub against him when he least expects it—especially when it's slightly naughty, like standing on line or at a business dinner. Here's one that drives some men wild: When you're out together, especially in a crowded place, whisper in his ear, "I'm not wearing panties."

If a more blatant surprise is appropriate, initiate sex at an unusual time: book a hotel for your lunch break; stop by his office, close the door and slowly strip; steal off to the bedroom for a quickie while the kids do their homework. Even if you've been planning the attack for days, it will seem excitingly spontaneous to him.

4. Don't automatically reject his advances. "Just say no" may work for drugs, but not for love. If he comes on to you at the wrong time, rather than respond with annoyance or criticism, remember how yin behaves in the propagation model: transform the situation into something you want. For example, tell him you're thrilled that he wants you, and if he'll just wait till you make that important business call and put the kids to bed, you'll meet him in front of the fireplace in the negligee he gave you for Valentine's Day.

5. Create rituals. Seduction doesn't always have to be new or surprising. There is something wonderful about the quiet gestures that couples develop over the years that tell each other "I want you" or "Now's the time." This private, familiar form of seduction is a yin process; when used with clever timing, it can create a yang explosion of erotic love.

6. Remember that men too enjoy being seduced. Their yin likes the lengthy, titillating process that women tend to favor.

YIN AND YANG
IN THE BEDROOM

Sex that is consistent with the principles of yin and yang is more enjoyable, meaningful, longer lasting, and health giving. "Yin and yang stimulate and respond to each other," the Yellow Emperor's teacher told him. "Yang without yin is joyless, and yin without yang is unexcited."

The ideal pattern of sexual interaction, as exemplified in the propagation model, goes like this: Regardless of who initiates the sex act (a yang function), the man gives generously, with true altruism; the woman openly receives him and transforms his contribution into the process of mutual lovemaking. If she is not receptive, nothing happens; but if she responds to him with enthusiasm, she fans the sexual flame and makes the experience more fulfilling for both. Once the woman gives the man her response, he receives it, processes it internally and gives back to her with even greater energy and creativity. This give-and-receive continues until they are both thoroughly nourished and satisfied.

Ideally, each partner should be comfortable in both yin and yang roles. However, it is absolutely crucial that they be skilled in the qualities of their primary trait. A man who is comfortable with his yang nature takes the time to learn what his woman needs and gives it to her graciously. If she needs an orgasm, he finds creative ways to satisfy her. If she needs cuddling, tenderness, or to hear "I love you" whispered in her ear, he gives her that. Remember, yin always gives back once it has received. When a woman feels she has been properly given to, she is inspired to give copiously in return.

A man may appear to be yanglike, but if what he initiates is self-oriented, he is not really being true to his primary trait. Suppose he comes home feeling horny after a difficult day, drags his wife to bed and pounds away as if sex were a race to the finish line. Yes, he's being aggressive and he's definitely attempting to create something, both of which are yang traits, but he's giving what *he* wants, not what his woman needs or can work with. She may have been in the mood for love. She may have yearned for him all day. But now she's turned off by his brute force and her body does not respond. Even if he succeeds in bringing her to orgasm, the overall experience will not meet her deeper yin needs. Instead of feeling closer to him, she will more likely feel frustrated and underappreciated.

If she's approached this way often enough, a woman will lose interest in sex because it has become emotionally unsafe and unsatisfying. The man will then feel that his woman is not giving him what he wants. In truth, the problem is not that she can't give; it's that she can't receive and work with what *he's* giving *her.*

A woman who is in touch with her yin nature is willing to explore her needs and help her partner fulfill them. On the surface, her receptivity may appear to be submissive, as if she were giving away her power by surrendering sexually to her man. But it is through the process of opening up and letting go that a woman fulfills her yin nature. The transformative power of yin can turn a sexual mouse into a real man: there is no greater aphrodisiac for a man than to feel he is desired by his woman. Knowing he has affected her strongly motivates him further, giving rise to inspired lovemaking.

If a woman is not true to her yin nature, she will not be genuinely receptive in bed but will merely go through the motions to get her man to stop hassling her. Alternatively, she might become extremely aggressive sexually, and, like many men, create brief, orgasm-driven sexual encounters. On the surface, this would seem to be a turn-on for a man. But, if it is taken too far or goes on too long, it can prevent him from acting in accord with his masculinity, since he has no one who can properly receive him.

It is important to recognize that yin is receptive, not passive. It doesn't just show up and let things happen, remaining disengaged. On the contrary, it is involved. It influences what it comes in contact with and is in turn affected by what it experiences. The Victorian woman who advised wives to lie back, close their eyes and think of England was not expressing a true yinlike attitude.

THE DO'S AND DO NOT'S
OF SUPERIOR SEX

Here are some basic—and enormously effective—do's and don'ts, based on yin and yang principles. If you apply them to your sex life, you will find yourselves growing in passion, love, health and vitality.

The Do's for Women

1. Do learn to respect what you are truly ready for. Pay attention to the pace at which your body responds to stimulation. If you are not aroused enough for sexual activity, let your partner know you need more time. Pushing your body to feel intensely before it is able is neither effective nor healthy.

2. Do bear in mind that you need to feel emotionally safe when beginning the sex act. True receptivity requires trust. While developing trust for your man is a joint project, it's primarily your responsibility.

3. Do help your man make sex work well for you. Enter the sex act knowing that he has to be educated about your needs.

4. Do let him fix what bothers you about your sex life. Yang loves to fix things. Give your man feedback so he knows how to give to you more effectively. If you have to express a negative, try to sandwich it between two positives: "I love it when you . . ." then "I wish you wouldn't . . ." then "I respond best when . . ."

5. Do participate fully in the level of sexual expression you can enjoy at any given moment.

6. Do occasionally take on the yang (assertive and explorative) role. Trading roles and responsibilities with your man will help you empathize with him, and it makes for very exciting sex.

7. Do let him know what you like about his sexuality and how he shares it with you. For example, tell him, "I love watching your arm muscles flex when you hold yourself over me."

8. Do let him know when you want to make love, even if he's busy with other things. There is no greater turn-on for a man than knowing his woman wants him.

9. Do remember that receptivity is more powerful than refusal. Appreciate that it is yang's role to stretch into new sexual territory. If what he initiates is uncomfortable for you, try to take it in and change it instead of flat-out rejecting it. This gives you more options and avoids hurting his feelings.

10. Do take responsibility for your own orgasm. Tell or show him what you need, or do it yourself. This takes the burden off your partner and helps you feel more in control of your experience.

11. Do confront him if he is avoiding intimacy by avoiding sex, or vice versa.

The Do Not's for Women

1. Do not let your man enter you when you don't want him to. According to traditional Chinese medicine, when your body responds and your psyche rejects, the push-pull can create a variety of gynecological problems in the long term.

2. Do not condemn or criticize him if he tries something new and doesn't get it right the first time—or even the second and third times. It is, in part, his job to expand your sex life and your job to let him know what works and what doesn't.

3. Do not service your man when your mind is elsewhere. You both deserve more respect, and this type of behavior will weaken your overall desire for sex. If your interest level allows you to participate only part way, find creative ways to help him achieve satisfaction. This can entail anything from stimulating him with other parts of your body besides your vagina to whispering in his ear while he masturbates. Direct communication and flexibility are very important.

4. Do not rush to orgasm. Rushing to orgasm is a yang trait. Being truly receptive means allowing things to happen, not forcing them.

5. Do not belittle the sex act by making it only his stress-relief valve. If your man wants to have sex as a way to reduce tension, transform what he initiates into a relaxing and intimate adventure. Use the raw ingredients he gives you to create a more meaningful experience.

6. Do not use fear or anger as a reason to avoid sex for an extended period of time. If you have such feelings, find a way to communicate them to your lover. Your power lies in being honest and sexual, not in avoiding issues and withholding sex.

The Do's for Men

1. Do respect your sexuality. Create time in your week that supports a good, active sex life. Restricting it to late at night when you or your partner is tired is not the best approach.

2. Do increase your sexual artistry, no matter how skilled you already are. Like a business, a lover must continue to grow and innovate to be successful.

3. Do begin making love with words and gestures long before you do so with your body. Her feminine nature will be more aroused and responsive when the time comes.

4. Do listen to what she has to say about your sex life. Help her communicate in a manner you can work with, so you feel inspired, not criticized.

5. Do occasionally allow yourself to take on the receptive role. Trading responsibilities with your partner will help you empathize with the position she is usually in. You might be pleasantly surprised by what happens.

6. Do take your time with her. Her body is designed to respond more slowly than yours. Allow her to open up at her own pace.

7. Do tell her what you appreciate about her sexuality, her looks, her actions in bed, her efforts to improve other aspects of your life together, etc.

8. Do approach the subject directly if you feel your partner is avoiding sex to avoid intimacy, or vice versa.

9. Do let her know if you are hurting as a result of anything she did or did not do regarding sex. Let her comfort and nurture you. Keeping secrets can sabotage sex.

10. Do give her what she wants, not what you think she should want. If she states, or implies, that she enjoys a particular activity, believe her.

11. Do be creative. Very creative. Surprise her in bed as often as you can dream up something new and different.

12. Do let her know what you want sexually. If she doesn't know how to satisfy you, show her. If she doesn't feel comfortable doing it, suggest baby-step alternatives; eventually, she may be ready for more.

13. Do behave like the man she first fell in love with. The skills you used when you first romanced and seduced her will still serve you well.

The Do Not's for Men

1. Do not make it difficult for your partner to tell you what she needs. She is training you to become a master at the art of loving her. Imagine how wonderful it will be to see her glowing more often, thanks to your willingness to learn.

2. Do not insist on all or nothing. If you think of fulfilling sex only as intercourse and orgasm, you limit your creative options and her ability to participate.

3. Do not have sex without paying close attention to how your partner is responding.

4. Do not have sex with your body while your mind is someplace else. Go into the experience honestly, and tell your woman how far you can go at that time. Let *her* take responsibility for her own sexual needs if you feel unable to do so.

5. Do not make love when you are exhausted, even if you feel a strong urge to do so. Feeling desirous when you are very tired is often a sign that you have used up your sexual strength getting through the day. Enjoy cuddling or "making out" with your lover, or just going to sleep.

6. Do not let work or other duties take all your attention away from your romantic life.

7. Do not have sex with a woman who doesn't really want it. Instead, find out how involved she can comfortably be and take it from there.

8. Do not put her in charge of your sex life. Switching roles is terrific, but on an ongoing basis it runs counter to the natural tendencies of yin and yang. She should not *always* be the one who initiates sex, or *always* be the one who directs the lovemaking activities. If she insists on having that much control, a serious discussion is warranted.

A SELF-NOURISHING
EXERCISE

As a first step toward strengthening your primary energetic aspect, you might take one to three minutes at least once a day to do the following exercise. It creates an opportunity to focus on the duality of yin and yang, and to make you more aware of your primary nature.

Find a picture of someone of the opposite sex whom you find attractive. It can be someone you know intimately or a perfect stranger, as long as it's someone you enjoy looking at and who embodies the qualities you appreciate most about the opposite sex. The person can be fully clothed or partially or completely nude. The exercise is not meant to arouse you sexually but to stimulate the deepest aspects of your sexual identity.

Choose a time when you won't be distracted. Let your eyes roam slowly over the entire picture. Luxuriate in the qualities of the opposite sex, the sparkle in the eye, the contours, colors and texture of the skin. Appreciate the differences between that gender and your own.

Breathe deeply and relax. Allow yourself to feel as if the person in the photograph is giving you exactly what you need to feel nourished and fulfilled, comfortable and warm.

Feel free to change the photo if the one you have chosen does not seem right after a time.

Although this might seem like a very simple exercise, it has been used with wonderful results by hundreds of my patients, many of whom suffered from chronic illness or sexual dysfunction. Absorbing strength from the opposite sex, even from a picture, is healing to all aspects of one's being.

THE TEN-MINUTE TRYST

Here's an exercise that works wonders. Take the first ten minutes of every day to be sexual together. As we will see in the next chapter, sexuality rules the heart, not the other way around, so beginning your morning with sexual stimulation can make you more openhearted the rest of the day. During the ten minutes, hold each other closely and focus your attention on how grateful you are to share erotic love.

I don't recommend hot, fast, orgasm-oriented sex unless both of you want that. The purpose is for both partners to enjoy ten minutes of sexual closeness before your responsibilities pull you apart. The man may be stimulated enough to have an erection, and the woman aroused enough to secrete moisture, but intercourse is optional. If you *do* have intercourse, move as much as is necessary to keep him inside, but not enough to trigger orgasm for either of you. Stimulating your sexuality without orgasm will give you greater strength—and keep the yearning for each other alive throughout the day.

Chapter 3

WIND BLOWS THE
TEMPLE DOOR AJAR
Energy, Attraction and Desire

*Whenever we try to pick out anything by itself, we find
it hitched to everything else in the universe.*

—JOHN MUIR

Have you ever wondered why your sex drive varies from one time to another? Why sometimes you're a hot-blooded animal in bed and at others you're more like a cold fish? Have you noticed that when you're physically ill or mentally troubled, or have just consumed a big meal, no matter how romantic the setting, sex seems about as exciting as raking the yard? Have you ever been alarmed to discover that, despite amorous intentions, you might as well be made of cardboard instead of flesh and blood—while the day before, in the same place with the same person, you performed like a dynamo? Well, according to traditional Chinese medicine, what makes the difference is the condition of *chi*—or, more precisely, sexual chi—in your body.

Chi is vitality itself, the stuff that differentiates a living being from a corpse. It is a synonym for life force. The more chi, the more life. The underlying power that allows life to express itself, chi is the medium through which growth and change occur. When condensed, chi forms matter; when dispersed, it creates energy.

Chi maintains the structural and functional integrity of the body. When our chi is weak, we are unable to accomplish tasks that require physical strength, as the stamina to do so is absent. Chi also drives the mind and emotions. It is the power behind creativity and intelligence, the exuberant energy behind our joy, the fortitude that allows us to feel

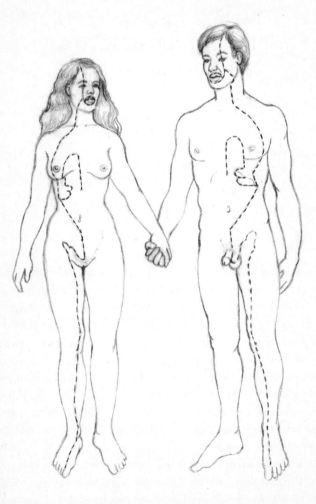

Channels, or meridians, through which chi (energy) passes

and cope with pain. Taking a number of different forms, chi flows constantly through our bodies, creating brain waves, causing the heart to beat, stimulating the nervous system, driving cell metabolism, generating thought and feeling, protecting us from harm, maintaining our sexual and reproductive systems. Rather than running through vessels that can be located anatomically the way that blood flows through veins and arteries, chi travels through meridians, or channels, which cannot be viewed with a microscope or an X ray. Western scientists are just beginning to identify what meridians are; so far, they have determined that they are, at least in part, pathways of electromagnetic energy.

When doctors of Chinese medicine diagnose patients, we assess how abundant chi is, its quality and how well it moves throughout the body. The overall picture is what I call an Energetic Profile, essentially a map of who the person is, based on the condition of his or her chi.

To a doctor of Chinese medicine, physical, mental, emotional and sexual symptoms are different expressions of one's underlying chi condition. For instance, when the chi governing our digestive system is strong, food moves into the body, gets broken down and is properly assimilated—as are the intellectual information we take in and the emotions we experience. But when digestive chi is weak or blocked, disease accumulates, just as bacteria and algae grow in streams where the water stagnates. We end up with indigestion, constipation or some other gastrointestinal problem. We might also get stuck in obsessive thought patterns or overwhelmed by feelings we can't digest.

THE CHI OF SEX

Sexual chi, or sexual energy, is concentrated in the kidneys and pelvic region. It is the fuel that powers the sex drive, the messenger that convinces us to abandon ourselves to erotic expression, the power that makes erections rise and vaginas wet. Healthy desire results from the smooth flow of chi through the meridian system and in particular the liver meridian, which runs through the genitals. When we are moved to share ourselves with another person, the body feels an initial erotic impulse. It draws on its reservoir of sexual chi and summons additional chi from other areas to the pelvis to assist in the process of making love.

Your body meets its daily needs by converting one form of chi to another when necessary. If it has to digest food, defend itself from illness or handle a challenging emotional situation, the body will mobilize chi for those purposes, leaving less for sex. That's why "I have a headache" can be a valid excuse for a low libido: headaches are a sign of too much chi in the head area, and that can leave too little in the genitals. If you push yourself too far, your body will be forced to draw on its storehouse of sexual chi. Do that too often and your sex drive will peter out. I advise my patients to live at the middle of their ropes, not the end, because burnout burns up sexual chi.

Sexual chi is weakened or strengthened every day of our lives by the lifestyle we lead. If you treat your body well and share emotional nourishment and good communication with your beloved, your sexual chi is more likely to be plentiful and strong. Thus it will flow properly through your system and your body will respond with vigor. If, on the other hand, you weaken your chi through unhealthy habits or inappropriate sexual behavior, the result can be sexual weakness or dysfunction.

If your sexual chi is abundant and moving through the system as nature intended, you can bet that your sexual urges will be in the service of health and happiness. However, when chi is weak or its flow is blocked by physical illness or energetic imbalance, you might misread sexual signals, just as you might misinterpret signals that urge you to stuff yourself with food when, in fact, your body doesn't need food at all but rather exercise, or sleep, or a sense of security. In short, what feels like sexual desire may be the body's way of saying something else, that it needs emotional intimacy, for example. Or, that it needs to move: when chi stagnates in the meridian that transports it to the genitals, the body needs movement to get the chi unstuck, but the urge to move can feel like a craving for sex.

Sometimes, what feels like lust is actually the body's way of telling you *not* to have sex. It's letting you know that your sexual chi has been depleted and you need to replenish it. The body needs to refill its tank, so to speak, but the signal it uses to call attention to the pelvic area can feel the same as "Have sex now!" For that reason, Chinese medicine advises not to have intercourse late at night when you're exhausted, as it can further drain the sexual chi you've been drawing on all day. The recommendation would be to go to sleep or make love without orgasm, a chi-strengthening concept that will be discussed in detail later in the book.

You can see that healthy chi is essential for a healthy sex life. But it's important to realize that the interaction moves in the opposite direction as well: healthy sex produces healthy chi. If you learn to master superior sex with the techniques and practices in this book, your storehouse of sexual chi will increase, making more of it available for healing and disease prevention as well as helping you to have abundant, high-quality sex throughout life. If, on the other hand, you engage in practices that deplete sexual chi, your physical and emotional well-being will suffer, and your desire and capacity for sex will diminish as you age. We tend to regard that decline as "normal." It is *not,* and it can be prevented by applying the chi-enhancing wisdom you'll find in this book.

THE MYSTERY
OF ATTRACTION

According to Chinese medicine, two people making love are sharing more than pleasure and more than emotional intimacy. They're sharing chi. She absorbs some of his predominately yang chi, and he takes in some of her predominately yin chi. This exchange of vital energy is considered the principal purpose of sex and the basis for its life-enhancing benefits. The chi exchange occurs in all sexual encounters. However, poorly matched couples and those whose sexual behavior lacks awareness and artistry, may end up depleting each other. Making love in accord with the principles in this book actually *generates* chi, adding to each partner's stock and energizing their systems. This is the basic dynamic that makes superior sex health-enriching to body and soul. On some deep, unconscious level, men and women know about the exchange of chi; it accounts for some of our mating behavior.

Did you ever ask yourself, "What does he see in her?" Have you noticed that some people tend to be attracted to the same type of lover over and over—even when each affair ends in disaster and they vow never to make the same mistake again? Have you wondered why the type of person who got your juices flowing at one time in your life now leaves you cold? Or vice versa? We tend to see the quirks of sexual attraction in terms of needs, neuroses, nurture and other psychological factors. Such explanations may be perfectly valid, but traditional Chinese medicine offers an additional angle: Whom we're attracted to—as well as whom we attract to us—is determined in large part by our Energetic Profile, the sum of the quality, quantity and movement of chi.

You see an attractive stranger at a party or on the street. Unbeknownst to either of you, subtle forms of communication pass between you. In an effort to direct you toward a mate who will heal and nourish you through the exchange of chi, your body voices its opinion about the candidate's Energetic Profile. If you're healthy and balanced—meaning you have an abundance of high-quality chi, effectively distributed—those signals will point you toward a beneficial liaison. If not . . . well, as you've no doubt noticed, sexual attraction does not necessarily mean that Prince or Princess Charming is good for you.

We are basically attracted to two kinds of people: our energetic opposites and our energetic mirrors. Either type of relationship can be heaven; either one can be hell. It depends on two things: how extreme the energetic imbalance is and how well the individuals adapt to their new situation as lovers.

How Opposites Attract

Someone with a deficiency of chi in one part of the body may be drawn to someone with plentiful chi in the same area, or even an *excess* of it, as a way to create wholeness. For example, a man whose job requires a lot of brain work may have a lot of chi concentrated in his head. He is likely to be attracted to—and *attractive* to—an athletic woman with abundant chi in her musculature. Or, he might lust after trophy girls whose heads are as empty as his is full.

Like everything else in the universe, chi consists of yin and yang qualities. Someone whose chi is deficient in either yin or yang might be attracted to someone with an excess of that quality. Shelley was a highly ambitious executive with strong masculine traits—determination, quick thinking, creativity, extroversion. She had burned up her yin chi as fuel for the yang that drove the engine of her success. So great was the imbalance that she developed chronic fatigue and debilitating respiratory infections.

Whom did Shelley attract on her climb to the top? Her energetic opposites, men whose lives were excessively governed by yin. Quiet, gentle and domestic, they offered her the qualities she had suppressed in herself because she viewed them as impediments. In every relationship, Shelley was the driving force while her men were the nurturers. They massaged and cuddled her at the end of the day, listened to her war stories and made sure she ate a decent meal. She needed this because her yin chi was so depleted she could not nurture herself.

Things might have worked out fine if one of Shelley's men had adopted some of her abundant yang behaviors and she had taken on some of his yin traits. The attraction of opposites is healthy for both parties when they respect each other's qualities and bolster their own weaknesses by adopting each other's strengths. This generates balance from within, which is healthier and more harmonious than becoming overly dependent on each other.

Shelley could not make the energetic role reversal work. Sexually aggressive, she criticized her lovers for not being strong or dynamic enough in bed, not to mention the rest of their lives. They would feel unappreciated, demeaned and beaten up emotionally, but it was always Shelley who initiated the breakup once she lost interest in—and respect for—her men. The one exception was a man who was balanced enough to be nurturing without sacrificing his yang assertiveness. He left Shelley, in large part because he felt drained by her. Because she drew on her sexual chi to support her hard-driving workdays, she had very little left at night. Her sexual voraciousness was her body's way of refilling its tank, so to speak, by siphoning off chi from her lover. The problem was, she had little chi to give back. When that happens, the partner whose chi is being drained comes to feel ripped off. He or she starts to pull away from sex, usually without knowing why.

Like Attracts Like

On an episode of *Seinfeld,* Jerry falls for a woman who's extremely similar to him. He exclaims euphorically, "Now I know what I've been looking for all these years: myself! I've been waiting for *me* to come along, and now I've swept myself off my feet!"

When we are drawn to those who mirror aspects of our own Energetic Profiles, the body is using sexual attraction to draw attention to its own chi patterns. Mirror attractions usually start out comfy and cozy, with a touch of wonder thrown in as the smitten ones discover the many things they have in common. If the relationship is to continue working, however, the couple must have enough differences to fill in the weak spots in their Energetic Profiles. Differences allow you to support each other when your respective weak spots are challenged. They also make life more interesting; differences are the spices that keep safety, comfort and understanding from tasting bland.

A mirror attraction will peter out quickly if the energetic weaknesses are extreme, creating a unit that magnifies the couple's strengths and weaknesses without any balancing qualities. If neither party adds anything new to the equation, one or both will start to feel bored, irritated, frustrated or incomplete. By the end of the show Seinfeld is engaged but having second thoughts. "I can't be with someone like me," he laments. "I hate myself."

THE ORGANS OF PASSION

When I work with couples, I often describe some of the ways they typically interact, based solely on my assessment of their Energetic Profiles. This seems miraculous to many of them: How could I possibly know how they behave with each other in the privacy of their homes? It's because behavior patterns and personality traits are revealed by the condition of chi in the body, and specifically in the internal organs.

Traditional Chinese medicine is similar to Western physiology in that the organs work together as a team. There are, however, major differences between the two systems, not only in what the organs do but also in what they actually are.

In traditional Chinese medicine an internal organ is defined as a set of functions, not as a material object with a specific location in the body. The term *kidney,* for example, does not refer simply to the twin organs in the lower back, but to a functional unit that also includes what we normally think of as the adrenal glands and the reproductive system. A healthy organ carries out its responsibilities smoothly and effectively; organ weakness results in illness and disease. And the duties of each organ system are not limited to the physical; rather, they extend to mental and emotional traits. It is through the functioning of the organs that the mind-body connection is forged.

Each organ is responsible for regulating a particular psychological quality, ranging from the negative extreme to the positive. The liver, for example, regulates warmth and kindness as well as anger. Emotional health in traditional Chinese medicine consists of the ability to go into and out of each emotion appropriately, according to the reality of one's circumstances. Organ weakness can produce either an inability to feel a certain emotion or a tendency to feel it too strongly or too often.

Through a freeway-like network of meridians, chi moves to each organ, providing the power that enables it to do its job—and *from* each organ chi moves to spread the effects of its labor in the service of maintaining our health, strength, emotional and mental capacity and sexual vigor. In turn, what we eat, how we think and process feelings and the way we make love can strengthen or weaken individual organs. Let's begin our survey of the organ system with a closer look at the kidneys.

The Sexual Organ

The kidney is responsible for all sexual and reproductive functions. The producer and distributor of sexual chi, it determines the foundational strength of our sex drive and our capacity to act on it.

Positive kidney qualities include calmness, wisdom and inner contentment, which explains why sex can make us feel peaceful and serene. The negative emotion associated with the kidney is fear. That's why sex, one of the most pleasurable and natural functions on earth, can make us so afraid—of failure, of pain, of looking ugly, of losing control and so forth.

The kidneys are also in charge of gender identity: when the kidneys function well, we are more likely to feel good about ourselves as women or men; when they are weak, we may feel that we don't measure up to standards of femininity or masculinity. Just ask a woman who is battling infertility (which is often a symptom of kidney weakness) how she feels about herself as a woman. Or ask a man who is struggling with erection problems, another kidney symptom, how he feels about himself as a man.

The kidneys are also responsible for the integrity of the brain and central nervous system. This has profound sexual implications in an age when people spend excessive amounts of time in cerebral activity. Have you ever noticed that mental stress saps your interest in lovemaking—and that no one says anything particularly smart when they're in the throes of lovemaking ("Oh God!" may be revealing, but it's not especially brilliant)? Mental energy and sexual energy come from the same pot: the kidney organ. When the brain withdraws too much of that energy, there's not much left over for the genitals. That's why long-term couples whose sex lives have sagged can become like honeymooners again when they vacation together. It's not just that they're well rested, although that's certainly important; it's that their minds are free of the constant demands of everyday life, which leaves them with more energy for sex.

Here are some of the attributes of the kidney organ and the four other principal organs—heart, liver, lung and spleen:

KIDNEYS

- Faith, wisdom, inner contentment
- Fear, terror
- Govern our sex drive, sexual stamina and reproductive ability
- Maintain the structure of the brain and nervous system
- Determine strength of memory

HEART

- Joy, happiness, loving inspiration
- Anxiety, hysteria, insanity

- Responsible for our personal identity
- Determines our view of reality
- Controls the blood vessels and the movement of blood through them
- Regulates the quality of sleep

LIVER

- Personal warmth, kindness
- Anger, rage
- Responsible for the smooth movement of chi throughout the body
- Regulates the intensity and flow of emotions
- Decision maker, differentiating the useful from the nonuseful, both chemically and emotionally
- Cleans the blood
- Regulates the menstrual cycle
- Responsible for flexibility of muscles, tendons and ligaments

SPLEEN

- Concentration, empathy
- Worry, obsession, lack of focus
- Metabolizes information so we can understand and cope with life's circumstances
- Transforms food into usable chi for nourishing the body
- Determines the strength of the digestive system

LUNGS

- Perseverance
- Sadness
- Responsible for bonding and attachment with other people
- Extract chi from the air so we can use it
- Govern the movement of fluids in the body

The Cycles of Being

The five organ systems influence one another through specific systems of interaction. The Shen Cycle, or Nourishing Cycle, describes how the organs support each other through a system of energy transference. It is portrayed as a circle of relationships, with the clockwise arrows pointing from the "mother" organ to the "child" organ. When the child organ is weak, the mother organ comes to the rescue with a wholesome serving of chi.

Obviously, each organ is both mother and child:

- The heart is mother to the spleen.
- The spleen is mother to the lungs.
- The lungs are mother to the kidneys.
- The kidneys are mother to the liver.
- The liver is mother to the heart.

The Ko Cycle, or Discipline Cycle, explains how the organs control and regulate each other through a system of checks and balances. If, for

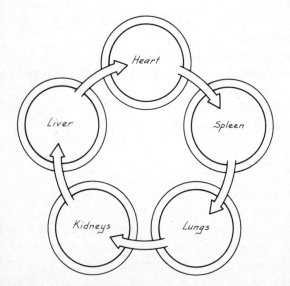

The Nourishing, or Shen, Cycle

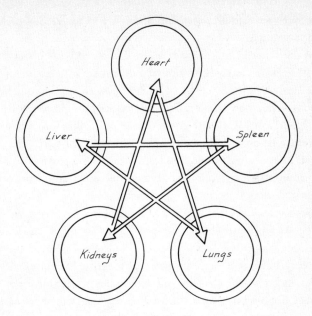

The Discipline, or Ko, Cycle

example, an organ is overstimulated, another steps in to calm it down. The cycle is depicted in the shape of a star, with arrows pointing from the controlling organ to its dependent organ.

Again, each organ serves in both capacities:

- The heart controls the lungs.
- The lungs control the liver.
- The liver controls the spleen.
- The spleen controls the kidneys.
- The kidney controls the heart.

The Organ of Perspective

In the Discipline Cycle, the kidney—the governor of our sexuality—controls the heart, the seat of the spirit and the organ that generates loving inspiration, joy and happiness. The interaction between the two explains why sex can lift our spirits and make us joyful. Sex makes the heart grow fonder.

On the other hand, the heart is also associated with anxiety. When the heart organ is weak, sexual arousal, or the mere anticipation of it, can make us feel anxious. Even the sweet afterglow of sex can quickly fade into anxiety. In a new relationship, the anxious thought might be "Will he call again?" or "Was I any good?" or "Am I falling into a trap?" In a long-term relationship, thoughts like "Was she faking it?" and "How long will I have to wait to do this again?" can crop up. Anxious feelings can be appropriate, of course; it's when they don't conform to reality that they reflect an imbalance in the heart organ.

The heart-kidney connection also explains why, when we've had good sex, we feel better about who we are. Our sex appeal and sexual capacity loom large in what we think of ourselves because the heart, which determines our sense of personal identity, is controlled by the kidney, which governs sexuality and determines gender identity.

A key responsibility of the heart is to maintain our sense of reality. When the organ is strong we tend to have common sense and a grounded, authentic view of the world. When it's weak or out of balance, we become prey to delusion. Hence, wild, jealous imagining can result from the kidney–heart dynamic. When one partner feels disconnected sexually, the other becomes anxious (the negative heart quality). Fear (a kidney quality) invades the mind: Is she really visiting her friend? Is he fooling around with that gorgeous new secretary?

The same system also produces romantic fantasies—erotic thoughts about an acquaintance or stranger, or reveries about some idealized lover. When the heart is out of balance the grass looks greener on the other side, no matter how green it actually is on your side.

The attributes of the heart and kidney organs also explain what appears to be a miracle. You're feeling pessimistic, the world seems rotten and foreboding. Then your sweetheart seduces you into making love, or you meet someone new and the promise of sexual bliss fills the air. Suddenly, your sense of reality flip-flops. The world becomes rosy. Your problems seem petty. You figure things will probably turn out fine after all. What happened is this: The sexual energy of the kidney was stimulated, and the kidney influenced the heart to change its perception of reality. This is how sex turns mountains into molehills.

That reality shift also explains why everything changes when sex is introduced to a relationship, because chi from the kidney affects the heart and alters our reality. A new lover might look like the sexiest movie star in Hollywood. He or she is more wonderful than everyone who came before and is beyond a doubt *right* for us. Even the pleasure-loving Chinese sages advised against having sex too soon with a new romantic interest. You lose perspective when sex is added to the chemical mix. (The exception to that rule, interestingly enough, would be a casual one-nighter in which both parties understand the purpose of the encounter and have no other agenda.)

The Emotional Organ

A warm, friendly woman who turns out to be hostile underneath. A nice guy who suddenly becomes abusive. What do they have in common? A liver chi imbalance. The liver is responsible for regulating movement in the body, including the flow of chi and all the emotions. It processes thoughts and feelings the same way it breaks down molecules into usable parts, separating what is needed from what can be discarded. In conjunction with its partner organ, the gall bladder, the liver acts as a decision maker. It distinguishes between the useful and the not-useful, the appropriate and the inappropriate. In addition, the liver is associated with warmth and kindness on the positive end of the emotional spectrum, and anger and hostility on the negative.

I'm sure you've noticed that when you're under a lot of stress or have experienced a psychological trauma, you don't feel very sexy. When you're forced to cope with more emotional input than you can comfortably handle, the liver gets overworked. Its mother organ, the kidney, comes to the rescue. And you know what happens to mothers who have to tend a sick child day and night: they get fatigued. So does the kidney organ when the liver needs an inordinate amount of support. The chi that the kidney would normally use to fuel the sex drive is used for coping. End result: a sex drive stuck in neutral.

By the same token, beautiful lovemaking can calm the liver and pacify negative feelings, turning anger into warmth. This is why many couples like to get passionate after a fight. The liver is also responsible for the flow of chi in the liver meridian, which delivers chi to the genitals, thereby freeing the person for even deeper emotional and sexual experiences.

A healthy, balanced liver not only moves chi efficiently through the genitals; it exerts a soothing influence on the heart, its child organ in the Nourishing Cycle. Individuals with healthy livers tend to have a more realistic perception of reality because their feelings are appropriate to their circumstances; those with inadequate liver function tend to have an overly dramatic sense of reality, often experiencing emotions in roller-coaster extremes.

The Discriminating Organ

Have you ever given your love to someone only to learn that he or she was unworthy? In your pain you realized that the signals were there all along; you just didn't see them. Perhaps you've had the opposite experience as well: failing to appreciate your lover or not recognizing signs of interest from a desirable stranger until he or she gave up on you. We are slow to catch on when the spleen doesn't do its job properly.

The spleen is responsible for digestion. Its function is to take in and metabolize material from the outside world—not only food and fluid, but perceptions and emotions as well. It determines how we think about and work with the information that comes to us. If the spleen's chi is strong, we digest food well and focus and think clearly. If it is weak, we can't digest food or information and do not concentrate well. We either lose discernment as the mind becomes disjointed, or we become overly intellectual, even obsessive in our thoughts.

In the Discipline Cycle, the spleen controls the kidneys. It regulates how much energy moves into the kidney system so we can act on a sexual impulse. You know how they say of certain men, "He thinks with his small head, not his big head"? Have you met women who keep falling for sexy heartbreakers even though their friends warn them to stay away? These people have spleens too weak to manage information and exert proper control of their kidneys, so they make the same sexual mistakes over and over.

When the spleen does not properly digest the romantic information that comes in, it sends foolish signals to the kidneys. Instead of sexual desire, you might feel disinterested, turned off or incapable of responding to someone who is a good match for you. This is analogous to what happens when you eat too much junk food. The spleen can't metabolize any more food, so delectable aromas from nutritious meals seem unpleasant and the sight of such a meal makes you nauseous. If the spleen is exhausted, it won't even let new data into the brain—including love or sexual overtures from another person. Unable to cope with new information, we simply write the person off or fail even to notice him or her. Greta Garbo's famous statement, "I want to be alone," was a typical expression of an overwhelmed spleen.

The spleen's job is made easier when the heart, its mother organ in the Nourishing Cycle, provides it with a solid sense of identity and a realistic view of the world. When the heart is *not* functioning well, it communicates a faulty perspective, warping the information the spleen takes in.

My patient Lee saw love where it didn't exist. She fell for and married a violent man. When her husband cheated on her or got drunk and beat her, Lee thought, "He really needs me and I've failed him," or, "I'm not giving him what he wants, so he has to get drunk or satisfy himself with other women." It took a lot of treatment, but we eventually got her heart and spleen healthy enough for Lee to realize that her life was on the line and she had better start working with a therapist and get out of the marriage.

Just as spleen weakness can make it hard to recognize that you are being treated badly, it can also keep you from feeling love. Many of my patients who are unhappy in their marriages actually have spouses who adore them. But their spleens can't metabolize what is being offered to them, so they appear unappreciative. As they become healthier energetically, they grow in their capacity to take in love.

The Persevering Organ

When the going gets rough it's the lungs that keep us going, just as, physically, they take in extra oxygen when we need to persevere in the face of physical challenges. Healthy lungs provide the strength we need to be vulnerable and the ability to press ahead in all aspects of life and relationships. They are the bonding organs. Strong lungs are helpful if a couple is to stay together through the ups and downs of life.

When we suffer a loss, the lungs enable us to feel the sadness and grief—and also give us the will to carry on. Like the proverbial chicken and egg, sadness can create a lung disorder, and a lung disorder can cause sadness. Patients who come to me with chronic respiratory ailments frequently have a deep core of sadness inside, often exacerbated by intense feelings of loneliness. In fact, psychologists often call asthma the separation disease because it crops up so often among the newly divorced.

The health of the lungs affects us sexually because they are the mother organ to the kidneys in the Nourishing Cycle. Many people observe that when they feel sad they don't feel sexy. That's because when the lungs are coping with sadness they can't fully nourish the kidneys, so the kidneys don't provide the body with enough chi to sustain strong, healthy desire. Others notice that they *do* want to make love when they're sad but lack the stamina to follow through. In that scenario, the kidney has enough chi to support desire, but not enough for performance. However, sad people sometimes observe that if they *can* have sex, some of their sadness dissolves; making love dislodges congested chi that's stuck in the lungs and moves it into the kidneys.

TEAMWORK

As you can see, each of the five organ systems affects our sexuality and the way we behave in the context of romance. If any organ has insufficient chi, or too much chi, the others are adversely affected. It is also true that if you improve the health of any organ, you enhance the others as well. With my patients, I look for the weakest links in the chain and address those first. This is because the weaker organs feel life's challenges most acutely and are most readily impaired. The weak link diminishes the health of the entire system, as all other organs try to compensate for the weakness. Since making love can be either beneficial or taxing to the body, energy-depleting sexual activities affect the weaker organs most adversely.

In addition to following the lifestyle advice in chapter 9, you can enhance the health of your organs by making a commitment to superior sex. High-quality lovemaking drives chi through the system, fortifying each organ. When your kidneys are energized by skillful, passionate sex, your mind becomes sharper, your nerves calmer, and the muscle and tissue in your pelvic region stronger. Through the Nourishing Cycle, the chi from your enlivened kidneys pacifies the liver, allowing for feelings of kindness and warmth. A healthy liver keeps the body limber, facilitates the movement of chi throughout the body and ensures the experience and expression of appropriate emotions. The heart is energized, aiding the circulation of blood through the system and inspiring joy, love and a brightened outlook. With nourishment from the heart, the spleen helps you derive maximum value from the food you ingest and process correctly the mental and emotional information you take in. With support from the spleen, the lungs distribute fluids efficiently throughout the body. Residual sadness diminishes in favor of perseverance and a sturdier bond with your beloved as you move the relationship forward. And the circle completes itself as strong lungs nourish the kidneys and strengthen your sexuality.

In the next few chapters you will find useful insights into and powerful advice on every aspect of sexual activity, from seduction to orgasm. I urge you to plunge right in and use this information, regardless of what may be going on in your relationship. You may find this a challenge if you are having emotional or sexual problems at the moment. But if you *can* be sexually intimate, I advise you to do it—not to cover up other problems but to help yourselves heal. While working out your difficulties, allow the power and magnificence of lovemaking to bring you closer and rejuvenate other aspects of your life together.

EXERCISES:
CULTIVATING YOUR CHI

Traditional Chinese medicine is concerned with three aspects of sexual chi:

1. To make it plentiful. A deficiency of sexual chi can lead to infertility and other reproductive problems, or to diminished desire, stamina or performance. In some cases it can actually lead to *excessive*

desire, as the body urges you to fill the lower abdomen with the energy it lacks by drawing it from a sex partner.

2. To help it move effectively when and where it is needed. If sexual energy does not move effectively it can stagnate, becoming unavailable for use. This can lead either to sexual apathy or sexual compulsion—the body's broken-record way of calling attention to the stagnation and getting the energy to move.

3. To ensure that it is of the appropriate quality to fulfill its functions. Quality refers to attributes such as moist or dry, hot or cold, yin or yang, rising or descending. If the energy in any particular area is of improper quality, it can't fulfill its function. Vaginal dryness, for example, is a sign that the yin chi quality of moisture is lacking; impotence is often an indication that the chi in the pelvic area is cold and descending (hot and rising creates an erection).

The exercises that follow, here and in later chapters, enhance sexuality and overall health by addressing all three aspects of chi. Many involve the breath, a vital component of Chinese medicine and the key to controlling chi. Scientific research has shown that breathing techniques can calm the mind, lower blood pressure, relieve stress, oxygenate tissue and produce other sexually beneficial changes. In traditional Chinese medicine, the kidney organ rules both sexuality and the central nervous system. Respiration affects both functions, because the lungs are the mother organs to the kidneys. Hence, controlled breathing can be used to manipulate sexual energy and also to heighten awareness and sensitivity.

These exercises will:

* enhance sensitivity to sexual stimulation
* reduce tension throughout the body
* increase control of body and mind by enabling one to direct and manipulate sexual chi
* increase blood circulation in the pelvic area
* improve the functioning of muscles involved in sexual activity
* build sexual stamina

All of which adds up to greater health and vitality, along with more control and skill during lovemaking.

For the best results, keep in mind these basic pointers:

1. If convenient, do the exercises in a well-ventilated room or outdoors.
2. Practice when you're relaxed and not in a rush.
3. Give yourself at least forty-five minutes to digest a meal before doing the exercises.
4. Wear comfortable clothing, with no constrictions around the midsection.
5. While doing the exercises, rest the tip of your tongue against the roof of your mouth, just behind the upper front teeth.
6. Maintain good posture. Avoid slouching or stooping. Keep your shoulders relaxed, not hunched.
7. Unless you're too congested to do so, breathe through your nose, flaring the nostrils to let more air in.
8. Eliminate distractions. Don't do the exercises while reading or watching television. They are best done with eyes closed, focusing easily on the breathing process.
9. As with any skill, consistency of practice is helpful. Try to do at least one or two sessions of fifteen minutes each week.

Deep Abdominal Breathing

Short, shallow inhalation prevents the lungs from filling completely and keeps stale air inside, depriving the organs of nourishing oxygen. Deep abdominal breathing improves overall respiratory efficiency. A valuable tool for relieving tension, it also heightens one's awareness of the lower abdominal region, which is the power plant for generating sexual energy and sensation. During sex, the practice can be used to fortify control, calmness and stamina, enabling men to delay ejaculation and of women to fully experience sexual sensations.

1. Allow a minimum of ten minutes for the exercise.

2. Lie flat on your back or sit with your back straight and feet flat. Rest your hands on your abdomen, just below the navel. The tips of your longest fingers should touch.

3. Breathe slowly and easily through your nose. Your belly should rise like an expanding balloon, and your fingertips should separate slightly. As your abdomen swells, your diaphragm (the muscle that runs across your abdomen, separating your lungs from your GI tract) will move downward. This allows fresh air to reach the bottom of your lungs.

4. When your belly is fully extended, continue to inhale and allow your chest to expand. Air will now enter the middle portion of the lungs.

5. Keep your chest, shoulders and neck relaxed. It is better to take in less air and stay relaxed than to breathe extra deep while tensing your muscles.

6. Exhale slowly through the nose, drawing in first your abdomen, then your chest. Push the last air out of your chest before inhaling again.

7. Take a few normal breaths before resuming, especially if you feel dizzy or tingly—signs of too much oxygenation that, if continued, can lead to hyperventilation. Simply breathe normally and the sensations will subside. (They seldom occur once one gets used to the exercise.)

8. When you are sure you're doing the exercise correctly, you can do it without placing your hands on your abdomen.

Four-Step Breathing

This exercise helps you gain more control of your breath, so you can manipulate it during sex to attain desired results. Once you feel comfortable with deep abdominal breathing, practice it in stages, adding five minutes to your allotted time:

1. Inhale, taking a slow, deep breath as described above.

2. Hold the breath for a few seconds, without straining. Breath retention enriches the blood and generates heat—i.e., energy—in the lower abdomen.

3. Exhale at a steady rate, preferably through the nose. When all the air is expelled, suck in your abdomen toward your spine, without straining. This will eliminate any final residue of used air.

4. Hold again. Pause for two or three seconds while letting your abdomen relax, then begin the next inhalation.

The four-step process is to be done in a smooth, steady rhythm. Exhalation should run slightly longer than inhalation, and the pause after the in-breath should be slightly longer than the pause after the out-breath. One system that's often recommended is: Inhale for a count of four, hold for four, exhale for six, pause for two. If you find yourself gasping for oxygen or expelling air with shotgun force, you're doing something too slowly or taking too long. Establish a rhythm that's comfortable for you.

ROMANTIC INSPIRATION

This exercise is a wonderful way for couples to begin the process of consciously harmonizing their chi. It involves, essentially, synchronizing your breath.

1. Create a soothing atmosphere. Soft light or candles are recommended. If you would like to have background music, make sure it's gentle and calming. Keep the room warm.

2. Lie together in bed, either in a face-to-face embrace or front-to-back, in spoon position. You can be dressed, partly dressed or undressed, but be sure to be comfortable.

3. Close your eyes and focus on the natural rhythms of your breath for a minute or so.

4. Become aware of your partner's breath.

5. Begin to coordinate your breathing. Breathe calmly and deeply in unison. By placing your noses near each other's ears, touching your chests or making a slight sound as you exhale, you can remain aware of each other's inhalations and exhalations.

6. There should be no strain involved. Find a mutually comfortable pattern by taking slightly longer or shorter breaths to conform to each other's lung capacity. If one's breathing pattern naturally shifts, the other should calmly adapt.

7. After breathing together in this manner for about five minutes, begin holding your breath after each inhalation. Simply retain the breath for a few seconds, without strain. Then do the same after the exhalation. Continue in this manner for another five minutes.

Like all breathing exercises, this one calms both body and mind, while revitalizing the system with fresh oxygen. Don't be surprised if you feel light and energetic afterward, and close to each other in a way you may not have experienced before. But the true value of this simple practice occurs over time. Done on a regular basis, it has tremendous value sexually. Think of it as preparation for superior sex, a way to develop subtle but powerful skills that you will later utilize during intercourse.

One of the reasons superior lovemaking bestows higher pleasure and more profound health benefits than ordinary sex is that it adds intention, discipline and concentration to what is often a purely instinctive, animal-like act. Coordinated breathing trains you to fine-tune your awareness of the nuances of your partner's body while also learning to regulate your own. As your skill and sensitivity develop, they transfer effortlessly to all sexual activities, facilitating the exchange of chi and making the two of you one.

Chapter 4

STAIRWAY TO THE STARS
Perfecting Foreplay

Women fake orgasms, men fake foreplay.

—ANONYMOUS

*He should seize her delicate waist and fondle her jade-
like body. Talking of being found together, with one
heart and a single intent, they should embrace and kiss,
suck tongues, press close and caress each other's ears and
head. Soothing above and stimulating below . . .*

—TAOIST MASTER

In *The Praise of Folly,* the fifteenth-century scholar Erasmus complained, "How a man must hug, and dandle, and kittle, and play a hundred little tricks with his bedfellow." Like a multitude of other men, he
might have felt more at home with the Manuans of the South Pacific,
among whom, wrote anthropologist Margaret Mead, "Kissing, fondling
and foreplay are regarded as the height of bad behaviour."

I don't know how the Manuans managed to do without foreplay, but
it's a vital part of lovemaking in virtually every other culture we know
of—including many in the animal kingdom. In fact, foreplay is indispensable precisely *because* it irritates men like Erasmus. As we've seen,

yang is goal oriented and quick to heat up, which means it can get impatient waiting for yin to become aroused. Thanks to society's new openness regarding women's sexual needs, many men have learned to restrain their yang hastiness and engage in the foreplay their partners desire. But too many men look upon it as a necessary evil, like a pregame show that one has to suffer through before the real action begins. Even among men who understand the female need for foreplay, there are many who think the only reason to caress, stroke, suck or fondle is to get a woman wet enough for intercourse—to prepare the receptacle, so to speak, as if foreplay were the equivalent of preheating an oven before shoving a casserole dish inside. But female readiness is not a matter of lubrication alone, and the activities we associate with foreplay are not just a means to an end but pleasurable and satisfying in their own right, and essential for obtaining all the rewards to body and soul that sex can offer.

Chinese sages in every recorded century stressed that skilled foreplay makes the sexual experience as a whole deeper, more enriching, more profound and more transformative—for *men* as well as women. A man who is creative and attentive during foreplay helps his beloved become a more receptive lover. The more complete her arousal, the more benefit he will receive from intercourse. "If you move up and down suddenly and violently, the joy of love will not be shared," states one classic text. "But when the man is desirous of the woman and the woman is desirous of the man, and their emotions are as one, then they will both be happy in their hearts. The woman is stirred to the quick and the man's 'stalk' is full of vigor."

Traditional Chinese medicine holds that the primary purpose of sex is to facilitate an exchange of energy between partners and a beneficial movement of chi within each body. Good foreplay brings all the organ systems into the sexual act and generates an abundance of chi. It also harmonizes yin and yang energies, both within each partner and between them, fostering health and the experience of oneness. By calming yang and invigorating yin, prolonged foreplay makes both partners more vulnerable, more sensitive and more open. Yin is not only the harder of the two forces to access, it is the more crucial as well: yin is what makes it possible for men and women alike to receive the energy exchanged during lovemaking and absorb its healing power. If intercourse begins too quickly, less yin chi will be involved, since yin takes longer than yang to move into the pelvic region. With her primary energy running slower than her partner's, the woman is unable to keep up and is less likely to end up satisfied—and the man does not receive the maximum benefit energetically because his partner's chi has not been fully activated and she has less to give.

Proper foreplay also adds variety to the sexual experience and brings the mind and emotions as well as the body into the act. This is especially important for couples who are in the process of learning more advanced intercourse techniques, and for those who are struggling to overcome sexual problems or incompatibilities. Pleasurable foreplay reduces the pressure to perform, and, for many people, helps to produce more reliable and satisfying orgasms. That in itself is a boon to health: orgasms not only reduce stress and tension, they also serve as a pump, bringing fresh, healing blood and chi into the pelvic region and shooting it back out to the rest of the body.

By making foreplay a joyful form of union in itself, you bring more of yourselves to the sexual experience. In turn, you take from it more pleasure and benefit.

A MATTER OF PRINCIPLES

Volumes have been written about foreplay techniques. The practices in this chapter were emphasized by the Chinese and can be especially powerful for modern lovers. Before we get to the specifics, a few important principles need to be mentioned:

1. *Forget the Golden Rule.* With foreplay, you don't necessarily do unto others what you would want done unto you. Instead, do unto your lover what he or she wants and needs. Whether the action is performed by the man or the woman, it's yang energy that takes the initiative, and as we have seen, it's important for yang to give *appropriately.*

2. *Cultivate variety and surprise.* Between you and your partner you have four hands, twenty fingers, four lips, two tongues, two sets of genitals and two virtual continents of skin rich in erogenous zones.

With all this, plus the objects in your environment, an imaginative couple has enough resources to keep from ever getting bored. Don't be a prisoner to foreplay routine.

3. Continue what works. While variety adds spice, every meal needs staples and everyone has certain dishes he or she looks forward to. So, balance the new with the familiar. Withholding your lover's favorite activity can be tantalizing, but don't disregard it just because *you* feel like trying something different.

4. Use all the senses. In Chinese medicine, parts of the body associated with sensory experience correspond to the five main organ systems: the ears with the kidneys, the tongue with the heart, the lips and mouth with the spleen, the lungs with the nose and the eyes with the liver. Stimulating the senses activates chi in the corresponding organ. Using all the senses during love play promotes the overall balance of the system.

Touch can stimulate *all* the organs since it stimulates the meridians on the area of the skin that is touched. Therefore, it is highly beneficial to touch each other all over, as it sends healing chi throughout the body.

While touch is perhaps the most arousing of the senses, the others are also important in artful foreplay. Seeing one's beloved undress can be highly exciting. Even more so are the visual signs of a lover's arousal. So, keep the room light enough to see each other. Savor the tastes of each other's saliva, sweat and genital secretions. Bring your ears into play with erotic or romantic music, and with sounds of your own pleasure—moans and groans, sighs and giggles, wails and shrieks. And don't neglect your noses. Smell is a powerful aphrodisiac, so make strategic use of perfume, incense, scented oils, fragrant air, and above all the natural scents of the male and female bodies.

5. Involve the whole body. One of the purposes of foreplay is to reduce chi stagnation in the meridians and remove blocks that keep chi from flowing to the pelvic area. When we don't fully experience our sexuality it's usually because our energy is stuck someplace else, most often in the head. Every kiss and caress invigorates energetic movement in that part of your lover's body.

6. *Pay attention to the breasts.* Kissing and caressing the breasts are important foreplay activities because the breasts are associated with three meridians: the pericardium, which is the tissue surrounding the heart; the liver, which is the channel that runs directly through the genitals; and the stomach, which runs about an inch and a half to the left and right of the genitals. When the breasts of either gender are stimulated, all three channels are enlivened.

7. *Quickies are okay.* As vital as prolonged foreplay is, there are times when it can be dispensed with. In long-term relationships especially, it's sometimes fun to satisfy the yang urge to burst out of the starting blocks and dash to the finish line. Many women find the change highly exciting, especially if the man—freed from what he may consider an unnatural pace and the pressure to do everything right—is particularly uninhibited. (Men, be aware that this may leave your woman unsatisfied, so be sure to let her know that next time—or later that same day perhaps—you'll make love at a pace more suitable to her yin nature.)

HARMONIZING
YOUR MINDS

*Sexual love is undoubtedly one of the chief things in
life, and the union of mental and bodily satisfaction in
the enjoyment of love is one of its culminating peaks.*

—SIGMUND FREUD

Good sex begins in the most erotic part of the body: the brain. As a prelude to a session of lovemaking, couples in ancient China would do things together—read poems about nature, play music, watch a performance, stroll, converse over tea, play backgammon, look at picture books. Such activities were considered important forms of foreplay, as they brought into harmony the thoughts, senses and emotions of the lovers before they even touched. "The man should harmonize his mood with that of the woman," said the Yellow Emperor's teacher, Su Nu. "Only then will his jade stalk rise." Such advice is not limited to the Chinese. A thirteenth-century European marriage manual instructs husbands to "engage her first in conversation that puts her heart and mind at ease and gladdens her . . . Speak words of love, some of erotic passion, some of piety and reverence . . . Hurry not to arouse passion until her mood is ready."

In our culture, this harmonizing phase is especially important because most couples spend their workdays apart. When I work with couples who complain of sexual incompatibility I often begin by suggesting that they develop a mutual interest, something to share besides finances and child rearing. This often revives the joy they once felt in each other's company but had lost to mundane concerns. By enhancing their sense of closeness, many a couple has rekindled their sexual flame.

Involving the mind allows more yin energy to participate, because yin starts in the head and moves down in its natural path of sexual expression. This brings out deeper aspects of each personality, making both partners more receptive. Because the ability to receive determines the power of love, the end result is a higher, more profound experience once the mental connection between partners gives way to a physical connection.

The importance of mental and emotional harmony can also be understood in terms of the organ system. Couples whose sex lives are lagging often fear that their marriage is in trouble. Pursuing an enjoyable interest together can diminish their apprehension. This has a positive effect on the kidneys, which control both fear and sexuality. Mutual interests also affect the kidneys through the other organs. Learning new information stimulates the spleen, which controls the kidneys in the Discipline Cycle. Having something positive to look forward to restores a couple's will to push past their reservations; this has a healing effect on the lungs, the mother organ to the kidneys in the Nourishing Cycle. Excitement stimulates the heart, which is controlled by the kidneys. And the sense of sharing stimulates feelings of warmth between partners; this soothes the liver, which is the child organ to the kidney and mother organ to the heart. Hence, harmonizing the two minds prepares the organ systems to contribute to the sex act.

When their kids had grown and left the nest, Suzanne and Frank discovered that just having fewer responsibilities and an empty house did not reinvigorate their passion. So, they turned their mutual love for film into creative foreplay. First, they made going to the movies something special by treating it as a date. Discussing what they'd seen put their minds on the same track, and the shared intellectual passion ignited their *physical* passion. Later, they turned up the juice by bringing cinematic characters home with them. Both partners would take on roles, then flirt with each other and remain in character all the way to the bedroom.

Dancing is a great way to harmonize your minds and spirits. As part of their wedding preparation, Alexis and Roger signed up for ballroom dance classes, and they haven't missed a step since. Even after the births of their three children, they continue to make time to go to clubs and learn new steps. On other occasions they turn up the stereo, push back the furniture and waltz or fox-trot until they can't resist a horizontal mambo. The ritual is especially powerful after a difficult day or a time apart, as it brings their thoughts and feelings into step along with their feet.

For some couples, finding something to share is a challenge. Peter and Andrea felt they had nothing in common besides their kids and their house. Because the house was as run-down as their sex life, I suggested they take a class in home remodeling. Every Wednesday night they learned about construction. Soon they were reconstructing their ardor for each other on Thursday mornings, a welcome and wonderful change for a couple who hadn't made love in the daylight for years. They ended up doing much of the actual work on the house themselves—and added a hot tub, just outside their bedroom door.

Mind Harmony Suggestions

1. Have a date night once a week. An old-fashioned date can restore romantic rapport. On those special nights, make an agreement not to discuss everyday matters.

2. Share your thoughts about each other. Tell your partner what you thought of when he or she came to mind that day. Then allow your partner to do the same.

3. Rebel together. Sometimes doing something naughty can make you feel like young lovers again. Begin foreplay on the kitchen table or in the backseat of your car overlooking the city or a lake.

4. Share the arts. Read poetry to each other. Bring home jokes or cartoons to share; laughter is a great harmonizer. Listen to music and look at art together. Erotic art is especially appropriate. The Chinese created the first books of erotica; called pillow books because they were stored in wooden pillows, they were given as wedding gifts to educate and inspire newlyweds.

5. Shop for sex toys. Build anticipation by going to a market, department store or shop that specializes in sexual paraphernalia, and pick up anything from a feather to whipped cream to a dildo. Browse through a catalog if you prefer to be titillated in the privacy of your home.

6. Name your genitals. Acknowledge the intimacy of your relationship by giving terms of endearment to your penis and vagina. Lending them a sense of character and personality can deepen your connection to each other's sex organs and help you communicate through them. We in the West have crude slang words. The Chinese have treated private parts with more reverence, creating dozens of poetic terms. Use some of the following or make up names of your own:

PENIS	VAGINA
Jade Stalk	Honey Pot
General	Jade Chamber
Weapon of Love	Mysterious Room
Crimson Bird	Golden Crevice
Flute	Valley of Joy
Heavenly Root	Cinnabar Grotto
Yang Peak	Yin Gate
Warrior	Lotus

SEXUAL MASSAGE

Studies have found that children who are deprived of touch are more likely to develop depression, hyperactivity and other psychological disorders, and touch-deprived older people deteriorate more rapidly, both physically and mentally. Research also suggests that touch promotes bonding, partly through the agency of oxytocin, a pleasure-producing chemical that we secrete in large amounts when we touch—or are touched—and that peaks when mothers nurse their infants.

Needless to say, there is an infinite number of ways for lovers to touch. In general, yin—the holistic aspect of our sexuality—enjoys having the entire body touched; yang is sharply focused and appreciates localized touch. Because of their relative proportions of yin and yang, women usually like to be touched all over during the sex act, while men enjoy being touched on the genitals as soon as possible.

Massage, one of the sexiest and most pleasurable forms of touching, appeals to the yin in women and men. The gentle movement of hands along the skin soothes the body and spirit and at the same time stimulates nerve endings. It's a great way to warm up to each other and create a calm, relaxed atmosphere for lovemaking.

Massage relieves energetic stagnation, which makes more energy available for sexuality. Tension is basically too much energy stuck in one place. If, for example, your shoulders and neck are tight, chi is congested in those areas and can't be put to other purposes, like supporting sexual strength and sensitivity. A good massage will release the stuck energy.

There are basically four types of hand movements that can be used during a sexual massage:

1. *Stroking.* With your fingers together, use your entire open hand to touch a large area of skin as you gently move up, down or across the body. The amount of pressure may vary from light to forceful.

2. *Grasping.* Gently pinch the skin and muscles between your thumb and four fingers. This is especially good when massaging the shoulders, arms and legs.

3. *Kneading.* Using your thumb, press down slowly on a particular point. Apply pressure for a moment, then release slowly. This is the basis of acupressure massage and can be used anywhere on the body. Try pressing on either side of the spine, about one inch from the vertebrae in the center. Begin at the shoulders and gently press every two inches or so all the way down the back.

4. *Pushing apart.* Place your hands on your lover, with the thumbs outstretched and the tips of the thumbs touching. Apply light pressure to the skin while pulling the thumbs toward their respective hands. Pressure can be increased as long as you use enough lotion to prevent pulling on the skin. This movement works well along the spine, chest, thigh and calf.

I recommend beginning every massage with stroking and then bringing in the other movements. Use varying degrees of pressure, depending on your partner's needs and preferences. As a rule, pressure enhances relaxation, while a light touch arouses and tantalizes.

With respect to duration, a long massage (more than fifteen minutes) allows you to deepen your partner's relaxation. You can take the time to increase the pressure gradually and pay special attention to areas of stored tension. However, be aware that *too much* relaxation may make the recipient feel too languid for sex. He or she might even fall asleep. A brief massage is often quite enough to soothe tension and connect two lovers through the sense of touch. If you have plenty of time, though, a longer massage, followed by a period of relaxation or even a nap, can launch you on a high-powered sexual adventure. Just don't expect your sweetheart to jump up from a lengthy massage hot and ready.

SEXUAL MASSAGE HINTS

1. Direct your hands from your partner's head, hands and feet toward the genitals. This supports the flow of blood and chi to the sex organs, which occurs naturally during arousal. Include direct mas-

sage to the genitals only if your partner welcomes it. Initially, stroke the sex organs gently, and give them no more attention than any other area. Making them the primary focus of the massage is more arousing than relaxing, and your partner may find it highly frustrating when you move your hands elsewhere.

2. Focus on the skin. Deep muscle pressure is highly relaxing, but perhaps *too* relaxing for foreplay. The nerves you want most to stimulate in a sexual context are closer to the skin. So use a tighter touch to excite and a firmer touch with more pressure to relax.

3. Make sure the room is warm, particularly if the person receiving the massage is undressed. Cold temperature tightens muscles. Many people tend to cool down when massaged, so have a blanket, sheet or towel handy to cover body parts that might get chilled while you are touching another area.

4. Encourage feedback. Everyone has personal likes and dislikes. Pressure that might feel wonderfully firm to one person can be painful to another. Encourage your partner to tell you if the pressure you're applying is appropriate, and to let you know when he or she wants it softer or stronger.

5. Lubricate. Kneading can be performed quite well without lubrication, but the other strokes work better with massage oil or lotion, especially if you are applying firm pressure or stroking large areas of skin. Bear in mind that lubricants that work well on the skin should not go into the vagina, so don't use oil near a woman's genitals. If you're planning to have intercourse after the massage, don't use it on the penis either. Vaginal lubrication such as KY jelly is fine for massaging the genital area, as it can safely enter the vagina.

6. Naturally, the person receiving massage should be in a comfortable position. That applies to the massager as well. Working in an awkward position not only diminishes the quality of the massage but also puts strain on your muscles; it might leave you needing a massage yourself.

7.   When massaging a woman, pay special attention to her breasts, if it pleases her. Because the breasts are on the liver channel, massaging them calms the emotions and moves sexual chi toward the genitals. Try grasping each breast in your hand (or both hands if necessary) and gently lifting. Pulling the breast up and away from the rib cage creates pleasurable sensations, as even small breasts can feel heavy to carry around all day.

A KISS IS STILL A KISS

What is a kiss? Why this, as some approve:
The sure, sweet cement, glue and lime of love.

—ROBERT HERRICK

Psychotherapists have told me that couples with marital difficulties often stop kissing on the lips—in some cases even though they still have intercourse! They say that's because nothing is more intimate than a deep passionate kiss. The ancients understood this; their texts consistently praise erotic kissing as both an essential aspect of foreplay and a delicious elixir in its own right.

Kissing was considered a powerful tool for creating closeness, emotionally and energetically. Because the lips and mouth are associated with the spleen, through kissing you allow your partner's chi into your system and absorb his or her affection. Bringing the tongue into play magnifies the effect, as the tongue is associated with the heart. Stimulating the tongue energizes chi in the heart, inspiring joy, uplifting the spirit and enhancing circulation: as we've all experienced, the heart races with a passionate kiss.

It is mainly the yin in us that is excited by long, luxurious kissing, because yin chi travels downward, descending from the mouth to the genitals. Whereas our yang aspect is moved to kiss *after* being aroused sexually, our yin aspect kisses in order to get turned on. That's why women usually want to spend more time kissing than men do. However, mouth-to-mouth kissing stimulates both the yin and yang in our bodies. Two major acupuncture meridians end in the mouth: the conception vessel, which rules the body's yin energy, moves up the front of the body from the perineum and encircles the lips; and the governing vessel, which rules yang energy, runs up the back of the body to the top of the head, then down to the upper lip. Kissing enlivens the chi in both these important channels. It harmonizes yin and yang, facilitates a healthful exchange of chi between the lovers and prepares their bodies for optimal enjoyment during intercourse.

In addition, the exchange of saliva was considered by sexual sages to be a great boon to health. Saliva contains antibiotic agents that are considered the immune system's first line of defense. But the elixirlike qualities that the Chinese attributed to the "jade liquid" when secreted during sexual arousal remain foreign to Western science. Saliva exchange brings to each lover the chi of his or her partner's primary trait: yin energy enters the man and yang energy enters the woman.

Blissful Kisses

You might think that kissing is a natural instinct and not a learned skill. Well, walking is a natural instinct too, but we can all improve our posture and gait with a little instruction. In both cases, it takes a period of regular practice to become really good at it. These tips will help you get the most out of kissing, both as a sexual stimulant and healthful elixir:

1. Keep your mouth, tongue and facial muscles relaxed. Tension reduces sensitivity and creates empty space in the mouth, which makes a kiss less sensual.

2. Stimulate secretions. Graze with your tongue around your partner's mouth, paying special attention to areas close to the salivary glands, under the tongue and adjacent to the rear teeth. This stimulates the healthful exchange of saliva.

3. Enjoy each other's fluids. The wetter the kiss, the more saliva— and therefore chi—is exchanged and the greater the benefit. If either of you is inhibited about taking in the other's fluids, an honest discussion and some reeducation are perhaps in order.

4. Be versatile. Experiment with different degrees of pressure, from feathery light to passionately firm, and with different ways of using your tongue—licking your partner's gums and palate, deep and shallow thrusts, etc.

5. Use your teeth. But use them gingerly. A light nibble or nip from time to time can be very erotic, but if you step over the line into pain you can spoil your beloved's most vulnerable moment.

6. Expand the range of your kisses. The pressure of lips and the caress of a tongue can be highly arousing anywhere on the skin. The body is one big erogenous zone; part of being a skilled lover is learning from your partner's responses exactly which areas of his or her body are most erotic. As with massage, when you kiss or lick your beloved, move from the periphery toward the trunk and toward the genitals from above and below.

The Chinese sages were great advocates of kissing, licking and sucking a woman's breasts. Because the liver channel extends to the breasts, stimulating them directly affects the flow of chi to the genitals. But arousing women was not the only reason the practice was recommended. It was considered an elixir for men. Sexually aroused women were thought to produce different secretions from the mouth, breasts and clitoris—the Red Lotus Peak, the Twin Peaks and the Purple Mushroom Peak, respectively. Men were advised to drink the "medicine of the three peaks" to enhance their overall health and potency. They contended that non-nursing women secrete a sweet, subtle liquid from their nipples. Called "white snow," this substance—possibly what we know as colostrum—is different from mother's milk and is said to have invigorating power.

THE JADE FOUNTAIN

*Why trouble with the pill of immortality when one is
welcome to drink from the jade fountain?*

—Hsu Hsiao Mu Chi

The Chinese considered oral sex the second most powerful way to
transfer chi from one person to another, the strongest being intercourse.
The prolonged connection of mouth and genitals and the absorption of
fluids from the opposite sex facilitate a potent exchange of energy. As
mentioned, the more chi that moves between partners, the more complete and unified they feel, and the more their health and well-being are
fortified by the primary trait of the opposite sex.

Whether they ejaculate or not, most men love having a women "go
down" on them. Some studies have found that over a quarter of circum-
cised men prefer that activity to intercourse, partly because it eliminates
performance anxiety and also because the mouth of a skilled woman offers tremendous variation in the pressure, texture and location of stimulation. Also, accepting oral sex puts the man in a receptive position. This
can teach him to be more vulnerable in general, making him more open
to pleasure in all aspects of sexuality. It can also increase his empathy for
women, who typically enter the sex act feeling more vulnerable than
men.

Women stand to benefit enormously from giving oral sex. While
traditional teachings held that men should ejaculate only during intercourse and not into the mouths of their partners, since less chi is exchanged that way, it was also understood that a woman takes in a
tremendous amount of yang energy when she ingests her lover's semen.
As we will see in a later chapter, semen contains a tremendous amount
of concentrated life force. Indeed, in ancient times, ejaculate was held to
be so powerful that emperors would have servants collect the semen of
healthy young men and mix it with herbs, and then consumed the tonic.
An orgasm represents a virtual explosion of chi. When a man climaxes in
a woman's mouth she receives that health-giving chi, and swallowing the
semen magnifies its impact.

I strongly recommend that women allow themselves to fully feel that burst of energy come into their bodies. When you swallow your man's semen, imagine it as an energizing, healing tonic coursing through your system. If you prefer not to swallow it, at least hold it in your mouth for a minute or two before spitting it out, and feel yourself absorbing your lover's vital energy.

Couples should bear in mind that when a woman gives a man oral sex, it brings out the secondary energetic trait in both partners—vulnerable yin for men, in-charge yang for women. This can make either or both of them feel uncomfortable. If discomfort arises, I suggest having short periods of oral sex, without the intention of bringing the man to orgasm, and gradually lengthening each session. The woman might also want to spend time exploring her man's genitalia, simply looking and touching without having to *do* anything. Letting the man have some control can also alleviate discomfort; if he guides his partner's motion or whispers instructions to her, neither one has to rely totally on their secondary trait.

What we call cunnilingus and they called "drinking from the jade fountain" was also highly recommended by the Chinese. Because the secretions that emanate from the "palace of yin" during sexual arousal were said to be nourishing and revitalizing, men were encouraged to partake liberally of this "moon flower medicine." I recommend that men luxuriate in taking in both the subtle essence of their women's chi and the physical elixir of their juices.

Through the ages most women have adored receiving oral satisfaction from skilled men, and countless numbers have quietly yearned for their men give to it to them more often. The prominent sex researchers Masters and Johnson considered oral sex the best way to bring a nonorgasmic woman to orgasm. Many of my patients have confirmed this, and those who *do* have orgasms during intercourse often say that oral sex is more reliable. This is, of course, because the clitoris—the most sensitive part of the vulva—often receives very little direct stimulation during intercourse but can be the focal point of oral sex. The tongue (the second strongest muscle in the body) can do things that a finger or penis cannot. Add a pair of supple lips and the mouth becomes an incredibly versatile instrument of pleasure.

For a woman, receiving oral sex is a terrific way to expand her range of sensations. It is also easier to control than intercourse, hence she can take charge of the pace of action. And, since there is no chance of the man's climaxing, the woman can relax and give her yin chi ample time to blossom. As a result, oral sex often feels more holistic, especially if the man caresses different parts of his lover's body while using his mouth on her genitals—something that is difficult to accomplish during intercourse.

In sum, the health benefits of giving and receiving oral sex are second only to intercourse. And, since it offers advantages that intercourse does not, it is a vital component of the sexual repertoire, both as an end in itself and as a form of foreplay.

Taste and Smell

If you need tips on how to administer oral sex, you'll find a plethora of books and videos with excellent instructions. Here, let's address the chief stumbling blocks to total enjoyment: taste and odor.

As a way to draw a mate's attention to the reproductive organs, nature designed the genitals to smell and taste like ambrosia. Men and woman alike secrete hormones called pheromones, whose purpose is to make us smell attractive to the other sex. The only reason a woman's scent would be consistently repellent is if she has a local or systemic health problem. Bacterial and fungal infections, constipation and insufficient fluid intake can create unpleasant odors. Women who want to improve their scent would be wise to drink plenty of liquids, add fiber to their diets, eliminate alcohol, cut down on caffeine and check with a gynecologist to be sure they do not have a vaginal infection.

What about douching and vaginal deodorants? Unless they are prescribed for a medical problem, don't use them. Patients of mine who douche frequently find that over time their vaginas smell worse and worse, and they need to add deodorants to their douches and douche more frequently. The continual washing destroys the body's natural disease-fighting bacteria. As a result, they become susceptible to infection, and the infections create a bad odor. Only with extended use of antibiotics and antifungal agents are their bodies able to replenish their defense systems and eliminate the foul odors.

Women often have an aversion to taste—not of the penis, which has no discernible taste unless it's unclean, but to semen. Some women, of course, are repulsed by the idea of swallowing male ejaculate, or even having it in their mouths, and wouldn't enjoy it if it tasted like honey. This attitude usually stems from thinking of semen as some kind of waste product. In truth, it's entirely nontoxic, and, as we've seen, is considered life-enhancing in traditional Chinese medicine. Semen can taste vile, bitter or salty, however, if the man has a local health problem or bad lifestyle habits.

One of the chief offenders is alcohol. If you want your man to taste better, ask him to drink more water and cut back on caffeine and alcohol. In fact, many clever women have used the taste of a man's semen as a way to solve another problem: they promise lovers who drink excessively that if they lay off booze for a week, they'll be rewarded with oral sex. A week without alcohol can dramatically change the taste of ejaculate.

Love Maps

Traditional Chinese medicine holds that specific locations on the genitals are linked to other parts of the body. You may have heard of foot reflexology, in which locations on the feet are massaged to stimulate healing in the heart, lungs, eyes and other organs. A similar reflexology system is located in the male and female genitals.

According to reflexology theory, stimulating a specific point on the penis or in the vagina energizes the chi in corresponding organs. This is one important way that sexual activity affects the body's health. To influence the organs in a balanced, holistic way, it is important to stimulate the entire genitalia. If you focus on one area at the expense of others, the corresponding organ can become overstimulated and eventually weaken.

For example, if a woman receives oral sex frequently, her clitoris and surrounding tissue may be stimulated exclusively, with the interior of her vagina remaining untouched. This can overstimulate her kidneys and

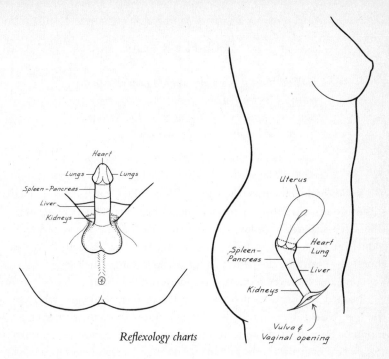

Reflexology charts

understimulate the other organs. The resulting imbalance could make her susceptible to kidney-related symptoms such as bladder conditions, memory loss, hearing loss, menstrual and gynecological disorders, infertility, back or knee pain and more. A man who receives frequent oral sex may have the head of his penis stimulated way in excess of the shaft. If that happens, the heart and lungs can become overstimulated, leading to symptoms associated with those organs: poor circulation, anxiety, respiratory conditions, sadness, etc.

For that reason, it is advisable to not receive oral sex too often without also having intercourse or manually stimulating the whole penis and the interior of the vagina. Also, *during* oral sex, the giver can make a point of getting around the entire area. Women can easily stroke and lick the entire penis; men can use their fingers to probe the vagina while using their mouths on the clitoris and surrounding vulva.

YOU HAVE TO HAND IT
TO HER

Half the time, if you really want to know the truth,
when I'm horsing around and with a girl, I have a
helluva lot of trouble just finding what I'm looking for,
for God's sake, if you know what I mean.

—J. D. SALINGER, *The Catcher in the Rye*

As with oral techniques, the range of possibilities for hand-to-genital stimulation is too broad to cover in detail here. Up-down, inside-outside, deep-shallow, high-low, gentle-firm—the combinations and individual preferences are virtually infinite. Remember, though, to try to stimulate all parts of the penis or vagina when using your hands.

One area deserves extra special attention: the G spot.

Named for Ernst Grafenberg, the German gynecologist who was the first to describe it in the 1940s, the G spot is about the size of an almond or fingertip and located on the front wall of the vagina, approximately two inches from the entrance. Although its actual existence was a matter of controversy for some time, researchers such as Beverly Whipple—not to mention countless women—have confirmed that the G spot not only exists but is exquisitely sensitive to pressure. So sensitive, in fact, that when their G spot is properly stimulated, many women have orgasms of great intensity and some ejaculate a milky substance through the urethra that is neither urine nor ordinary vaginal lubrication.

There is no explicit reference to the G spot in Chinese sexual texts. However, it is reasonable to assume that the ancients knew about it since the intercourse positions they recommended most for satisfying a woman are precisely those singled out by modern researchers for stimulating the G spot (see chapter 5).

Every woman and her lover should get acquainted with the G spot. The best positions in which to locate it are with the woman on her hands and knees and her partner behind her, and with the woman on her back with her legs raised and parted. Making sure the vagina is well-lubricated, the man should insert one finger up to about his second

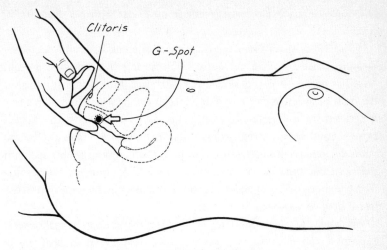

The best position for finding the G spot

knuckle. Pressing gently against the front wall of the vagina—i.e., toward his lover's belly—he should probe for a small area that feels slightly tougher and bumpier than the smooth tissue that surrounds it. It might be hard to find. In some women, the G spot is located only a half-inch or so from the vaginal opening, and many women have to be well aroused before the spot swells enough to become obvious to the touch.

Don't expect instantaneous combustion; the G spot is not like a button you press to start a fireworks display. Women respond in highly individual ways to the initial probing. Some are turned on immediately, some feel no sensation at all, others notice a slight numbness in the area, and some feel so irritated they push the man's finger away. Some feel a need to urinate because the location is quite close to the bladder. Both partners should accept whatever happens with patience and should persevere, knowing that the woman's reaction might vary each time the G spot is stimulated.

The exploratory phase should be gentle, calm and loving. Couples should adopt a mood of tranquillity, respecting the vulnerability of the woman's position. Her attention should focus on the physical sensations, and he should avoid getting so turned on that he becomes overly forceful. Consider this exploration an end in itself, rather than a means to an end.

The G spot can open the door to a different kind and degree of pleasure. Once a woman feels comfortable having the area touched—and once her partner becomes skilled at it—she may find G spot stimulation the most pleasurable part of making love. It can be stimulated with a finger, either by itself or along with manual or oral contact with the clitoris—a combination many woman find incomparable—and also by the penis during certain intercourse positions. Women who are blessed with the right combination of anatomy, attitude and adroit lover may ultimately experience ejaculatory orgasms that the Chinese compared to the joyful flow of a river in springtime.

Indeed, the sages considered this orgasm the ultimate sexual experience for a woman. As we will see, they delineated several levels of female orgasm, each one offering a different degree of benefit, as orgasmic contractions pump lifegiving blood and chi through the body. The ejaculatory orgasm represents the highest level, the completion of the female sexual cycle. At that moment, she is at once the ultimate receptacle for her partner's chi and the most generous giver of her own chi.

ANOTHER WINDOW

For most of us, the anus has been hidden from awareness as well as sight. Because of its role in excretion, it's thought of as dirty, a place to avoid. In fact, the anus can be a highly erotic area for both men and women. Some of the muscles and nerves in the area directly affect the genitals. By stimulating the anus, you open another door into the pelvic region, expanding the ability of sex to move chi through the receiver's system. Awakening the erotic potential of the anus expands the range and intensity of sensation and makes the buttocks, hips and perineum more powerful instruments of love play. For many people, anal stimulation has psychological value as well, enhancing their respect for their bodies. If the body part that you find least attractive can provide you with pleasure, the rest of you becomes that much more sacred.

You might want to approach anal stimulation gingerly at first. Most people feel more comfortable having the area touched *after* they've been turned on by genital sensations, so wait until foreplay is well on track and your lover is already aroused. Begin with a gentle touch, simply laying a finger or two lightly on the exterior of the anal sphincter while simultaneously attending to the genitals with your other hand or your mouth. The idea is not to penetrate but to remain still until your lover is ready for you to move your finger. Then stroke the area with a feathery touch, applying no force or pressure. Once the anus is regarded an acceptable erogenous zone, proceed with gentle, shallow penetration.

Any time either of you intends to stimulate the other's anus, make sure to take certain hygiene precautions. The anal area is usually cleaner than we imagine it to be and is normally not a place where one encounters feces. Nevertheless, there are exceptions, and the region is a prime breeding ground for bacteria. The giving partner would be wise to have smoothly trimmed nails, wear a latex glove or finger protection and apply a lubricant before insertion. The receiving partner may want to wash the rectal area thoroughly before beginning. In fact, rubbing each other all over with a warm washcloth is an excellent addition to a couple's foreplay ritual. Afterward, the giving partner should wash up immediately, even if all precautions have been taken. Never place your fingers near the vulva after touching the anus, as doing so can cause infection.

Many of us carry a great deal of residual tension in the anus, so be patient if your partner's muscles contract when you touch the area. When he or she is reassured by your loving caresses that the activity is safe, those muscles will relax. Playing with your partner's genitals while stimulating the anus helps by providing a familiar pleasure that distracts the attention and reduces resistance to the unusual sensations in the anus.

Men in particular are often hesitant to let themselves enjoy anal stimulation. They think that feeling pleasure in that way might mark them as latent homosexuals. This is unfortunate nonsense. In fact, men stand to gain even more than women from the practice; because it places them in a yin position, they may become more receptive to pleasure in general.

Hand to Gland

A skilled lover can use the anus as the gateway to a man's prostate gland. In Chinese medicine, the prostate plays a greater role in maintaining sexual vigor than is recognized by Western physiology. Prostate massage is often used to strengthen a man's sexual chi or to inspire its movement, especially if chi has become congested in the gland itself. Many men with acute prostate irritation are told by urologists to have more erections and ejaculate more often to stimulate the gland and facilitate blood flow. The Chinese sages would suggest direct stimulation on a regular basis, not only to improve the health of the prostate but to increase potency and produce more powerful orgasms—the gland expands and contracts during ejaculation as it pumps seminal fluid into the penis.

A walnut-sized organ located just under the bladder, the prostate can be located by inserting a finger into a man's anus and curling it toward the front of his body. This is essentially what an internist or urologist does when performing a prostate examination. At the beginning, insert your finger only a short distance and stop for a while. Ask your partner if he feels comfortable (in fact, ask for feedback at every stage). It's quite normal for the man to contract his muscles, as a kind of protective reflex. If that happens, don't force anything. To relax the man and distract his mind, play gently with his genitals. Encourage him to take deep breaths and relax. When you're sure he's calmed down and is used to the anal sensation, slowly move your finger deeper inside. Proceed gently and lovingly in stages, stopping now and then to be sure he's comfortable.

Eventually, you will feel a round, smooth surface. This is the prostate gland. At first, simply rest your finger on it without moving, so your lover feels just gentle pressure. Then massage it gently, perhaps vibrating your finger slightly while your partner takes a series of deep breaths and relaxes completely. He will delight in the myriad new sensations. You can slide your finger over the gland, applying gentle pressure along the way. If at any point he feels pain or the need to urinate (this is common, as are false alarms), remove your finger slowly and easily. Stroke his belly, buttocks or genitals to soothe him as you withdraw your finger.

Once your partner is more at ease with prostate massage, you can simultaneously use your mouth or free hand on his penis. Eventually, if you are dexterous enough, you can even stimulate his prostate during intercourse. This can produce orgasms of incredible power. It also puts the man in the position of giving and receiving equally at the same time. This creates an inner balance of yin and yang, bringing deeper aspects of his being into the experience. The more yin gets involved in a man's sexual process, the more pleasure he is capable of feeling and the more chi he can absorb from his partner. Also, men whose partners are well skilled in massaging the prostate gland often find it much easier to experience the internal, nonejaculatory orgasm described later in the book.

TOYS ARE YOU

You give toys to your children, you give toys to your pets, so why not give toys to yourselves? The ancient Chinese did. In fact, they invented sex toys. The first recorded use of dildos refers to ivory objects carved in the image of a husband's penis, to be used by the wife when her man went off to war or on a diplomatic mission. The husband's portrait was carved at the bottom end—the part not inserted into the vagina—presumably as a reminder to the wife. In addition to dildos, the Chinese used penis rings to help maintain erections (some had little bumps to arouse the clitoris), little balls inserted in the vagina that stimulated the G spot when the woman rocked back and forth, and a variety of other paraphernalia.

Toys can be a great addition to your sex life. They make sex more playful, reducing self-consciousness and inhibition. They create new sensations, thereby expanding a couple's range of pleasure. And they create a sense of anticipation and surprise. Don't limit yourselves to the items sold in sex shops. Take advantage of everyday objects: soft fabrics like silk or satin, feathers and feather dusters, facial tissues, powder puffs, paintbrushes, foam rubber, sponges and washcloths dipped in warm water, ice cubes, Popsicles, cucumbers, whipped cream, pudding, lettuce leaves, fans, oils, lotions—all these and more can be turned into erotic toys if you improvise with flair. Just be sure to keep all foods containing sugar or oil out of the vagina as they can cause infection.

WHEN LOVE PLAY
UNLEASHES EMOTIONS

You're in bed, you've been smooching and sucking, fondling and stroking, and all of a sudden your beloved starts to cry or pull away. Paradise is suddenly lost. If this has ever happened to you, you no doubt felt startled and bewildered, wondering what in heaven's name you did wrong. Well, you might not have done *anything* wrong; in fact, you probably did a lot of things right. The early stages of great lovemaking can touch off an outpouring of unsolicited emotion.

The explanation lies in the Nourishing Cycle. Sexual arousal stimulates the flow of energy from the kidney to the liver, which controls the emotions, and from the liver to the heart, the organ of love. The body tries to release any energetic stagnation that impedes the flow of energy through these key organs. As a result, powerful emotions get unleashed. The feelings may be associated with your relationship, or they may have nothing to do with it. They might relate to something that happened at work, or with a friend or a parent. They might be connected to old fears or bad memories, or just be an explosion of raw emotion, with no particular focus at all. For a variety of cultural and energetic reasons, women are more likely than men to experience a surge of emotion during foreplay—especially when their G spot is stimulated and they are not used to it, since a great deal of emotional memory is stored in that area.

If this happens, let your partner air her feelings. Be a good listener: pay attention and show that you care about how she feels. If you can't do that, you might as well get dressed, toss the flowers in the trash and start planning for your next opportunity. She must let her stirred-up emotions out, or her body won't let yin energy move downward from her heart to her genitals.

When a man unleashes a flood of emotion, he is less likely to understand what's going on or verbalize his feelings. Instead, he might express the feelings physically. Suddenly, he'll feel like eating, or he'll lose his erection and become self-conscious. This is because uncomfortable emotions send yang energy into retreat, bringing up feelings of powerlessness and yinlike vulnerability. The man also loses some of the sharp focus that yang energy provides, including the drive to make love. If he doesn't realize what's actually going on, he may withdraw.

At such times, it's imperative for the woman to reassure him and make him comfortable. It takes a great deal of courage for a man to hang in there when the balance of yin and yang is altered. If he is able to enter into those awkward, discomforting feelings and acknowledge that he feels insecure, alone or disturbed—that is, if he can respect his yin energy and express himself honestly—his sense of male power will soon return.

Many women have trouble being supportive in such situations. They say they want men who are vulnerable and open to their feelings, but sometimes they get frightened out of their wits when they're actually with one. Deep inside, they don't really want their hero to get soft on them. Women, please bear in mind that if you don't truly allow your man to express his yin energy, you could end up with a brute who is insecure underneath. If he is able to accept his yin as well as his yang, the relationship will provide room for *you* to express both qualities as well.

Whether you're a man or a woman, if your partner goes through a sudden upsurge of emotion during foreplay, let him or her do whatever is necessary to go through it completely. Once it's over, you can help him or her return to sex by encouraging the appropriate feeling: as we saw in the previous chapter, women open sexually when they feel the heart qualities of happiness and excitement; men get sexy through the kidneys, when they feel brave as opposed to fearful.

IMPROVING YOUR SKILLS

Couples fail to achieve harmony and happiness, Su Nu told the Yellow Emperor, when "the woman is not able to determine her husband's desires and the husband does not understand the nature of women." If you want to be a great sexual artist, you have to be taught, and if you want to be loved *by* a great artist, you have to teach your lover. One way to learn is to discuss each other's foreplay needs, desires, quirks and proclivities. These tips can help you and your partner communicate about foreplay:

1. Set aside time for discussion. For the most part, it's easier to discuss what you would like to do *in* bed when you're *out* of bed. Once you're naked and horizontal, it can be difficult to speak openly; physical vulnerability accentuates emotional vulnerability.

2. Create the right atmosphere. Make sure you're calm and comfortable. Dim lighting is often a good idea, as you might feel less naked while revealing the naked truth. Some people prefer being in a restaurant or other public place.

3. Treat the subject with respect. Don't just dive into it as soon as you get together after having been apart for some time. Touch on other topics of discussion before engaging in this sacred subject.

4. Speak about what you would like your partner to do in bed. Avoid criticizing what has already been done.

5. Demonstrate. Sometimes a verbal description is not enough. An illustrated book on anatomy or sex education might help; you'd be surprised how little some people know about the genitals of the opposite sex. You can also demonstrate some of your preferences directly on your partner. Things like the softness or firmness of a touch, the nuances of a stroke and the position of a tongue when you kiss can be simulated.

6. If you are too shy to discuss this topic at all, try writing your sweetheart a letter. Be specific when you write down what you like.

7. Give yourselves permission to communicate *during* foreplay as well. If your lover does something that causes pain or discomfort, it's important to let him or her know immediately. But do it gently; everyone's feelings are vulnerable in bed. It's also a good idea to use moans, sighs, words or signals you both understand to let your partner know when you *like* what he or she is doing. And you can teach your lover to do things even better by gently directing his or her hand or mouth.

Love Signs

Each partner can benefit greatly from careful observation of the other's responses. Like jazz musicians, you can eventually come to know each other's melodies so well that you will be able to improvise without thinking about what to do and when to do it. You'll be able to lose your individual selves and function as a harmonious unit to create something new and exciting every time you make love.

To help emperors and noblemen become masters of the boudoir, the ancient teachers listed the various signs of female arousal. These include, in no particular order:

- Her face becomes flushed.
- Her throat becomes dry.
- Her nipples harden.
- Her nostrils widen.
- She perspires profusely.
- She sighs and moans.
- She breathes rapidly.
- Her vagina becomes moist.
- She grasps for the man and holds him tightly.
- She quakes and quivers.
- She stretches her legs and presses her thighs together.
- Her belly distends.
- She arches her body.
- Her secretions become copious and spread over her buttocks.

These reactions indicate that the right quality of sexual chi has entered various parts of the woman's body—the blood, bones, muscles, skin and key organs—in the right amounts for making love. This is necessary if the woman is to achieve her full potential for healthy sexual pleasure, and the couple is to achieve the highest levels of orgasmic ecstasy together. It should be noted that each woman expresses arousal in a highly individual way. It's important to learn your lover's particular pattern of responses and elicit her entire spectrum.

The longer a couple has been together and the older the man gets, the more attention he requires to become aroused. More important, if you want to bring the entirety of a man's being into the sexual experience—his heart and soul, not just his genitals—extended foreplay is essential. He may not realize it himself, but he stands to benefit a great deal from slowing down and lingering instead of rushing pell-mell to intercourse. He too has yin energy that contributes to the experience and healing capacity of sex; it needs to catch up with his yang.

His performance stands to benefit as well. While an erection itself is the quintessence of yang, *maintaining* it is a yin function. Hence, efficient male arousal requires an abundance of smooth-flowing yin chi, which is facilitated by skilled and knowledgeable foreplay. According to the ancient Chinese, before intercourse begins, the penis should achieve what were called "the four attainments." Said Su Nu to the Yellow Emperor, "If the jade stalk is not aroused, the sexual chi of the man and woman is not in harmony. If it is aroused but not yet enlarged, the muscle chi has not yet arrived. If it is enlarged but not yet hard, the bone chi has not yet arrived. If it is hard but not yet hot, the spirit chi has not yet arrived." In other words, the penis should be aroused, enlarged, hard and hot before intercourse begins. The four attainments ensure that the penis is enlivened by all four types of chi, bringing the fullness of male strength and stamina to the act. This portends greater pleasure for the woman and opens the man to a deeper, more transformative and complete experience, one that is more moving, emotionally and spiritually. If all four kinds of chi are *not* in the genitals, the man is more likely to drain himself of vital energy during the sex act. This depletes kidney energy and can lead to kidney-related problems ranging from memory loss to decreased vitality to sexual dysfunction to prostate swelling.

Needless to say, having the four attainments is not, by itself, sufficient reason to begin intercourse. The readiness should be mutual. The ancients contended that a man could be weakened by beginning intercourse before the woman is completely ready. Said one: "If the woman's secretions have not yet issued forth and her private parts are dry, but the man forces his way, then the jade stalk simply pierces in vain and it is a useless waste of spirit." What that means is, the man can't fully receive chi from his woman, since she is not adequately primed for giving. He gives up sexual energy to his lover with his orgasm but does not receive as much in return.

The rule of thumb for men is, delay the moment of penetration as long as possible. True, it is possible to delay too long. But that is much less likely to happen than starting too soon, so it's safer to err on the side of tardiness. If you penetrate her too quickly, she might end up frustrated; if you delay it, a delicious yearning will build up within her, and the ache of anticipation can make the act explosive.

When a Climax Is Not the End

Whenever possible, delay penetration until the woman has had an orgasm. The level of excitement that we in the West think of as a woman's climax consists of vaginal spasms and contractions of the muscles surrounding the clitoral bulbs. Unfortunately, we tend to think that once a woman has had one orgasm, she, like a man, is finished. In traditional Chinese medicine, the ordinary clitoral orgasm is not considered a peak at all but rather an intermediate stage, with greater heights still to be attained. It is a sign that the kidney organ is filled with chi. Once that level of orgasm has been achieved, the woman is primed for the more intense vaginal orgasms that are possible with artful intercourse. The orgasmic response is like a pump. It draws blood and chi into the pelvis and then shoots it back out. The process cleanses and heals tissue, and stimulates the secretion of pleasure-giving endorphins. Multiple orgasms multiply these benefits. They also give the woman access to deeper and deeper layers of self-nourishing yin energy. That's why orgasmic women tend to feel sexually healthier and more self-confident. And the lucky man who gives his woman multiple orgasms receives a more powerful dose of chi in return.

One reason the Chinese believed that intercourse should not even begin until the woman has had an intermediate orgasm is that it dispels fear. You'll recall that fear is the emotion associated with the kidneys. Orgasm cannot take place if the woman is afraid since fear keeps the kidney from filling with sexual chi. Once she's achieved this level of orgasm, the fear is gone. This allows her to open fully to the sexual experience, lose herself in the process and unite with her lover in the sacred embrace of love.

In short, for a skilled couple, an orgasm during foreplay is not a signal to stop but to begin a new phase of lovemaking. While some women want to be penetrated immediately after a clitoral orgasm, many need to rest for a few minutes; the vagina may be so sensitive that further stimulation can feel painful. In either case, if the woman is willing to move ahead and explore more deeply the magic and power of her sexuality, the couple can soar to new heights.

FIVE MINUTES TO THE EDGE

Here is a simple but highly tantalizing foreplay technique. Each partner takes a full five minutes to titillate the other as much as possible without bringing him or her to orgasm. You may start out either naked or clothed, standing or sitting or lying down. But the recipient has to be completely receptive and refrain from doing anything to the other partner. At the end of the five minutes, the giver stops whatever he or she is doing, no matter how much the recipient wants to continue. Then they trade places. You can add to the titillation by gently stroking your partner's thighs with a soft, feathery object. *Only* the thighs. Come tantalizingly close to the genitals, but don't touch them. Move away, come back, move away, come back and so forth, but stay on the thighs without touching the genitals for the full five minutes.

You and your partner can take turns an equal number of times, filling each round with greater sexual tension and pleasure, bringing each other closer and closer to the edge. Or, you can limit yourselves to one turn each, intensifying the sexual stimulation rapidly during that five minutes. Establish the parameters beforehand. No matter what variations you choose to adopt, however, always take each other only as far as the brink, never beyond.

This wonderful game gives both partners the chance to experience their sexual self without the pressure of doing anything or climaxing. It is particularly good for men who tend to ejaculate quickly and for women who have difficulty having orgasms. For many couples, the game changes their perceptions about what they are capable of experiencing during sex. Greg and Debbie, for example, had been married for twenty-three years and had always enjoyed their sex life together. After a series of five-minute games, they had intercourse and Debbie not only had an orgasm but her first ejaculation.

Use this practice only after you and your partner have become familiar with what turns each of you on. Five minutes can feel like forever if you are not pleasing each other. Also, remember the value of surprise; doing only what he or she expects will reduce the level of excitement that this game can offer.

EXERCISE: LOCKING IT UP

Here is another breathing exercise to add to your chi-cultivation practice.

According to Chinese anatomy, there are several passageways, called "gates," through which chi enters and leaves various areas of the body. They can be opened and closed by the action of muscles and breath. In the following exercise you will learn to lock three separate gates during your breathing practice. This strengthens key muscles, increases the flow of energy and blood to the pelvis and helps move chi from the genitals to nourish other organs, all of which enhances control and sensation, adding variety and intensity to the sexual experience. In the beginning, I recommend that you practice each lock separately in descending order:

1. *The Neck Lock.* Sit comfortably, with your back straight and well supported. Hold your head upright and keep your shoulders from hunching. Tighten your throat muscles by pulling your chin down toward your Adam's apple, creating the sensation of closing your throat. Imagine pushing the back of your neck forward to the front. Hold the position for three counts, then slowly relax.

2. *The Abdominal Lock.* Suck the lower abdomen inward and upward. Imagine that you are pulling your belly button in toward your spine and upward. Hold for three counts. This has a beneficial effect on the kidney organ system.

3. *The Anal Lock.* Contract your anal sphincter as if you were holding in a bowel movement. Hold for a count of three, then squeeze more firmly so that you feel muscles contract higher up in your rec-

tum. Hold for another three-count. Release the lock in reverse order, relaxing first the higher muscles, then the lower. The anal lock strengthens the muscles and increases blood flow in the pelvis, enlivening all the organs, nerves and glands in the area.

Once you feel comfortable with all three locks, practice closing them together. When you have mastered that, incorporate the practice into your breathing exercises. Simply close the locks while retaining your breath after inhalation, and release the locks as you exhale.

Chapter 5

INSIDE THE JADE CHAMBER

Mastering the Art of Intercourse

> *Of all the things that make mankind prosper, none can
> be compared to sexual intercourse. It is modeled after
> Heaven and takes its form by Earth; it regulates Yin
> and rules Yang. . . . Thus the four seasons succeed
> each other; man thrusts, woman receives;
> above there is action; below, receptivity.*

—Taoist master

The Hendersons were an affectionate couple. During our initial meeting together, they constantly held hands and touched each other. When I asked how often they had intercourse, I was not surprised by the initial response: "Almost every night." Then came the punch line: "Almost on Monday, almost on Tuesday, almost on Wednesday . . ."

They were joking, of course, but not entirely. Even though they had once been passionate and were still very much in love, the Hendersons did not have sex very often. When I asked them why, they rounded up the usual suspects: lack of time, fatigue, the pressures of career and parenting. When I pressed them, another factor emerged: boredom. Intercourse had become monotonous. They were using the same techniques and following the same routines they had when they first got married. Even their fantasies were monotonous. They could imagine having sex in different places or seducing each other under different circumstances, but the act of intercourse itself always fell into the same patterns and positions.

I ask couples like the Hendersons these questions: Would you keep listening to music if it never varied in tempo, tone or rhythm? Would you watch the same movie repeatedly, once or twice a week for years? Would you eat the same meal every day? If not, why would you make love the same way every time?

The art of intercourse contains possibilities that few couples imagine and techniques they don't even realize exist. The ancient Chinese discovered an enormous variety of intercourse positions and thrusting techniques. To them, the value of mastering this repertoire went beyond the enhancement of pleasure; intercourse techniques were known to have powerful ramifications for health and well-being. By mastering the art of intercourse they were able to work with sexual chi the way engineers use the energy created by waterfalls or nuclear reactors to light up cities. By practicing the techniques in this and the following two chapters, you will be able to light up your sex life, now and into your golden years. You will not only open the door to greater pleasure, you will be healthier and stronger and you'll ensure the future of your sexual relationship.

HAVING A HEAT WAVE

Expressions like "red-hot lover," "hot babe" and "in heat" were not invented in a vacuum. We use terms like *steamy, blazing, torrid* and *on fire* to describe passionate encounters because the heat we feel is literal. Like a car engine, the body revs up when sparks ignite between sexual partners, and it gets hotter and hotter as the pistons fire away. Think of it: When you get into bed you have to pull the covers over you to get warm; then you start making love, and before you know it you're sweating as if in a sauna, tearing off your pajamas and tossing off the covers.

During intercourse a tremendous amount of heat is generated—because of the friction in the genital area and a complex series of electrical and chemical events in the nervous system. Heat is a transmutable form of chi. The body converts it into other forms of energy, such as chemical and electrical. In turn, the chemistry of the blood and the electrochemical reactions of the nervous system generate more heat, producing a variety of reactions that we experience as passion, pleasure and intense emotion.

We in the West don't know what to do with the energy generated by intercourse except to throw off the covers and get "hot and heavy" with it. The ancient Chinese learned to harness it and move that heat energy through the meridian system to all the internal organs and the central and peripheral nervous systems. Their techniques, which you are about to learn, make it possible to use sexual chi for healing purposes, store it for future use and convert the chemistry of ordinary pleasure into the rocket fuel of sexual ecstasy.

I advise you to explore the techniques we are about to discuss with light hearts, a spirit of mutual exploration and patience. Don't put any pressure on yourselves. Just as it takes time to accomplish your other goals as a couple—completing your education, raising healthy children, improving communication, attaining a comfortable lifestyle, etc.—it takes time to master sexual techniques. Enjoy the process.

THE SACRED TRANSITION

For Chinese sexual sages, the transition from foreplay to intercourse was sacred. In addition to sublime works of art that illustrate the moment of penetration with delicate, erotic beauty, the ancient texts abound in poetic descriptions, such as this one from *The Mystic Master of the Grotto* (the grotto refers to the vagina): "He immediately drags his hardened jade stalk [penis] lengthwise against the doors of the jade gate [vagina], a sloping luxuriant pine tree nudging at the entrance of an unexpected valley. The jade stalk throbs, pulls, grinds and bridles. He kisses her mouth and seeks her tongue. Now he gazes at the jade face above, now he looks at the golden gulch [upper vulva] below. He strokes and pats the front of her abdomen and breasts, massages the sides of her examination hall [vulva]. When he is aroused and she is enchanted, he at once uses his Yang peak to assault vertically and horizontally, now impinging on the jade vein [lower vulva] below, now pressing at the golden gulch above, now stabbing at the sides of the examination hall, now resting on the right of the jewel terrace [clitoris]."

A lover's range of choices is as wide as that of a composer. Intercourse can begin with dramatic intensity, like Beethoven's Fifth Symphony, or quietly and gently, like Debussy's "Prelude to the Afternoon of a Faun." Like the opening movement of a musical composition, the first minute of intercourse can state a theme. The statement might be "We're eternal lovers united in an intimate embrace," or "Let's waltz slowly into ecstasy," or "We lust for each other and we're going to boogie our brains out." One partner might say with his or her style, "Trust me, I'm in control," or "Take me on an adventure," or, "Let me show you something new," or "Please reveal another part of yourself."

Artistic lovers pay special attention to the sacred transition and use it to add variety and surprise to their lovemaking. If what you're accustomed to doing works well, don't stop doing it. But consider adding a change in tone, texture or tempo from time to time. The important thing is to approach the moment of penetration with forethought, awareness and a sense of purpose. This is beneficial to both yin and yang energy. It gives yang a mission beyond its own satisfaction and gives yin an opportunity for greater participation. It helps women in particular feel more comfortable as they open up to the sexual experience. In general, an exciting start helps to ensure a glorious climax and the sweet elixir of intermingled chi.

Here are some tips for getting the most out of the sacred transition:

Transition Tips for Men

1. Rather than always entering your woman to the same depth and at the same speed, surprise her with something different. Do this often enough and she'll approach making love flush with anticipation.

2. Enter her only to the two-inch mark (the part of the vagina the Chinese called "the wheat bud"). Play around at that depth, like a dolphin dancing in the waves, then retreat and titillate her vulva with

your penis before entering her again. This extends the transition into a lovely, teasing duet.

3. Enter her quickly and deeply, then pull back almost all the way and pause. This will startle her a bit, but she will be delighted as you briefly hover close to the vaginal entrance before you resume thrusting.

4. Sustain penetration as long as possible by entering very, very slowly. Keep the speed of your entrance consistent from beginning to end. This can make the sublime transition last for what seems like hours. Be sure she is lubricated from top to bottom to ensure a smooth ride.

5. Change the speed of your initial thrust. Begin slowly, then, once you are inside an inch or so, suddenly speed up. Or, enter quickly, then pause and continue very slowly, making her wait for what feels like an eternity to be filled all the way.

6. Enter at a rather severe angle from the top or bottom, or from side to side. This will bring to her first moments of intercourse unusual and highly pleasurable sensations. Make sure you proceed slowly and that your partner's outer labia are well lubricated.

7. Prepare her body for penetration by parting her legs slowly. Enter her while she gently resists with counter pressure, increasing the tension in her inner thighs. You will both love the feel of this, provided she is well lubricated. Maintain steady pressure; don't use sudden, jerky movements. Let her provide variation by increasing and decreasing the tension in her thighs.

8. Place your hands on either side of her vulva and pull her labia slightly farther apart as you penetrate. This increases the tension around the opening to the vagina, providing a new, heightened sensation. For you to access her in this way, she needs to have her legs wide open or raised.

9. Bob back and forth as you enter her. Move forward two inches, then back one inch, then forward two and back one and so on. It

may take three or four repetitions to get all the way inside, but the journey will be lovely.

10. Don't enter at all, just knock on the door repeatedly. Place your penis at the opening of her vagina and push very gently. As the head begins to enter her, pull back. Repeat this several times, until she is panting to have you inside.

Transition Tips for Women

1. Vary the degree of tension in your vaginal muscles. For example, contract the muscles of the outer portion of the vagina (but not so tightly as to cause discomfort) and have your partner enter you slowly. As he penetrates, relax the muscles. You will feel like a flower opening in the spring.

The easiest position in which to adjust your muscle tension is lying on your back. Once you become skilled at controlling the muscles of the vagina you will find it easier to do in other positions. The next chapter contains exercises that will help you accomplish this.

2. Change the angle of your legs. This alters the direction of penetration and the accessibility of your vulva, allowing for many new sensations. If you are on your back, you can place your feet on his shoulders, wrap your legs around his waist, extend your legs straight out on the bed, cross your ankles and so forth.

3. Press your hands against your partner's hips or groin so that he can enter you only to the depth you desire. After several strokes, without warning, move your hands so that he plunges deeply into you.

4. Slowly change the angle of your pelvis as he enters you. For example, start with a straight back and move into an arched posture. This is a subtle change, but it produces pleasant results and does not require new positions or a great degree of assertiveness.

5. If you are on top, in the assertive or controlling position, insert your partner's penis into you from a severe angle by leaning forward or back. Go slowly so as not to put too much pressure on his penis as it rubs against your vaginal wall. Be sure you are well lubricated before doing this.

WANTED, DEAD OR ALIVE

In a sexy twist on an old adage, Mae West once said, "A hard man is good to find." Well, most women would certainly agree. Intercourse is virtually defined as a man entering a woman with an erection and withdrawing without one. But hardness isn't necessarily a prerequisite. In fact, there is special satisfaction to be gained from the occasional use of soft entry—what the ancient Chinese, in typically colorful fashion, called "In Dead, Out Alive."

In addition to providing a fresh twist to your sexual agenda, the technique has several advantages:

1. One of the changes that can occur as couples age is that the man takes longer to gain an erection due to the gradual loss of yang energy to life's demands. This can be traumatic for those who don't anticipate it or realize how common it is. One advantage of In Dead, Out Alive is that a couple can gain experience in beginning intercourse without the need for an erection.

2. It reduces performance pressure on the man. When having an erection becomes a goal rather than a natural event, it adds a measure of tension, which invariably makes an erection problem worse than it already is. Just as the more you try to fall asleep the less sleep you get, the harder a man tries to get hard, the harder it is to get hard. Adding soft entry to your repertoire reduces performance anxiety considerably. It also reduces the sense of failure and shame that a man feels when he doesn't get an erection. Men find it a great relief to learn that their wands can still make magic even when they dangle. The result is more relaxed intercourse even when you *don't* practice this technique.

3. It provides an entirely new set of sensations. Because a soft penis feels different from an erection—and also from a finger or a

tongue—the technique expands a couple's range of pleasure. A soft penis can feel wonderful to a woman, both when it strokes the vulva and when it's nestled inside the vagina. In addition, as the man begins to become erect, his partner has the unique experience of feeling his penis become engorged while inside her. Many women find this extremely arousing.

The technique also brings new sensations to the man. Men are used to becoming hard in a woman's hand or mouth, or without any direct contact at all. The feeling of the penis expanding as it pushes against the walls of a vagina is a different kind of pleasure entirely.

4. As we will discuss momentarily, many women prefer shallow penetration in the early stages of intercourse. Soft entry has the advantage of making deep penetration—for which the women might not yet be ready—impossible.

5. It makes the woman more aware of her vagina. This is a subtle benefit. To fully appreciate the unique sensation of soft entry, the woman has to pay closer attention to her vaginal sensations. The heightened awareness and concentration that result can enhance her ability to create varied sensations in the future.

6. It can make a man more receptive. Since hard is yang and soft is yin, the technique makes the man more vulnerable in the context of intercourse. This effect is amplified when the technique is performed with the woman on top and when she controls the penis during insertion.

How to Do It

Soft entry requires special handling. Either the man or the woman has to gently stuff the penis into the vagina. The Chinese recommend that the woman be in charge. This enables her to give herself pleasure by manipulating the penis as she wishes, perhaps using it to stroke her clitoris or vulva before insertion or between insertions.

The easiest position to be in is with the woman on top. Straddle his waist while facing him. Cup your hand so the palm faces up and clasp the base of his penis between your index finger and middle finger, firmly but not hard enough to hurt him. Grasping the penis in this way also helps assure that any blood that has already entered the organ will stay inside. This helps maintain enough rigidity for insertion. You might want to use your other hand to part the lips of your vulva.

The female superior position offers maximum maneuverability. If the woman were to lie on her back she would have to tighten her abdominal muscles in order to reach down to hold the penis. This would have the undesirable effect of tightening her vagina, making insertion slightly more difficult. If you do choose to lie on your back, propping your head and neck on pillows will help.

The position that gives the man the best handling ability is with the woman on her back, with her hips close to the end of the bed and the man standing or kneeling between her legs. Being supported by his legs frees up his hands and gives him more stability. He should grasp his penis at the base and hold it gently but firmly from both sides. This will make it slightly rigid. It is also important for the woman's vagina to be relaxed and moist.

Once the penis is inserted, as long as it remains soft or semierect it's usually a good idea to keep holding it at the base. This keeps it from slipping out and allows it to be manipulated into the most pleasurable angles.

The Chinese called the technique In Dead, Out Alive because they advocated withdrawing after erection is attained and before ejaculation. As we will discuss in the next chapter, nonejaculatory sex is a central feature of ancient sexual teachings. For now, suffice it to say that when the man refrains from ejaculating on first impulse, the encounter can last much longer and the pleasures of initial penetration can be repeated. When a man does not dissipate his sexual energy through ejaculation, he continues to have a high level of interest and anticipation, and his partner can experience ongoing delight and multiple orgasms.

For couples who are not ready to pursue the Out-Alive option (or are not interested in doing so), the In-Dead portion can simply be enjoyed on its own. When erection is achieved, intercourse can continue in the usual manner. But it should not be assumed that as soon as the man becomes hard, thrusting has to become hot and heavy. He might feel a greater urgency to reach orgasm once he has an erection, but the use of control and variety should not be automatically abandoned.

Another option is for the man to withdraw (come out alive, so to speak) and for the couple to change position or reverse roles. If, for example, the woman had been in control, the man might now assume the yang role. You might want to discuss in advance what you will do if and when the penis becomes "alive."

THRUSTING:
THE INS AND OUTS
OF INTERCOURSE

When it came to pelvic thrusting, the ancient Chinese made Elvis Presley look as if he were standing still. The Taoists described an amazing variety of thrusting styles, in typically poetic terms, such as: "He moves his jade peak out and in, hammering at the left and right sides of the examination hall, as if a blacksmith is shaping iron with his five hammers." Or this: "Thrust down to the jade substance and pull up by the gold gully [clitoris], as though slicing off stones to find beautiful jade." Thrusts can be deep or shallow; light or forceful; intense or superficial; probing, teasing or coy; straight ahead or at an angle. They can be slow or fast, gradual or sudden, repetitive or varied. Then there is the possibility of pausing, which adds an element of anticipation, mystery and grandeur.

By drawing on the full range of thrusting possibilities, sexual artists can enhance their pleasure as well as their overall health and vitality. Expanding your repertoire of thrusting techniques helps to ensure that the entire penis and vagina are stimulated, thus invigorating all the organs of the body equally through the reflexology system. It can also extend the duration of intercourse, which activates a greater amount of chi and enhances all the benefits that superior sex bestows on both partners. Fast, deep, repetitive thrusting—the kind most men habitually use—tends to speed up the male orgasm because it provides a lot of intense stimulation to the entire penis. Varying the depth and speed gives a man greater ejaculatory control as well as a variety of ways to tantalize and delight his partner.

Monotonous pumping can also have a numbing effect on the woman, especially if foreplay has been insufficient and she is not aroused enough to respond to the intense sensations. Overstimulation can lead to a loss of sensitivity. A pleasant massage, for example, can feel annoying if the same section of skin is rubbed over and over again. After a while, the nervous system simply tunes out. Hence, no matter how exciting they are at first, the same thrusts repeated endlessly will soon lose their sparkle. In fact, couples often find themselves rushing to climax to avoid the tedium of that same in-and-out feeling.

By creating ever-new sensations, varied thrusting also increases the potential for pleasure, leading to powerful orgasms and all the benefits to body and soul that they bring. Just as painters can create endlessly new canvases by utilizing the complete repertoire of brush strokes, colors, textures and shapes, creative lovers can use thrusting variations to transport each other to the stars and moon. Let's look at some basic ways to add shade and texture to intercourse.

The Long and the Short of It

To help physicians locate acupuncture points, and to aid in sexual instruction, the ancient Chinese divided the vagina into eight sections according to their distance from the opening. Each yields different sensations and is the focal point of specific thrusting styles. Characteristically, the Chinese gave each section of the vagina, from the entrance to the cervix, its own name (the basic unit of measurement, the *tzun,* is approximately one inch, or two centimeters, in length).

- 1 tzun: Lute String
- 2 tzun: Water Chestnut Teeth
- 3 tzun: Little Stream
- 4 tzun: Black Pearl

- 5 tzun: Valley Proper
- 6 tzun: Deep Chamber
- 7 tzun: Inner Door
- 8 tzun: North Pole*

While counseling the Yellow Emperor on the art of thrusting, Su Nu pointed out that remaining superficial limits pleasure, while thrusting too deeply without restraint may injure the woman. Between the two extremes lies a wide range of possibilities, divided into two basic categories: shallow (roughly the first four inches) and deep (more than four inches).

Run Shallow, Run Deep

Basic to every pattern of thrusting advocated by the sexual masters is this principle: Start with predominantly shallow thrusts, add occasional deep thrusts, and increase the proportion of deep thrusts as the level of excitation builds. There are several reasons why this makes sense. One is to prolong intercourse while maximizing pleasure. Not only does persistent deep pumping hasten the male climax, it is also less stimulating for the woman in the early stages of intercourse. Deep thrusts can be tremendously exciting once a woman is highly aroused, and especially just prior to orgasm, but if she has deep thrusts imposed on her before she is adequately warmed up, she might have trouble keeping up with her partner and be unable to participate fully. In essence, he will be doing it *to* her instead of with her. And if she is *really* not ready for deep thrusts, her body might feel very little throughout the act. This can eventuate in chi stagnation, causing gynecological problems and resentment toward her lover.

In traditional Chinese terms, deep thrusts are yin and shallow thrusts are yang. You might think it would be the other way around, since deep seems to suggest more aggressiveness and power. But in Yin-Yang Theory the inner part of the body is yin, whereas everything on the surface

---

*The cervix and surrounding tissue.

is yang. Because the purpose of intercourse is to unite yin and yang, it stands to reason that men, who are primarily yang, would rush to the deeper portion of the female body, which is yin. It also stands to reason that women would benefit from having the yang areas of their genitals aroused first, since the yin portions heat up more slowly.

Let's look at some hard facts about anatomy: The nerves in the outer portion of the vagina are more sensitive to touch; the nerves deeper inside are more sensitive to pressure. In the earlier stages of intercourse, shallow thrusting is better for a woman because it directly stimulates the areas of the vagina that are most responsive to touch. When the head of the penis, with its soft ridges, moves back and forth along the first few exquisitely tender inches of the vagina, the woman receives intense pleasure and stimulation. This builds up heat and excitement, setting the stage for her to get maximal pleasure from the stimulation of deeper portions of the vagina. Another advantage to shallow thrusts is that, depending on the angle of penetration, they can be used to stimulate the G spot.

For women, the urge to be filled up is like hunger. Shallow thrusts arouse the appetite for deep penetration, just as an appetizer makes a diner hungrier for the main course. Superficial thrusts also serve as a tease. When the man pulls out nearly all the way, the woman's body may react as if he is leaving. Sometimes the vagina instinctively contracts, as if trying to keep the penis inside. This not only heightens the woman's emotional expectations but also creates a pleasurable physical sensation by increasing friction. She can enhance this feeling by intentionally contracting her pelvic muscles.

If done with consideration and the intention to please one's partner, teasing can be quite romantic and erotic. The longer that shallow thrusting is sustained, the more suspense is created, and the more intense the ultimate satisfaction. A skilled man can create in his woman an almost unbearable sense of yearning and anticipation. When, after lingering on her doorstep for a long time, he finally enters the inner chamber, she becomes, in essence, much more welcoming. She has been made hungry, and the deep penetration sates that hunger. Energetically, her yin has become involved and is now ready to unite with his yang in a powerful exchange of health-giving chi. Anatomically, the pressure-sensitive nerves deep inside the vagina have been aroused and are now capable of responding with greater pleasure.

The sexual masters recommended alternating shallow and deep thrusts. When the vagina is filled up entirely, any air that might have entered is forced out. If, after deep penetration, the man pulls out partway and thrusts superficially, the vacuum created by the lack of air and the movement of the penis creates a slight tugging sensation on the inner walls of the vagina. This increases the pleasurable sensations from pressure-sensitive nerves deeper within.

Naturally, during intercourse the head of the penis and the outer portion of the vagina always receive the most friction. Shallow thrusting accentuates the effect. In the early stages, this has great advantages: it not only focuses friction on the most sensitive parts of the genitals, but it activates the woman's kidneys and the man's heart and lungs (see reflexology charts on page 93).

Because the head of the penis is connected to the heart and lungs, stimulating the area draws yang chi upward, facilitating its natural movement. Deep thrusts stimulate the *base* of the penis, which activates the kidneys and draws the yin aspect of the man's sexuality downward. Combining deep and shallow thrusts creates a circle of movement through the organ system, invigorating both yin and yang.

A similar process takes place in the woman's body. Shallow thrusts stimulate her vulva, which corresponds to her kidneys. This pulls chi downward, in the yin direction, and enlivens the sexual and reproductive organs. As the proportion of deep thrusts increases, the innermost areas of the vagina are stimulated, as is the corresponding organ—the heart. This creates a circle of chi from the heart to the genitals and back. Again, yin and yang are brought into balance.

Overall, the ancient Chinese found that alternating shallow and deep thrusts creates the most beneficial stimulation of all the organs through the reflexology system. The sexual texts describe a number of thrusting patterns. My advice is to begin experimenting in a flexible manner but to follow these basic principles:

1. In the beginning of intercourse, use several shallow thrusts for every deep thrust. You might find it easier to start with a small ratio,

such as three shallow–one deep, and increase to five-and-one, seven-and-one and nine-and-one as you become more skillful.

2. As intercourse progresses, increase the number of deep thrusts. For example, six shallow–two deep or nine shallow–three deep and so on.

3. One of you should be in control. While communication is essential before, during and after intercourse, it's best if one partner takes the lead at any given time. This allows the receiving partner to relax and go along for the ride. It also allows for more variety, spontaneity and surprise.

Because he is wielding the thrusting instrument and is usually on top, the male partner is typically the one in control. One way for a woman to take charge of thrusting when in the receptive position is to put her hands between her legs and either cup the sides of her vulva or make two fists. This enables her to use her hands to keep her partner from entering too deeply. Another method is to place her hands on his hip bones and apply different levels of pressure to hold him farther away or let him in deeper. She can also change the angle of her pelvis in different ways—by arching her back, for example.

4. Men should always remember that shallow works best for building excitement in the woman, and deep works best when she is aroused and wants to be sated. As a rule, when she's warming up, tease her more; when she's really hot, satisfy her more. It is usually not very difficult to recognize when your partner is ready for deep thrusting. She may press her pelvis toward you and move her body in such a way as to draw you further into her. She might grab your behind with her hands, or wrap her legs around you and pull you closer. But you don't have to yield to her desire immediately. You might want to keep the tease going as long as you can, until the room is spinning and she's practically begging to let loose with total abandon. The more you tantalize a woman, the more satisfied she will ultimately feel.

5. Once you're experienced in varying your thrusting depth, try to vary the pattern within each lovemaking session to keep the element of surprise alive. You might start out with an entirely different pattern, for example, or interrupt a rhythm to try something new.

6. Bear in mind that varying your thrusting pattern may require more control and willpower than you can manage at first, especially for the man. Because yang chi creates structure and organization, men typically settle on something that "works" and then use it over and over again. When you introduce these new skills, start at a comfortable level, practice without pressure or unrealistic expectations and work your way gradually to a more varied repertoire.

And don't be too mechanical or rigid about counting. You don't want to lose the spontaneous joy of sex or the pleasure that comes from letting the lower parts of your body take over from your brain. Like any new skill, patterned thrusting requires conscious attention in the beginning stages, but it soon becomes second nature. If you keep it up (pun intended), you and your partner will soon be moving together like Fred Astaire and Ginger Rogers, without counting the beats. It's well worth the effort.

The Sets of Nine: Something to Shoot For

If you'd like something to aim for, here it is. Dr. Stephen T. Chang, author of *The Tao of Sexology,* recommends a thrusting system that he says will energize all the organ systems and produce a balanced infusion of vital chi throughout the body. It also mobilizes a great amount of sexual chi, adding strength and staying power to the act. Over time, practicing a disciplined technique like this makes lovers better sexual artists. It expands their repertoire, improves their control and boosts their confidence.

The Sets of Nine technique works best when performed slowly. It begins with a sequence of nine shallow and one deep, then continues by subtracting one shallow thrust and adding one deep thrust in successive sets, like this:

SHALLOW STROKES	DEEP STROKES
9	1
8	2
7	3
6	4
5	5
4	6
3	7
2	8
1	9

Getting through a full set takes a great deal of control on the man's part. The techniques for delaying ejaculation in the next chapter will improve your staying power. Meanwhile, don't feel as though you've failed if you accomplish only a small part of the Sets of Nine. If, for example, you find it more comfortable to repeat one of the patterns, do so. If at any point you both find yourselves overwhelmed by desire and want to relinquish yourselves to unfettered thrusting, by all means let go and enjoy it to the hilt. If, on the other hand, you get through a complete set of nines and want to continue, go ahead and start over. Highly accomplished sexual artists are said to do numerous sets of nine without ejaculating.

Stillness Moves Us

In music, rest stops between notes build suspense and power. The same is true of intercourse. Stillness creates a delicious sense of anticipation. It also increases one's awareness of the sensation of motion, just as silence in music raises one's awareness of sound. Stillness is a yin quality. It has a natural appeal to women and to the yin aspect of men, providing balance to the yang of motion. In addition to removing the urgency from the sexual act and calming the lovers' bodies, strategic pauses extend the duration of intercourse and give yin chi more time to heat up. As mentioned earlier, the more yin that is brought into the act, the greater the ability to receive love, pleasure and chi from one's beloved.

When to Pause

1. When you want to tease your partner in a loving way. Just as shallow strokes increase the hunger for deep thrusting, a pause increases the hunger for movement.

2. When you're trying to maintain a slow pace or prolong intercourse. A brief respite interrupts the stimulation and gives you a chance to cool down if you're overexcited.

3. When you're tired. A pause allows you to rejuvenate yourself.

4. When you feel the need to regain your sense of control.

How to Pause

What does sexual silence entail? Pretty much whatever you want it to. Here are a few suggestions:

1. Stop moving, whether for a few seconds or several minutes, while remaining coupled in intercourse. This can produce exquisite feelings of closeness and intimacy, even if the erection diminishes.

2. Withdraw entirely and snuggle together for ten seconds. A brief respite from the meal enhances the appetite. You then get to enjoy once again the sacred transition into intercourse.

3. Withdraw and do things normally associated with foreplay— kiss, hug, caress, engage in oral sex.

4. Use the pause in intercourse to bring the woman to orgasm orally, manually, or through her own masturbatory efforts. Then resume intercourse to create higher levels of orgasm for her.

After the pause you can take up where you left off or start something entirely new. In any case, you get to enjoy once again the beauty of gradually building up excitement.

Be aware that during a pause the man may lose his erection. In some instances, he might not get it back so easily, especially if he is tired, distracted or recovering from an illness. It would be self-defeating to make staying erect, or becoming erect again quickly, a necessary goal. The erection is more likely to return in an atmosphere of calmness rather than tension. Make it okay either not to resume intercourse at all or to try the in-dead-out-alive technique described earlier in this chapter.

The main point is, once intercourse begins it does not always have to be carried to its usual conclusion in a linear fashion. Sex isn't necessarily an express train. You can make as many stopovers as you like, for as long as you like.

THRUSTING SPEED

Goal-oriented yang wants to move fast and reach its destination. This is especially true with younger men, whose sexual chi consists of proportionately more yang. The yin tendency is the opposite: women usually favor slower thrusting in the simmering early stages of intercourse. This doesn't mean that men are always jitterbugging while their women want to waltz. The yin aspect of men enjoys slow dancing, and many men are sensitive enough to put the brakes on their natural tendency to please their women. It's also true that yang-oriented women prefer to pump fast and furious right at the outset.

Thrusting preferences tend to change with age. One of the advantages of a long-term relationship is that over time couples become more alike in terms of sexual energy. As they approach middle age, men burn up their primary aspect and their yin exerts a larger influence on their sexual behavior. They become more patient and find it easier to move slowly during intercourse. This change suits most women just fine. In many cases, they need *less* time to heat up, for their yin energy has dissipated because of childbirth and the stress and strain of daily life. As they age, many women take pleasure in approaching sex in a more yanglike way, initiating the action, taking control and thrusting faster.

Long before age brings their energetic profiles closer together, wise partners learn to recognize and obey their bodies' signals. Take, for example, my patient Carla and her husband, Ned. A very aggressive woman, Carla is in a demanding, stress-riddled profession, and most of her workday is fueled by her yang energy. On some nights, she would arrive home still in high gear and jump her husband's bones with the energy and fervor of a sailor on shore leave. Other times, she would recognize that her body had become yin deficient and needed to be balanced. On those occasions Carla was drawn to more traditional sex, in which she played the coy, receptive partner who yielded to her man's control. This helped to revive her yin.

Two problems cropped up when Carla was in her yin mode. One, when she wanted Ned to take charge, he would often go too fast, reaching full thrusting speed way ahead of the pace that Carla's body needed. Two, Carla was conflicted: as a young, independent feminist, she felt there was something wrong with wanting male-dominated sex. Both partners had something to learn: Ned, that he could take control without *losing* control; Carla, that nurturing her yin needs in bed was a way of creating balance, and did not mean that she was belittling herself. On the contrary, she was accessing her deeper strengths.

The Slow Ride to Orgasm

Couples are often surprised to learn that female needs are usually best served by starting intercourse with slow thrusts. This is largely because many women have never actually done it that way. Another reason is that as women heat up, they naturally begin to thrust faster while displaying various signs of high arousal. It's easy for a man to conclude that fast thrusting is a major turn-on for his partner.

As heat builds up from the friction of intercourse, the yang aspect gradually takes over. That's why, just prior to orgasm, men and women alike thrust hard and deep and fast. In terms of the propagation model, the woman has received the man's contribution and has transformed it into mutual lovemaking; now she is able to contribute what she has created in the form of intense passion. Instead of merely *allowing* him to thrust deep and fast, she joins in the effort, helping to make her and her partner one as excitement builds and the exchange of energy is most powerful. The man's dynamic in the propagation model is this: He has been contributing; now, when the woman heats up and starts thrusting rapidly, he is also in the receiving position. For him, orgasm represents the point of transition from the sensation of contributing to the sensation of being fully receptive.

For a man, learning to adapt to a woman's thrusting needs can pay off handsomely in the long run. Eventually, when your partner begins moving faster and faster, she won't be merely accommodating you; her body will *want* to move quickly. When that happens, the rapid thrusting you've been craving will be infinitely more satisfying because you and your partner will be in sync. The energy that has built up between you will penetrate deeply into both of you. Your entire bodies, not just your genitals, will be involved in the lovemaking. So will your souls: what had already been a pleasure will take on the qualities of ecstasy.

As you become more adept, you might want to mix up the speed of thrusting. If you're moving slowly, slowly, slowly, suddenly surprise your lover with a series of rapid thrusts. If you're pumping quickly and moving closer to orgasm, you might want to suddenly slow down for a while before speeding up again. Remember, any tune can be played in different tempos.

THE RIGHT ANGLES

Changing angles—up or down or side to side—is another way to vary the art form. Each angle stimulates different parts of the genitals and therefore generates its own type of excitement and sends healing chi to different organs according to the reflexology system. In fact, the usual thrusting angle—straight ahead, with the penis filling the cylinder of the vagina like a piston—can be the least stimulating for women, particularly if it's the *only* angle that's used. Varying angles also creates more pleasure and health benefits for the man by applying pressure to different areas of the penis.

In general, if you think of the circumference of the vagina as a clock, the most sensitive area is at twelve o'clock (the ceiling) and the least sensitive is at six o'clock (the floor). The ceiling of the vagina, of course, includes the famous G spot, which can be exquisitely sensitive.

For this reason, I recommend finding ways to angle the penis upward. At the same time, by angling *downward* in the right way—and perhaps using a hand to press the penis down—you can produce interesting sensations on the perineal muscle that runs between the vagina and anus.

A downward angle can also create delicious sensations on the clitoris. Many women don't have orgasms during intercourse because their clitoris does not receive sufficient stimulation. One way to remedy this is to stimulate it during intercourse with either the man's or woman's fingers. Another is to angle the penis in a sharp, downward direction so the partners' bodies are more parallel than perpendicular. When the man's pubic bone (the hard area of his abdomen, just above the shaft of the penis) is aligned with the woman's mons (the fleshy pad just above the vulva), deep thrusting is virtually impossible, but the clitoris—which sits just below the mons and above the vaginal opening—can be directly stimulated by the shaft of the penis. If you use that angle, try rocking in a gentle, rhythmic motion, with a minimum of movement.

Since every woman has her own preferences in vaginal sensation, I tell my male patients to experiment with various angles to see which elicit the most pleasure. They are often surprised by what they discover. For example, many women love to feel a man's testicles bump against them as he thrusts, and certain angles allow for that. Also, some angles stimulate parts of the vulva, which can be far more exciting than many women realize. If, for example, the man tilts so that he enters his partner at a slight sideways angle, he can glide along the side of the labia minora (the inner lips of the vagina), creating a new set of sensations for both partners. Men can accentuate this effect by using their hands to cup the vulva and pressing inward while thrusting—in essence, squeezing the labia around the penis.

The woman can alter the angle of penetration by raising or lowering her legs, tilting her pelvis, or twisting slightly to one side or the other. Perhaps the best position in which the woman can explore different angles is crouching on top of the man, with her feet flat on the bed on either side of his hips. Essentially, she squats, lowering herself onto his penis with her knees pointing upward. This enables her to maneuver her entire body weight, allowing for a wide range of motion and enabling her to change the angle of her pelvis. Another good position has her lying on her back with him perpendicular to her—while standing at the foot of the bed, for example. But even in the most ordinary positions, with a little practice, women can learn to adjust the angle of penetration.

Remember, when trying something new, it's always best to use slow, shallow thrusts. This reduces the risk of injury from overzealous pounding at a precarious angle.

TAKING A POSITION

When asked toward the end of his life if there was anything he would have done differently if he could, Groucho Marx replied, "Try more positions."

He should have read the ancient Chinese treatises on sex; they expound more positions than a politician trying to win votes. Even an imagination as fertile as Groucho's would be boggled by the diversity in those texts, and by the erotic illustrations that accompany the descriptions.

While it would be foolhardy to attempt to master the full range of positions, it would be equally foolish to settle on one and ignore the pleasures to be found in others. Each position lends itself to certain movements, angles and depths of penetration. Therefore, each creates a specific set of physical sensations. They also elicit different emotional and psychological experiences; seeing each other's faces, for example, is different from having the man view the back of the woman's head while the woman sees the wall.

A couple's position preferences depend on their likes and dislikes, their personalities and their attitudes about issues such as openness and control. Their physical conditions also play a role, since some positions require more flexibility or strength than others. Height, weight, shape, distribution of muscle and fat, and the length, width and placement of the sexual organs also help determine which positions are comfortable, or even possible. It's important to honor these differences and use only positions that are suitable for both partners. I trust you will have better luck than the late actress Tallulah Bankhead, who once complained,

"The conventional position makes me claustrophobic, and the others either give me a stiff neck or lockjaw."

Trying different positions will not only add fun and adventure to your experience of intercourse, it will also increase your pleasure and amplify the benefits of sex to your overall health and well-being.

One of the Yellow Emperor's female tutors taught him nine fundamental positions. Each was given a name based on the behavior of creatures in nature. Later, other commentators added more postures, some of which require the agility of an acrobat. What follows are the basic nine, along with some of their more attainable variations. Don't simply follow the descriptions as if they were instructions for using a new gadget; adapt them to your own preferences and needs. When you add to these positions the assortment of thrusting depths, angles and speeds that are available, intercourse becomes limited only by the boundaries of your imagination and sense of adventure. If all this knowledge had been available to Groucho Marx he would have died with no regrets.

1. The Dragon Turns   The woman lies on her back, legs barely parted, with her thighs on the bed. The man lies on top of her. She raises her pelvis to receive his jade stalk (the penis). While this position limits the depth of thrusting, it lends itself to romance because it enables lovers to see each other's expressions, gaze into each other's eyes, kiss and embrace. Different sensations can be achieved if the woman makes subtle adjustments: moving her legs closer or further apart; pointing her feet straight up or splaying them to the sides. Also, raising her pubic bone while pressing her back to the bed increases the tension across the pelvic muscles and thighs, which can enhance sensation.

2. Treading Tigers   This is the basic rear-entry position, the one Shakespeare must have had in mind when he referred to a couple "making the beast with two backs." The woman leans on her hands and knees as if crawling. Her head is low and her buttocks are raised. The man kneels behind her, wraps his arms around her waist and "inserts his penis deeply—piercing her innermost center," as the Chinese texts describe it. They move back and forth, "advancing and retreating, like tigers attacking." There are, essentially, three op-

The Dragon Turns

tions: He pushes while she remains still; she pushes back toward him as he holds still; they both push.

In a variation called *Donkeys in Spring*, the woman bends over with her hands touching the floor or the seat of a chair and her legs slightly bent. The man stands behind her. The tension in her hip and pelvic muscles helps to hold her up while she leans over. It also makes the vaginal opening tighter. Obviously, this position requires

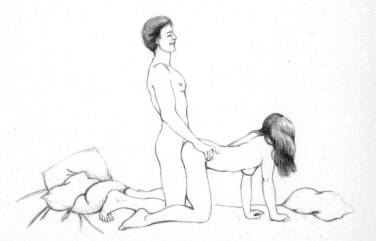

Treading Tigers

a certain amount of flexibility on the woman's part, along with the ability to raise her haunches high. Alternatively, she can be on her hands and knees near the edge of the bed while her lover stands on the floor. This increases the couple's ability to vary the angle and depth of penetration. By crouching slightly, he may be able to rub his penis against her clitoris. By standing higher (on tiptoe, perhaps, or on a phone book), the man can angle with shallow thrusts to stimulate her G spot.

3. Monkey Attacks The woman lies on her back with her legs raised and resting on the man's torso. He kneels between her legs and pushes her legs straight back toward her chest. This raises her buttocks and lower back off the bed. (One variation instructs the man to push her feet back with his left hand, while using his right hand to insert his penis.) The description then gets sexy: He pierces her "perfumed mouse" deeply with his jade stalk, and her "fluids pour like heavy rain." While thrusting, he holds up her buttocks with his hands. This position is excellent for a man with a narrow penis, if the woman's legs are held close together. To tighten her vaginal opening further, she can cross her legs while they are in the air.

One popular variation is called *Wild Horses Leaping*. In this posi-

Monkey Attacks

tion, the woman's feet are thrown over the man's shoulders. This severely restricts her freedom of movement but allows the man to thrust very deeply, at angles that are highly arousing to his beloved. Also, by leaning forward and angling his body so that it's more parallel to hers, he can stimulate her clitoris with his belly. The position is especially good for a woman with a long vagina and a man with a short penis.

4. Cleaving the Cicada   The women lies facedown with her legs extended. The man lies on her back and inserts his jade stalk, raising her buttocks so he can "tap at her red pearl" (the labia minora). The position allows for only shallow thrusting, but it can serve as a delicious tease and can turn into Treading Tigers when you get very excited. It is said that in this position the woman becomes so aroused that the inside of her vagina throbs and her vulva spreads open.

Here is a delightful way to get started in this position. Begin with the man giving his lover a light sensual back massage. Kiss her lovingly on her buttocks and the back of her thighs. Without penetrating, "dance at the palace door," using your penis to touch her labia with light, feathery strokes while your fingertips gently stroke her back. This will be an encounter she will not soon forget.

5. Mounting Tortoise   The woman lies on her back and raises her legs with knees bent (as opposed to Monkey Attacks, where her legs are straight). Kneeling, the man pushes her feet until her knees reach

Cleaving the Cicada

Mounting Tortoise

her breasts, then enters her. The position allows for a wide range of mobility. He is advised to alternate deep and shallow thrusts, and when his lover "shakes and rises" and "exudes copious fluids," he should penetrate to the deepest point.

This position is especially good if the woman's vagina is naturally narrow or the man's penis is very wide. If that is the case, the woman should be as relaxed as possible when the man enters her. The man can help by spreading her buttocks or labia apart with his hands.

In a variation called *Sea Gulls Soaring*, the man stands at the edge of the bed, lifts the woman's bent legs high and penetrates.

6. *The Phoenix Soars*   The woman lies on her back with her hands palms-down on the bed and raises her legs, with her knees pointing straight up and her thighs perpendicular to her torso (as opposed to Monkey Attacks and Mounting Tortoise, where her legs are pulled back). The man kneels between her thighs, supporting himself by placing his hands on the bed on either side of the woman. When he inserts his jade stalk, she begins moving. This position works espe-

The Phoenix Soars

cially well if the woman controls the movement and the thrusting is rapid, "with their buttocks attacking each other."

7. *Rabbit Lickings Its Fur*   Here we have the man on his back, legs extended. With her back to his face, the woman straddles him, placing her legs on either side of his body. She inserts his penis into her and "moves voluptuously," bending forward with her head lowered and her hands resting either on the bed or on his legs. Among other

Rabbit Licking Its Fur

things, this position is good for women who like to massage their clitoris during intercourse but are too shy to have their men watch.

In a variation called *Mountain Goat Hugging a Tree,* the man sits up (preferably with his back supported by pillows) with his legs extended. From this position he can reach around and stimulate her clitoris and vulva. He can also spread open her vulva from underneath.

8. *Fish Joining Scales* Another woman-on-top position, only this time she faces him. The man lies on his back, legs extended. She straddles him and moves her pelvis forward to insert his penis. The texts recommend that she not sit down all the way, thereby keeping penetration shallow. One translation says that the jade stalk should "lightly sport inside her . . . like an infant playing with its mother's breast." In general, movement should be controlled by the woman.

In one variation, *Fluttering Butterfly,* it is specified that the woman should rest her feet on the bed and lean forward, supporting herself with her hands; this alters the angle of penetration. If she lies almost parallel to him and rubs her pelvis against his, she can stimulate her own clitoris without using her fingers.

Fish Joining Scales

Cranes with Necks Intertwined

9. Cranes with Necks Intertwined   The man sits either cross-legged or with his buttocks resting on his heels. Wrapping her arms around his neck, the woman sits on his lap, facing him, with her feet on the bed beside his thighs or hips. After penetration, he holds her buttocks to help guide her up-and-down movements as "the jade stalk stabs her wheat bud and strives to strike her seed." One of the advantages of this position is that it allows for stimulation of the clitoris and sensitive front wall of the vagina as it rubs against his lower abdomen. If she leans back and rests her weight on her hands, she can maneuver her G spot into position for stimulation.

One variation, *Shouting Monkey Embraces a Tree,* is easier on the man's knees: he sits with his legs extended.

Taking Sides

The nine positions appear to have one glaring omission: there is no side-by-side posture. A few centuries later, another Taoist master rectified that with what he called *Fish Eye-to-Eye.* In this position, the man and woman lie facing each other, taking pleasure in their lips and tongues. She raises one leg above his side. Supporting the leg with his hand, he inserts his jade stalk and they rock back and forth together.

Another side-by-side position is known as *Mandarin Ducks Joined*. Instead of facing each other, the man is behind the woman. She bends both legs and raises the upper one. He supports her raised leg with his upper leg and inserts his penis from the rear.

In Chinese literature, the descriptions of the positions include colorful images of female arousal, such as "her fluids pour like a fountain." They also call for the man to stop "when she rejoices" or "when she reaches the zenith of pleasure." This is consistent with the ancients' emphasis on female orgasm and the retention of male semen. Illustrating the Chinese view that good health as well as pleasure can be gleaned from the act of love, the descriptions end with phrases such as "A hundred illnesses will vanish" or "The seven injuries are cured." Great pleasure and better health are in store for you, too, if you put yourself in these positions.

PHYSICAL BARRIERS

Adjusting your position is the best way to solve problems of incompatibility due to the size, shape and position of the genitals.

One Size Does Not Fit All

Bigger is not necessarily better. However, size *does* matter in another sense: it's important for his penis and her vagina to fit well together. If they are incompatible, problems can arise and adjustments must be made.

In ancient China, when parents chose spouses for their children, one thing they considered very important was genital compatibility. Even when the children were five or ten years old, the parents would use a traditional method of facial diagnosis to determine what the size and shape of their offspring's genitals would be when they grew up.

If a man's penis is wider than his woman's vagina, she may need a great deal of time and stimulation before her vaginal walls can stretch enough to accommodate it, or else tissue can tear, resulting in pain and even bleeding. In some cases, the girth just *can't* be managed, even with gobs of lubrication and every effort to relax and stretch the vaginal walls. Women who endure this discomfort repeatedly can also end up with bladder infections; because the penis causes the tissue around the urethra to torque, love juices can work their way into the urinary tract and bladder.

If his penis is too *long* for her vagina (or her vagina too short for his penis), her cervix can take a painful pounding during intercourse. If his penis is too *narrow* for her vagina (or her vagina too wide for his penis), neither partner may receive enough stimulation. If his penis is much *shorter* than her vagina, the woman may miss the feeling of being filled up, and the nerves deep within the vagina, which are most sensitive to pressure, will not receive adequate stimulation.

In most cases, couples can compensate for physical incompatibilities with the right intercourse positions. I recommend that you experiment with the positions in this chapter and improvise your own variations until you find what works for you. Here are some specific suggestions:

1. If his penis is wider than her vagina, it's crucial to allow lots of time for foreplay. If possible, allow the woman to have an orgasm— preferably with fingers or a sex tool inside—before penetration. This will help loosen her. The man should enter straight, not at an angle, and move slowly, avoiding sudden movements, until she warms up and widens. She can help by trying to relax as much as possible, breathing deeply and slowly as he enters.

In some instances, incompatibility of width is not a permanent anatomical problem. Rather, it's the result of fear or post-traumatic tension on the part of the woman, causing the walls of her vagina to tighten. If the relationship is new, she may just need healing time and lots of gentle loving before she can trust her man enough to truly open up.

2. If the penis is longer than the vagina, the woman can lie on her back with her legs straight and her ankles touching, or as close to- gether as possible. The man is on top of her, with his legs placed

outside hers or resting on top of hers. Thrusting in this position keeps the penis from penetrating too deeply. Another solution is to have the man lie on his back while the woman lowers herself onto his penis. This allows her to control the depth of penetration. Leaning slightly forward rather than sitting perpendicular to him will accentuate the effect. She should remain on her knees and not squat, as squatting puts pressure on the pelvic floor muscles, shortening the vagina even more.

It is also a good idea to prolong foreplay. With arousal, the vagina balloons upward, increasing its length. If the man enters too soon, this may not have occurred.

3. If his penis is too narrow for her vagina, the woman can compensate by learning to intentionally contract her muscles. The exercise that concludes this chapter will help considerably. She should also avoid opening her legs too wide. The man can learn to thrust at different angles, side to side and up and down.

Two rear-entry positions are particularly advantageous for this match. One has the woman on her hands and knees, with her legs fairly close together. The second has the woman on her back but twisted slightly at the waist. In other words, her upper back is flat on the bed and her hips rotate sideways. Her bottom leg remains straight or slightly bent, and her upper leg is bent at a ninety-degree angle from the hip and also at the knee. This compresses the vaginal area. The man kneels behind her buttocks, with his body perpendicular to hers, keeping his knees wide apart so he can get close enough to enter.

4. If his penis is short in comparison to the length of her vagina, try positions that shorten her vagina. For example, the woman can lie on her back with her knees up around her shoulders. Or, the man can lie on his back while the woman squats on him. Rear-entry positions in which the woman is on her elbows and knees are also good, especially if she arches her back or raises her behind while lowering her chest. Bearing down slightly as if having a bowel movement will further shorten her vagina.

The Shape of Things to Come

Genitals not only vary in size but shape. Some penises actually curl when erect—upward toward the belly, downward toward the scrotum, or to either side. If the penis does not naturally straighten out during intercourse, discomfort or injury can result for either partner. The solution is to try positions that provide a natural bend to the vagina, so it conforms to the curled penis. Two helpful positions are: (1) The woman lies on her back on the bed or a table and the man stands on the floor at a ninety-degree angle to her. Placing her weight on her elbows or hands, she raises or lowers her torso to find the most comfortable angle for penetration. (2) The woman is on her hands and knees with her back arched. The man enters from the rear.

Another variation in penile shape has to do with the proportions of the penis. The Chinese identified three distinct types of organs: (1) cylindrical, in which the circumference of the head is the same as that of the base, (2) wider at the base than the head, (3) wider at the head than the base. The third type provides some extra stimulation as the penis moves in and out of the vagina. Some women notice that when making love to men with the second type of penis, and sometimes also the first, thrusting does not provide enough friction for them to reach their full potential for arousal. Here are some suggestions (these can be followed by any couple for whom lack of sensation during intercourse is an issue, regardless of penis shape):

1. Emphasize superficial thrusts so that the outer third of the vagina receives maximum attention from the ridges on the head of the penis.
2. Use severe angles to thrust directly against the walls of the vagina. In other words, aim at the top, bottom or sides (without angling so sharply that the penis bends uncomfortably).
3. Use penis rings. Rubber or plastic rings sold in sex shops are used to keep blood in the penis when it is erect, thereby keeping it from becoming flaccid. If you get the right size ring, you can place it just behind the head without discomfort. This will mimic the feel of a penis with a larger head, providing the same kind of pressure variations during thrusting. At first it may be necessary to thrust gently, until you learn to keep the ring in place.

Location, Location, Location

The placement of genitals can also produce incompatibility. For some women, the vulva is closer to the front of the body, higher up toward the pubic bone. For others, it is further back, closer to the anus. Also, some penises are located higher up on the abdomen, while others are positioned lower down. If, for example, a woman whose vulva is low has intercourse with a man whose penis is high, their pelvic bones might bang together during intercourse, resulting in pain or discomfort.

It is very important for such couples to realize that the discomfort is no one's fault. It is not caused by a lack of skill or compassion. It's simply the result of anatomy. The solution is to patiently try different positions and find some that work for you.

In some women, the urethra is located especially close to the opening of the vagina. This makes them prone to bladder infections, especially if their partners have extrawide penises. And someone who gets bladder infections after having intercourse may quickly lose interest in making love. The missionary position makes such women more vulnerable to infection. Instead, try positions in which the woman is on top, seated in an upright position. Also, try to angle the penis toward the upper wall of the vaginal interior, in the area of the G spot. This applies less pressure in the area around the urethra. However, bear in mind that this doesn't work for everyone: because the bladder rests above the G spot, the extra stimulation can cause additional irritation. If that is the case, use manual techniques to stimulate the G spot, not intercourse. (Chinese herbal formulas can help treat and prevent bladder infections without the side effects associated with antibiotics. See Appendix.)

EXERCISE:
WORKING THE PC MUSCLE

When you have to urinate but can't do so because you're stuck in an important meeting or can't bear to miss a minute of the movie you're watching, what do you do? You hold it in. What you're actually doing is contracting the pubococcygeus muscle, which sits on the floor of the pelvis. Squeezing the PC muscle, as it is called, closes the urethra, which stops the flow of urine. Strategically located and vastly underrated, the muscle has many other functions besides keeping you from peeing in your pants. It affects the genital organs of both sexes, as well as the uterus in women and the prostate gland in men. Keeping the PC muscle strong and learning to control it can be a great boon to your sexual health and vitality.

The muscle was brought to the attention of the Western world when gynecologist Arnold Kegel discovered that incontinent women could gain control of their urine by alternately contracting and relaxing their PC muscles. The system of exercises he developed proved to have unanticipated sexual benefits. What Kegel and other scientists discovered had actually been recorded by the Chinese many centuries earlier, and the benefits described in the ancient texts went far beyond anything imagined in the West.

Because PC exercises increase blood flow to the genitals, many men who practice them find they have firmer, more reliable erections. They also develop much greater staying power, delaying the moment of ejaculation and experiencing more intense orgasms when they climax. The exercises are also said to improve the functioning of the prostate gland and enhance its contribution to sexual strength, which, in traditional Chinese medicine, is considerable. Studies indicate that men with weak PC muscles are more likely to have problems with their prostate glands and seminal vesicles.

Women who strengthen their PC muscles find that they have orgasms more easily and reliably, and feel them more intensely. The practice also helps keep the vagina tight, youthful and healthy. And, by enhancing control of the vaginal muscles, the exercises enable women to create a wider variety of sensations for themselves and their partners during intercourse. Researchers have noted that women with weak PC muscles are more likely to be sexually dissatisfied.

For both sexes, PC exercises greatly enhance the ability to control sexual energy. For one thing, traditional Chinese medicine holds that the genitals are like tunnels through which chi can enter the body through intercourse but can also escape. A strong PC muscle helps keep chi within the body, where it can be put to use to heal and strengthen the system. In addition, squeezing the muscle creates a kind of pumping action that propels chi up from the pelvis, helping you avoid stagnation disorders and move life-enhancing energy throughout the body—and, during sex, between you and your partner.

One of the great advantages of PC exercises is that you can do them just about anyplace, anytime—while driving, watching TV, even during a business meeting. They are so imperceptible that no one will know you're doing them, and so simple and localized that they're not likely to distract you. All you do is squeeze the pubococcygeus, then relax it.

You might want to begin when you urinate, by simply trying to stop the flow. Do this for a few seconds two or three times during each urination. When you've mastered this, begin contracting and releasing the muscle at other times as well.

You may notice that you feel the contraction not only in the portion of the perineum closer to your genitals but in your anus as well; the same action usually tightens the sphincter muscles. This is okay. Just make sure you're not *only* squeezing the anal sphincter. One way to tell is by holding in your urine, then relaxing the anus. If you're still keeping the urine inside, you're squeezing the PC muscle.

I recommend doing two types of PC exercises: slow and fast. In the slow version, squeeze the muscle slowly, then, when you reach maximum contraction, hold that position for a count of three. You may find it difficult to hold for that long; like any muscle, the pubococcygeus can't remain in a contracted state if it's weak or out of shape. With practice you will be able to hold it longer. (As you get better at it, increase the holding period, until you can slowly count to five.) After holding, let go, rest a moment, and repeat the sequence. You may find that you're bringing in your stomach and leg muscles, and perhaps hunching your shoulders, to help during the squeeze. Try to keep those other muscles relaxed.

When you are comfortable doing slow contractions, start coordinating them with your breath: breathe in as you squeeze, hold the breath while you maintain the contraction, and exhale as you relax the muscle.

The fast method is more like a quick pumping action. Squeeze and relax the muscle in rapid sequence. You might want to begin with five quick squeezes followed by a moment of relaxation. Work your way up to thirty contractions between rest periods. As with any muscle, the strength of the PC must be built up gradually. If at any time you begin to ache down there, give it a rest.

When doing the rapid squeezes, you might feel tingling or other unusual sensations in the genitals or other parts of the pelvic region. You may even feel horny. These are good signs. They mean that more energy and blood are flowing into the area.

If you and your lover apply the information in this chapter with patience and diligence, intercourse will become more varied, more intensely pleasurable and more physically and emotionally satisfying than ever before. But there are yet higher levels to be attained, should you choose to reach for them. The practices you've just learned will make you experts in the art of love; the next chapter will help you become masters.

Chapter 6

HEAVEN COMES TO EARTH
Making Love Divine

Skill makes love unending.

—Ovid

*Correct practice of sexual intercourse can cure every ailment
and at the same time open the doors to liberation.*

—Taoist master

Throughout the centuries, lovers and poets have rhapsodized about an intimacy so deep, a connection so intense, that individual identities merge into one inseparable whole, without boundaries, like two ice cubes melting into a single pool of water. The idea of two becoming one may be the stuff of sonnets and love songs, but from an energetic perspective the idea can be taken quite literally.

The genitals of both sexes are passageways through which chi is expelled from the body. During intercourse, the sex organs become two-way channels; through them, chi passes into and out of each partner's body. With superior lovemaking, the exchange is not just a simple give and take, like a business transaction in which two people trade commodities of equal value. Rather, sexual passion generates an abundant flow of new energy, just as the merging of sperm and egg produces a new entity. Lovers experience this as oneness.

At its highest level, as practiced by two loving souls who have mastered the techniques in this book, intercourse creates such a complete and continuous exchange of energy that the feeling of union soars to a level most romantics have only imagined—one that lifts us out of our animal nature and closer to the divine in us. It is this transcendent quality of superior sex that led the Taoists to view sexual energy as a spiritual force and sexual intimacy as a holy ritual, a vehicle to enlightened states of consciousness like prayer or meditation.

In more prosaic terms, the friction of intercourse produces heat energy, which stimulates the kidney organ and moves chi through the system. Additional life force pours into the liver and heart (as in the Nourishing Cycle; see chapter 4), igniting powerful emotions associated with those organs: warmth, tenderness, joy, love. As physical excitement builds, the intensity of those feelings soars. With ordinary sex, this elevated experience tends to be short-lived, crashing to Earth after the brief spasm of male ejaculation. But for couples who work with the techniques in this book, the surge of unifying emotion is more powerful, more pure, more enduring. With continued mastery of sexual energy, yin and yang unite more perfectly and the sense of union transcends human coupling to encompass a merging with all of life. The chemistry of love becomes pure alchemy, turning pleasure into ecstasy. At this level of mastery, all the benefits to health and well-being that we have so far attributed to satisfying sex are greatly magnified.

THE GOLDEN CIRCLE

From the pelvic area, where it is created and stored, sexual energy can be directed to the rest of the body through energetic channels. The goal of this exercise is to make you aware of the path through which chi naturally moves and to cultivate the ability to stimulate and control its flow. Once you are able to work with this energy you can begin to manipulate it during sexual activity to enhance your pleasure and strengthen your entire system.

1. Sit in a comfortable position, close your eyes and let the tip of your tongue rest just behind your upper front teeth.

2. Focus your attention on your pelvic girdle. This area is shaped like a bowl: the front is your pubic bone, the sides are your hip bones and the back is your sacrum (the lowest triangular bone in the spinal column). Feel those bones with your hands so you know where they are, then imagine the bowl.

3. Visualize this bowl as filled with warm golden honey.

4. Imagine that the warm honey can flow up a tube through your spinal column to the crown of your head.

5. Imagine that the honey can flow down the center of your body, a few inches in from the front, and return to the pelvic girdle.

6. Breathe in as you visualize the warm honey rising up the spine.

7. Hold the breath for five seconds when you complete the inhalation and the honey has reached the crown of your head.

8. Breathe out as the honey flows back down the body.

9. Hold the breath for a moment when you complete the exhalation and the honey has returned to the pelvic bowl.

10. Do not strain during this exercise. If your attention wanders or you have difficulty coordinating your breath with the visualization, simply stop the process and relax a moment before resuming. It won't be long before you can run through the entire cycle easily and smoothly.

This ancient practice connects two acupuncture meridians mentioned on page 87, the governing vessel and the conception vessel. Both pathways originate in the lower pelvis and move down to the perineum, between the genitals and anus. From there, the conception vessel moves up the front of the body and the governing vessel runs up the back. They meet again at the upper lip. The Golden Circle moves sexual chi through these two vital channels, connecting them in a single continuous loop. This harmonizes yin and yang energy in the body. As chi circulates in this manner, it nourishes the organs and stimulates the glands, enhancing health and sexual vitality and enlivening our capacity for feeling, thought and awareness.

One point should be emphasized: Obviously, the intention is to move *chi* through the system, not imaginary honey. In reality, energy moves far more rapidly than anything we can visualize. However, in the early stages of working with chi, imagination can help you sense the energy flow that naturally exists. This is an essential step toward moving the energy through intention alone. Once you've been doing the exercise for some time, you can dispense with visual imagination because you will *feel* the actual flow of energy around the orbit.

I recommend starting with three Golden Circles and working your way up to nine. When you feel comfortable with that, you can add sets of nine until you're doing as many as eighty-one orbits.

Once you get used to the Golden Circle, combine it with PC contractions and breathing exercises into a single practice:

1. Sitting comfortably with your back straight, focus your attention on your pelvic bowl. Using deep abdominal breathing, inhale as you contract the PC muscle and visualize the honey moving from your pelvis up your spine.

2. Hold your breath while focusing your attention on the energy in your head.

3. While holding your breath, keep the PC muscle contracted. Or, perform the three locks.

4. As you exhale, relax the PC muscle (and the locks) and bring the energy back down to your pelvis.

The coordination of these actions is a powerful way to cultivate control of sexual energy. Shortly, you will learn how to put them all together in the context of superior sex.

THE EVER-FLOWING WELL

In addition to specific techniques for manipulating chi, sexual energy control entails both partners maximizing the potential of their primary energetic nature—yin for women, yang for men.

When it comes to muscles men are the stronger gender, but sexually speaking, women win hands down. As the ancient Chinese observed, male vitality in the bedchamber is strong but fleeting—as thin as oil on water and as frail as a willow branch that bends with the wind. But, because women produce children on behalf of the species, they have been endowed by nature with an abundance of sexual chi. This endowment enables them to enjoy sex for long periods of time, have repeated orgasms without getting exhausted and give generously of their sexual chi without depleting their energy or harming their health. That's why rulers from the Yellow Emperor to Mao turned to women not just for pleasure and intimacy but rejuvenation.

Like all things governed by yin energy, female sexuality is hidden, sometimes even from women themselves. Its depth and power tend to be underappreciated. Not that a woman's supply of sexual chi is inexhaustible. It too has limits and will wear out over time, due to menstruation, pregnancy and childbirth. One study of 100,000 women, reported in a European medical journal, found that the more children a woman has the more likely she is to develop one of several life-threatening diseases. The loss of life-enhancing sexual chi during reproduction makes certain parts of the body more vulnerable to illness. This is why doctors of Chinese medicine use herbs, acupuncture and other treatments to tonify the chi of pregnant women and new mothers. But overall, women are less likely than men to lose interest in sex later in life, and in virtually every culture they live longer than men, all because they have more sexual, or kidney, chi.

It's Better to Receive

The cultivation of yin sexual energy is related to the ability to receive and transform, as suggested in the propagation model. A receptive woman takes in and absorbs sexual energy from her man and mixes it with her own to create a more satisfying and intimate experience for both partners. The more genuinely receptive a woman is, the more sexual chi she has available to her. As a result, her body is stronger and more vibrant, and her capacity to heal and nourish is greater.

A patient of mine named Gina was typical of the many women I've treated who have blocked their natural receptivity. She came to me because she had dysmenorrhea (painful menstruation) and cysts on her ovaries. She had been married for less than a year. When I asked about her sex life, she said she adored her husband and enjoyed making love to him. She started to add something, then stopped and looked away. "When you begin to have sex with him," I asked, "does a small part of you wish that you were someplace else?" She admitted that such feelings occasionally cropped up. She sometimes resented her husband's advances, although she did not know why, and had to grit her teeth and convince herself it was okay to give in. As their lovemaking continued and she became excited, the negative feelings would dissipate, but if the arousal diminished, they would return

I asked Gina about this because I see many women with gynecological problems accompanied by a subtle—and sometimes not-so-subtle—resistance to sex, even with the men they love. If a woman blocks the energy coming into her, her *own* energy does not get healthfully involved in the sexual process. This can result not only in an unsatisfying love life but also in illness. If the resistance becomes chronic, an energetic wall—a kind of sexual iron curtain—gets erected. The chi that ought to pass from one partner to the other during intercourse does not move smoothly. Instead, some of it stagnates. Stagnation causes things to grow where they shouldn't and cells to reproduce inappropriately. Chinese medicine contends that stagnation can make a woman vulnerable to benign and malignant tumors of the breasts and reproductive system, as well as endometriosis, polyps and other gynecological disorders. Lack of receptivity can also rebound and create health problems for the woman's partner; if the energy that the man is naturally giving out does not find a willing recipient, it can back up into his own system and stagnate, causing symptoms such as prostate swelling, testicular pain and urethral irritation.

Resistance to receptivity has many possible causes. Often, it's based on fear stemming from painful past experiences or having been taught that sex is immoral or dangerous. Sometimes it stems from anger toward the woman's mate or dissatisfaction with the way he makes love. Many women block their natural receptivity because being open to penetration feels like a weakness to them rather than a strength. It makes them feel vulnerable to hurt. While understandable, this attitude amounts to a misconception that devalues the essential power of yin. Yin is inherently vulnerable, which is why it needs the protective coating of yang. But yin vulnerability implies openness, not weakness, passivity or helplessness. Women who become martyrs or victims of abuse are usually so yin *deficient* that they turn into pathological give-aholics. Strong yin energy is receptive and *discerning*. It enables you to choose a worthy lover and determine what is appropriate to receive from him.

Whatever the cause, for a woman to achieve true receptivity she must have respect for her sexuality and take pride in it. For many, this entails overcoming cultural values that disparage overt female sexuality and regard women who enjoy sex as somehow wicked.

The Transformative Power of Yin

Women often neglect the transformational skills that their natures bestow upon them. When their lovers do something in bed that they don't like, for example, they think they have only two choices: accept it or reject it.

Outright rejection creates anger, resentment and often retaliation. The other option is not much better: when you open your legs but not your heart, you are not being truly receptive. That energetic curtain is drawn, which not only leads to the health problems described earlier but also makes your man feel rejected even if you don't appear to be rejecting him. As a result, his sexual chi does not move up his body and his heart remains closed.

Instead of just rejecting or complying, a truly receptive woman turns what her man initiates into something she really wants and is able to work with. Because yang energy is energized by an enthusiastic yin response, your man will be more motivated to give to you—and have much more to give—if you are genuinely receptive.

Becoming More Receptive

Here are some ways to cultivate sexual energy by enhancing the power of yin receptivity:

1. *See what's in front of you.*   Chances are, your sweetheart gives you more attention, interest and affection than you realize. Look for the small, subtle signs of love.

2. *Appreciate your womanhood.*   In order to work effectively with sexual energy, it's important to be familiar with and friendly toward the organs of your femininity. It is amazing how many women have no idea what their genitals look like, and how many think they are ugly and smelly. I recommend that you use a hand mirror to take a long, loving look at your vulva. Sometime when you're sexually aroused, rub yourself with your hand and smell the natural odor of your secretions on your fingers. While you're at it, taste yourself. And, if appropriate, the next time your gynecologist examines you with a speculum, ask to have a look inside.

3. *Massage your breasts.*   Many women are critical of the other symbol of femininity, their breasts. They think they're too small, too big, sag too much, or stick out too straight. Done in a loving manner, the following exercise can be healing, physically and emotionally. Said to enhance the secretion of female hormones and assist with blood and lymph circulation, this ancient practice has helped women keep their breasts healthy for thousands of years. It will also help acquaint you with a truly beautiful aspect of yourself.

Create a soothing atmosphere. With your breasts bare, lie down or sit up in a comfortable position. Rub your hands together until they are warm. Then place them on the lower portion of your breasts, below the nipple. Gently massage in a circular motion around the entire breast, avoiding the nipples. Rotate the right hand clockwise and the left counterclockwise. Do nine circles and then change directions, moving clockwise with the left hand and counterclockwise with the right. Repeat the sets of nine as many as four times in each direction.

4. Take charge of your pleasure. Pay attention to what you feel as you make love and initiate steps to make it better. If you're not sure what pleases and displeases you, it's time to start finding out. With your man's help, try new activities in bed to discover what you like. Browse in a bookstore for new ideas. And use self-pleasuring as a learning tool. By touching yourself you can discern exactly what feels good and when, so you can inform your lover with confidence.

5. Flex your muscles. Using your vaginal muscles during inter-course will improve your control and heighten pleasurable sensations for you and your lover. Begin by gently contracting your muscles—as in the PC exercises you learned in the previous chapter—to tighten their grip on your man's penis. Stop thrusting for a moment so you both can acclimate to the new sensation. Then relax your muscles and squeeze them again. Repeat this squeeze-and-relax sequence a few times. When you resume thrusting, squeeze gently for as long as it's comfortable. Avoid sudden movements and don't tighten too much as the additional pressure can make both of you vulnerable to injury.

Once you become more adept and your muscles grow stronger, you can extend the duration of the contractions and perform them in an infinite number of exciting ways. A gentle, prolonged contraction brings one kind of excitement; firm squeezes produce another; a series of quick, pulsing contractions creates something entirely different. Some women eventually develop the ability to make their vaginas practically vibrate. In fact, the Chinese texts describe experts who could voluntarily create the same vaginal tremors that sometimes occur spontaneously during orgasm. Naturally, this skill takes a great deal of time to master, but you might find it well worth the effort. Simply imagine the walls on either side of the vagina as fluttering butterfly wings. At first, you're not likely to feel any actual movement, but with practice many women begin to feel a fluttering sensation inside. You can also experiment with different pelvic movements to go along with the contraction patterns.

6. Recycle his energy. Have you ever noticed that when your lover ejaculates you feel revved up, as if you had just received a jolt of stimulation and want to keep going? This is caused by his sexual energy moving into you. A man releases a tremendous amount of chi when he ejaculates. By moving this infusion of chi through the Golden Circle you can incorporate that life force into your own system to fortify your sexuality and health. This is especially helpful at times when your man ejaculates before you are fulfilled; it can turn what might be a frustrating experience into a strengthening one.

You have already learned how to draw sexual energy up from the pelvis and circulate it through the meridian system. Simply use the same practices during intercourse, as your lover climaxes inside you.

7. *Work with your man.*   Your own ability to receive fully and maximize the exchange of energy with your partner depends in large part on his confidence and sexual control. Pay close attention to the next section of this chapter, and work patiently and creatively with your beloved to help him realize his sexual potential.

CULTIVATING STAYING POWER

As we have seen, the key to a man's sexual ability is to give appropriately. Where intercourse is concerned, the most important thing a man can give a woman is *time.* Delaying the moment of the male climax leads to deeper satisfaction, more intense orgasms for both partners and a stronger and a more healthful exchange of sexual energy, with all its ramifications.

When a man lasts long enough for his lover's yin to fully awaken and participate in the process of lovemaking, he gives her a magnificent gift. Healing chi is liberated and released into her system. This helps unblock areas of her body where energy may have congested, reducing the likelihood of stagnation disorders, especially gynecological conditions such as tumors, fibroids and cramping. Naturally, the longer he lasts, the more likely she is to have orgasms, and not just the ordinary kind but a series of climaxes and perhaps the ejaculatory orgasms we described earlier.

The more orgasmic a woman is, the more healthy the blood flow into and out of her pelvis.

Emotionally, with chi moving effectively in and out of her organs, she experiences a surge of joy and an infusion of inner peace. Her muscles and tendons become more flexible, as does her personality; women who start having superior sex tend to become less rigid, less controlling, less fearful—about life in general and their gender identity in particular. They open up in every way.

According to the propagation model, a man who gives his woman such a gift should receive something wonderful in return once she has processed and transformed his offering. If he is receptive, what he receives is glorious indeed. For one thing, he gets to enjoy watching how joyously satisfied he has made his beloved. Being yang oriented, men derive gratification from the responses to their actions. For another, he gets a longer, more sustained aerobic workout, improving circulation in general and especially in his pelvic area, where local tissue is infused with oxygen and nutrients. Nerves in the pelvic region are enlivened as well, enriching subsequent sex with heightened sensation and stamina.

The ability to last longer also generates within his system a greater amount of chi. Sex is like a vacuum that draws more and more energy into the pelvis the longer it lasts. This surge of chi not only enhances sexual performance but also helps prevent and heal disorders of the bladder, genitals and prostate. Tension and other symptoms of stagnation dissipate elsewhere in the body too, as congested chi is released to support the sexual function. This, along with a surge of endorphins and the powerful release of a long-delayed orgasm, produces an exceptional degree of calmness and well-being. The longer the act, the more yin chi enters the kidney organ, which conquers fear and energizes the mind and nervous system. Add to that the abundance of chi that flows back to him from his lover's overflowing well and he is infused with life-giving energy. This fortifies his long-term health, keeps him young and vigorous, and reinforces his sexual strength—which is how superior sex begets more superior sex.

What lasting longer in bed does for a relationship often seems like a miracle to couples who develop the skill. As I indicated earlier in the book, hundreds of my patients have discovered a rebirth of joy, passion, generosity of spirit and devotion to a shared future after learning to unite in prolonged sexual bliss.

Here are some techniques to help men cultivate the ability to delay ejaculation:

1. Recognize your point of no return. Ejaculation is an involuntary reflex. As the contractions of the perineal muscles move semen through the urethra, you begin to feel sensations that tell you that you are going to come. Soon you reach a point of no return, after which expulsion is virtually inevitable. Any effort to delay or avoid ejaculating must be made prior to that moment. Therefore, it's important to observe your sensations closely and recognize when you are reaching the brink.

2. Adjust your thrust. In general, men have greater control with slow thrusts rather than fast. Many also find that shallow thrusting gives them more control. If you're approaching the point of no return, pull back and slow down. You can also make other adjustments to reduce the level of sensation—change angles, for example, or grind in a circular motion rather than pump in and out.

3. Take a pause. One way to delay ejaculation is to stop thrusting. Either remain inside your woman, withdraw partially or pull out completely. When you resume thrusting, your arousal level will be further back from the brink. Don't worry about losing your erection; if it goes away it will probably come back, and if it doesn't, try the soft entry technique described on pages 115–118.

4. Breathe, squeeze, lock and draw. Utilize the deep abdominal breathing, PC muscle contractions and Golden Circle techniques— alone or in any combination—to draw energy upward from the pelvic area. Together, they constitute a powerful way to forestall ejaculation and simultaneously pull sexual chi upward.

When you are close to the point of no return, stop thrusting and breathe slowly and deeply (the opposite of the short, shallow breaths that take over as orgasm approaches). Contract your PC muscle and imagine sexual chi moving up the Golden Circle from the pelvis. If you find yourself teetering on the edge of ejaculation, you might want to suck the air into your lungs with a sense of urgency. This abruptly draws the energy and sensation away from your genitals.

5. *Press the perineum.* If you probe along the perineum, you will find, midway between the scrotum and anus, a slight hollow. When you are about to ejaculate, press firmly—but not too firmly—on that point with your forefinger and middle finger. This can effectively prevent ejaculation by inhibiting the contractions that move semen through the urethra. Taking several slow deep breaths while pressing on the point can enhance the effect.

You do not have to withdraw to use this technique, although in the awkward early stages you might want to do so. Also, if you have difficulty reaching your perineum, your lover can do it for you. Simply show her where to press before you make love and arrange a signal so she knows when to do it.

Incidentally, the location is also an important acupuncture point, *hui-yin,* which sends chi upward within the body. I treat the point in my medical practice to help impotent men regain the capacity to have erections, as it awakens the yang chi that's responsible for raising the penis.

6. *Put the squeeze on it.* Perhaps the method of ejaculation control most commonly used by sex therapists is the squeeze technique introduced by Masters and Johnson. It serves as a kind of emergency

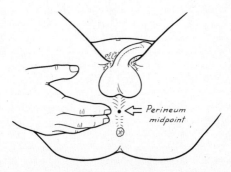

Location of the perineum

brake to stop the flow of semen at the last moment. If you feel the point of no return approaching, withdraw and squeeze your penis, either at its base or at the juncture of the shaft and the head. Simply place your thumb on the front of the penis and your first and second fingers on the back, then squeeze. This will forestall the ejaculatory reflex.

If you find it awkward or impossible to free up one hand to perform the squeeze, have your partner do it instead. Let her know that the penis can withstand more pressure than she might imagine. Show her in advance how much pressure she can use.

Additional Tips

When practicing techniques for developing ejaculatory control, keep the following in mind:

- Practice by masturbating. To develop your skill before you and your lover work on it during intercourse, or to advance in this area

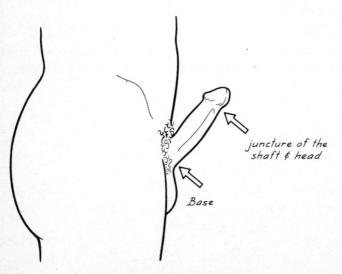

Pressure points for halting ejaculation

while single, you might want to practice on your own. Arouse yourself as you normally would but stop well before you reach the point of no return, then begin breathing deeply. Fill yourself with air from your belly to your head, allowing the air to push against the inner walls of your body as if you were a balloon. Inhale and exhale like a bellows, keeping your attention on the breath filling your torso.

You can bring yourself to the edge several times, using deep breathing to keep from going over. After each pause, bring yourself closer to the point of no return. You may, for example, start off by getting 70 percent to the finish line, then get 80 percent there, then 90 percent and so forth, until you can hold back even at the 99 percent point.

• Remember, withholding ejaculation is not considered easy. The Chinese said that a man who could have nonejaculatory intercourse ten times in a row with an orgasmic woman would become immortal. Since there are no thousand-year-old sages walking around, we can assume that even the experts found this skill difficult to master. If you experience the discomfort known among men as "blue balls," you might want to employ a simple exercise recommended by modern doctors: Gently try to lift an immovable object. This is said to ease the discomfort.

• Enlist your partner's cooperation. Ejaculation control should be a mutual goal, since it stands to benefit the woman as much as, if not more than, the man. Your lover should know exactly what you are trying to accomplish and why, and be willing to support your commitment. She can help you develop control either during intercourse or while masturbating you by performing the ejaculation control techniques in this section.

• Relax. Approach lovemaking calmly and maintain that calm even in the heat of arousal. Unbridled passion lends itself to abandonment and quick bursts of pleasure; it is more likely to hasten ejaculation, not delay it. Inner calm promotes control and makes possible the achievement of prolonged ecstasy.

• Satisfy your partner. Use various foreplay and intercourse skills to make sure your woman does not end up frustrated while you are learning ejaculatory control. A happy lover is a more helpful lover.

Also, if she hungers for release it will be harder for you to refrain from ejaculating, since her sense of urgency will heighten your arousal. If, on the other hand, she is sated but still aroused, her yin energy will pour into you, cooling the yang rush to ejaculate.

• Do it more often. The longer the gap between lovemaking sessions, the stronger the urge to come, and therefore the more difficult it is to practice ejaculation control.

• Be patient. Like any skill, ejaculatory control takes time to master. You will undoubtedly ejaculate at times when you'd rather hold out. Be easy on yourself, enjoy the experience and try again next time. You have a lifetime of pleasure in which to perfect your skills.

THE ESSENCE
OF MALE ESSENCE

Semen must be regarded as a most precious substance.
By saving it, a man protects his very life.

—PENG-TSU

The ancient Chinese took ejaculatory control a step further, advocating a higher and more difficult goal: not ejaculating at all. This is not some form of religious self-denial. On the contrary, it is in the service of ecstasy, intimacy and high-level energy exchange for the couple, and health, vitality and longevity for the man himself.

Come Again?

The tablespoon or so of semen that's emitted when a man ejaculates contains a tremendous amount of protein and nutrients, along with up to 500 million sperm cells. The precious fluid also contains a vital essence called *jing*. Once expelled, this essential life force is as useless to a man as water down a drain, unless he has a truly receptive partner who can recycle the energy and return it to him in some form.

Athletes and other men who need to perform at optimal physical levels have often claimed that ejaculation can weaken performance. Players and prizefighters are often sequestered the night before an event and ordered by their coaches to stay away from women. Nowadays, most people think of such ideas as old wives' tales. But, one thing is undeniable: After ejaculating, a man's once-insatiable yearning for union with a woman suddenly disappears and he's likely to collapse into sleep. Perhaps we should call it *going*, not coming. Meanwhile, his woman may have had an orgasm too. In fact, she may have had several. But she's ready to keep on making love, or cuddle, or go out dancing. Why? Because she did not ejaculate semen and thus did not dissipate as much sexual chi.

Every man is born with enough jing to produce a specific amount of ejaculate in his lifetime. As a man gets close to using up his allotment he will still be able to ejaculate, but he will begin to show signs of sexual weakness, such as lowered sex drive, reduced semen volume and less firm erections. In our culture, such changes in a man's sexuality are considered natural consequences of aging. To the Chinese they are preventable symptoms that can result from insufficient sexual activity, squandering one's sexual allotment through profligate sex, or depleting it through excessive thinking and stress. Some sexual chi is inevitably lost through the strain of daily living. But a man who practices the energy-conserving techniques in this book can postpone sexual decline in much the same way that a man who exercises sensibly can keep his body strong and limber well into old age. He will also be stronger in the short run, both sexually and in terms of overall health and well-being, because the life force that heals and sustains his body is being preserved.

Emission Possible

If expelling semen can weaken the body, does it follow that a man should never ejaculate? Not at all. When the Yellow Emperor asked his teacher, Su Nu, if he should refrain from sex to preserve his chi, she replied, "That would be a grave mistake. If you were to abstain from intercourse, your spirit would have no opportunity to expand, and yin and yang would be blocked and cut off from each other. . . . If the jade stalk does not stir, it dies in its lair. So you must engage frequently in intercourse."

The ancient Chinese did not believe that ejaculation is bad. In fact, not ejaculating enough can cause serious chi stagnation in the kidney organ system, which can lead to tumors, swelling, infections and other problems in the pelvic region, especially in the prostate gland. Also, because of their energetic connection with the kidneys, the liver and heart can be weakened, leading to emotional and spiritual imbalances. As a rule, men who feel a strong need to ejaculate but do not have the opportunity to do so become ornery, edgy and aggressive—just the way a boxer wants to feel when the bell rings. In traditional Chinese medicine terms, energy becomes congested in the kidney, which makes that organ less effective at controlling the emotions of the heart. This leads to a disturbance of spirit and personal identity.

The sexual masters knew that there is another alternative besides frustration on the one hand and ejaculating whenever the desire arises on the other. "To be aroused but not ejaculate is what is called 'returning the jing,'" Su Nu explained. "When jing is returned to benefit the body, then the tao of life has been realized."

The pleasure and relief we associate with the male climax is due in large part to *orgasm,* not to ejaculation as such. As modern science has confirmed, there *is* a difference. Ejaculation refers to the discharge of semen through a simple reflex action. Orgasm is a neurological event that produces intense feelings of pleasure and release. That these are two separate events has been observed in laboratories: scientists can trigger orgasm without ejaculation by stimulating certain parts of an animal's brain with electricity. In human life, the distinction is evidenced by two opposite observations: (1) men sometimes ejaculate without having the pleasurable sensation of orgasm, and (2) men throughout history have— either through training or accident—experienced orgasms without the emission of semen (the updated Kinsey Report observed that some men "experience real orgasm which they have no difficulty in recognizing, even if it is without ejaculation").

Chinese sexual teachers trained men to achieve intensely pleasurable orgasms without ejaculation. This releases the life force in semen so it can be redirected internally to bestow a myriad of benefits to body and soul, essentially magnifying the blessings of health, vitality and longevity that good sex offers. Through extended practice of ejaculatory control techniques, a motivated man can eventually achieve this goal. Be assured that a man who learns these techniques can reap the benefits of non-ejaculatory sex without the physical discomfort that an untrained man would experience.

Until then, men are advised to engage in moderate ejaculation, at a rate that's appropriate for their health and age. Chinese teachers had conflicting ideas about how often a man should ejaculate. One school of thought used this formula: age multiplied by 0.2 equals the number of days one should allow between ejaculations to protect one's body. For example, a twenty-year-old can ejaculate every four days (20 times 0.2). At age twenty-five, the ideal interval would be five days; at thirty, six days; at forty, eight days; and so forth. By following this formula, the Taoists believed, a man would not use up his sexual energy prematurely. He would, in effect, expend a certain amount of chi and then replenish his reserves by having intercourse (which generates more chi) without ejaculating, before emitting his seed the next time. Other texts follow a similar formula, and some also claim that the rate of ejaculation should vary with the seasons: more in spring, less in summer and autumn, and seldom if ever in winter. All schools of thought agreed on this basic point: The stronger and younger a man is, the more he can ejaculate without the deleterious effects of depleting sexual chi.

How often should *you* ejaculate? I suggest observing your own experience. As a rule of thumb, if ejaculating leaves you feeling lethargic and moody, you should probably do it less often. If you ejaculate under appropriate circumstances, and at intervals that are right for your physical condition, you should feel lighthearted and loving afterward.

The Joy of Retention

To most men, sex without ejaculation sounds more like torture than pleasure. However, those who learn the art of orgasmic, nonejaculatory intercourse find it revitalizing and health enhancing. They also discover that it produces extended, ecstatic orgasms for themselves and their partners. However, this goal must be pursued properly, or else it can cause illness and unbearable frustration. I remember a sincere young man who came to see me because his testicles had become as hard as marbles. He had read (*misread* is more like it) a book about Taoist sexual philosophy and decided to quit ejaculating. Sexually active, he used willpower and physical restraint to keep his semen to himself. But, he did not develop the skill to recirculate the chi that built up during the friction of intercourse. The energy became congested and stuck in his genitals, resulting in hardened testicles. I recommended that he start ejaculating on a regular basis and learn to circulate the energy he generated during sex through his system. Otherwise, he would develop more serious symptoms.

This distinction—merely suppressing ejaculation versus not ejaculating and moving sexual chi inward and upward—can't be emphasized enough. It is also important to reiterate that not ejaculating does not mean doing without the pleasure of orgasm. On the contrary, the nonejaculatory orgasms revered by the Taoists are vastly superior to the ordinary variety.

With ordinary sex a man becomes increasingly aroused, reaches a peak and climaxes while expelling semen. He then retreats sexually so his body can recover. By contrast, a man who has mastered sexual energy control is able to have a *series* of nonejaculatory orgasms. The Chinese called these by various names, such as the superior orgasm, the extended orgasm and the heavenly orgasm.

The extended orgasm is experienced throughout one's body, not just as a spasm in the genital area. Intensely pleasurable, it produces feelings of extraordinary joy and spiritual bliss. In *Taoist Secrets of Love,* Mantak Chia, a leading teacher of Chinese sexual practices in the West, describes it this way: "When the exchange of [chi] reaches a certain intensity and balance, the solid bodies of the two lovers begin pulsating as if charged with electricity. The feeling of having solid flesh disappears. You are suddenly a pillar of vibrating energy held in exquisite balance by your lover's field of energy. This is a total orgasm of body and soul."

As implied by the word *extended,* this higher level of orgasm also lasts longer; if ordinary orgasm is a quick burst of pent-up pressure from a fountain, the superior orgasm is a prolonged journey on waves of ecstasy.

And, whereas men usually withdraw after ejaculating—going to sleep emotionally as well as physically—those who master nonejaculatory intercourse continue to be loving, affectionate and emotionally connected to their lovers. Because so much chi has been generated by intercourse, the nerves become highly sensitive. Hence, kissing and touching become more exquisitely pleasurable than ever before. As the Taoist master Peng-Tsu promised centuries ago, such a man's love for his woman will increase, "as though he could never get enough of her."

Mastering Nonejaculatory Sex

Sexual masters are able to have extended intercourse while drawing the highly charged energy up to their heads to trigger ecstatic orgasms—all with very little physical effort, using mental concentration. Needless to say, it takes a great deal of time and effort to attain that level of skill. If you care to experiment with nonejaculatory sex, simply practice the techniques described earlier for developing ejaculation control and see if you and your lover find it appealing.

When practicing nonejaculatory masturbation, bring yourself close to orgasm, stop stimulating yourself and use the combination of deep breathing, PC squeeze and Golden Circle to draw the energy up and out of the genital area. Perform only the first part of the Golden Circle, however. Pull the energy up to the crown of the head and either leave it there or bring it down as far as the abdomen, not all the way to the genitals.

You might also want to do this when practicing nonejaculatory sex with your partner, as soon as you stop making love. In fact, both of you are advised to perform these practices after making love, to circulate the chi you have absorbed from each other. They are especially useful for men in the early stages of practice: it's not uncommon to feel some pressure in the scrotum after having intercourse without ejaculating. This is natural and nothing to worry about; it simply takes time for the body to adjust. Drawing the built-up sexual energy from the pelvis to the head can help prevent chi stagnation and dissipate any feelings of frustration that might arise. A gentle massage of the perineal muscles can also help.

At times it might feel frustrating not to ejaculate. You may want to give up, telling yourself that the whole idea is just mumbo jumbo from a culture half the globe and many millennia removed from your own. Your partner's enthusiasm may also flag, as many women derive great pleasure from making their lovers ejaculate and have difficulty adjusting to this new concept. I recommend that you focus on what you stand to gain, not the temporary discomfort. The payoff for skillful nonejaculatory sex is a new depth of intimacy, higher levels of ecstatic pleasure, better health and greater sexual and physical vitality.

Also, remember that you can ejaculate soon enough if you want to. In fact, I suggest that in the early stages you schedule a lovemaking session *with ejaculation* for later the same night or the next day. It is easier to maintain your willpower if, in the heat of the moment, you know you will soon have the opportunity for release. Eventually, you'll reach the point where ejaculating becomes a conscious choice, not a necessity, a habit or an accident. And when you can *choose* to do it, it becomes far more enjoyable.

RIDING THE WAVES OF PASSION TOGETHER

The breathing and visualization exercises you have learned can become lovemaking techniques of the highest order when performed in unison with your lover during intercourse. Best practiced in a calm, quiet state, the techniques can be initiated at the beginning of intercourse or after a period of active, passionate thrusting. The latter allows the friction of intercourse to arouse sexual energy so it can be moved effectively through your bodies.

This form of advanced lovemaking is not about building to a crescendo in a linear fashion; it's more like surfing—riding a wave to the top, dipping, leveling off, rising again, dipping, coasting and so on until you choose to float to the beach in an explosion of mutual bliss.

The techniques are best performed in an intercourse position in which you and your lover can be face to face. You want to be able to embrace, look in each other's eyes, kiss if you choose to and be aware of each other's breath. One highly favored position has the woman straddling the man, as in Cranes with Necks Intertwined, which is described on page 139. Most couples can remain in this position for some time without discomfort, especially if the man sits on a chair or pillow. It has the added benefit of keeping your backs straight, which facilitates your awareness of the upward movement of chi. The idea is to create a prolonged experience, so it's important to be comfortable. Make sure neither of you places too much weight on the other, and keep plenty of pillows around for support.

1. *Coordinate your breathing.* Once you are in a comfortable intercourse position, begin practicing the synchronized breathing technique described on page 72. Breathe calmly and deeply in unison.

2. *Circulate the energy.* Once you settle into the rhythmic unity of coordinated breathing, perform the Golden Circle exercise together, drawing upward the intense energy that has built up in the pelvis. Use the PC squeeze as you begin the in-breath. Feel or visualize chi rising up your spine to the crown of your head. Hold your breath for a few moments as you focus your attention on your head. As you exhale, allow the energy to come back down to the genitals. Repeat the cycle with each inhalation. You can add to the effect by touching your foreheads or lips together.

3. *Give and receive chi.* Now you will circulate energy between you, with each partner bestowing upon the beloved the power of his or her sexual chi. When you begin to inhale, imagine you are drawing energy from your partner's genitals into your own. As the in-breath continues, pull the energy up your spine to the head. Hold the breath a moment. Press your foreheads or lips together, then release the breath through the nose while imagining that you are sending energy through your forehead or mouth into your lover's body. As the exhalation continues, imagine the energy moving down the center of your partner's body to his or her genitals. With the next in-breath, begin the cycle again.

4. Invert the cycle. As a variation on the above, instead of both partners inhaling and exhaling at the same time, one inhales as the other exhales. If you find it comfortable to do so, you might want to perform this technique mouth-to-mouth, with each partner breathing in the other's exhalation. On his in-breath, the man visualizes energy moving into his penis from his partner's vagina, then up his spine to his head. When he exhales, he sends energy out through his mouth or forehead into his partner and imagines it moving from her head down to her genitals. On her in-breath, the woman takes in chi from her lover through her forehead or mouth and breathes it *down* her body to her genitals. On her exhalation, she releases her energy through her vagina into her lover's penis and visualizes it moving up his spine.

The same process can be done with the directions reversed: the man draws energy down his body and the woman pulls it up through hers. When drawing the energy down, however, do not perform the PC muscle squeeze, as that propels chi in the opposite direction.

Giving and receiving chi

Additional Points

1. In the early stages, you may want to rehearse these techniques without penetration, or even without taking your clothes off, just to get the coordination down. (An excellent way to feel closer to your mate, this can also be used as a meditative practice or during the ten-minute morning tryst recommended at the end of chapter 2.)

2. Stay relaxed but aroused. That apparent contradiction is the key to sustaining ecstasy. Overexcitement may cause the man to have trouble withholding ejaculation. If that happens, be still and use any of the control techniques on pages 160 through 164. On the other hand, if you relax too much, the sexual charge may diminish, causing you to lose focus. If that happens, introduce some genital movement; thrust slowly a few times or grind in a circular motion.

3. As you master the process, you will find that you need to use imagination and visualization less often, because you are able to feel the actual movement of energy more vividly.

4. If, at any time, you both want to suspend the practice and abandon yourselves to heavy thrusting and ejaculation, go ahead and enjoy it. More than likely it will be more exciting than it was before you began to practice these techniques.

5. Eventually, couples who make love this way on a regular basis find that both the man and woman have intense, prolonged, full-bodied orgasms—or a series of them—without the man ejaculating. That is a most worthy goal. However, it's important to allow yourselves the luxury of awkwardness and mistakes along the way. Unrealistic expectations will only lead to disappointment. Enjoy your journey to the fullest. Each step of growth will inspire lovemaking that is healthier, more intimate and more pleasurable than before.

EXERCISE:
SEXUAL HEALING

Thousands of years ago, the Chinese developed visualization techniques to help heal the body, a practice whose efficacy has been documented by Western science. Now that you have learned to mobilize and maneuver sexual chi, you and your lover can direct it to parts of the body that need support. By aiding the flow of chi into and out of a weakened area, you fortify the body's natural healing ability, allowing it to restore the proper level and quality of chi.

If you or your partner feels pain in some area, or knows that a particular organ or body part needs to be strengthened, do the following exercise together. You can treat it as an interlude during intercourse or as a separate practice, in which case you can press your bodies together without penetration. If either of you has a serious illness, the latter option may be preferable.

1. You can be in any position that's comfortable, as long as your bodies are parallel to each other.

2. Begin with a series of four Golden Circles, using PC contractions and deep breathing to get the chi moving.

3. When you are ready, allow a stream of chi to leave the circle and enter the organ or body part you wish to heal. Simply visualize or feel the energy move to where it is needed.

4. With each in-breath, draw fresh chi into the area you're healing.

5. Exhale through your mouth while imagining that pathology from the unhealthy area is being expelled with the out-breath.

6. During this dual practice, you and your partner can each attend to areas of your own bodies that need healing. Or, you can focus in unison on an area in one of your bodies, thus magnifying the intensity of the healing energy.

These additional options can enhance the process:

• When you draw chi into the area, visualize the energy taking the form of light. The light can be any color that feels appropriate at the time, and if the color changes, let it change. Breathe normally as you focus on the light bathing the unhealthy or injured body part.
• If the area is hot, imagine the energy moving in and out of it as a stream of cooling water. You know it's hot if the skin is reddened by inflammation, if it's swollen or if it's very sensitive to the touch.
• If the area is cold, imagine the energy as a warm fire. You know it's cold if it wants to be touched, or if it feels better with a heating pad or hot shower.

The practice should be done for at least five minutes, but not more than twenty. Consistency brings the best results, especially if you are attempting to use sexual energy to help heal chronic or serious conditions.

Chapter 7

BOULDERS BENEATH OUR FEET
Obstructions to Passionate Love

This is the monstruosity in love, lady—
that the will is infinite and the
execution confined; that the desire is
boundless and the act a slave to limit.

—SHAKESPEARE

He that will not apply new remedies
must expect new evils.

—FRANCIS BACON

Yُou and your lover are on the path to excellent health and sublime passion through superior sex. But no matter how diligently you apply the information in this book, life still has a way of placing obstacles in the way. Illness, injury or energetic imbalances can diminish the body's sexual capacity. Fear, resentment and pain from the past can rise up and sabotage the heart's best intentions. This chapter focuses on common obstacles to healthy sexuality and offers fresh ways of dealing with them.

Western science has done a commendable job of classifying sexual dysfunctions and analyzing the various impediments to erotic fulfillment. In most cases, the root of a problem is traced to either a physical or psychological cause, and the attempted solution consists of some combination of medical, psychotherapeutic and behavioral interventions. From the traditional Chinese medicine point of view, there is virtually always an energetic component as well, usually a chi deficiency or chi stagnation problem in the pelvic area. In fact, many conditions are *entirely* energetic, with no psychological or physiological origin to speak of, although the energetic problem will have an impact on both the body and the mind. Unfortunately, when they don't find a medical cause, most doctors assume the problem is strictly mental, and the unlucky patients are left feeling that they're psychologically unsound.

In some cases, sexual dysfunction can be seen as a form of bodily communication. Just as the body uses hunger and desire to make statements about its needs, it can let you down sexually as a way of telling you something you feel or believe deep within but have not consciously admitted to yourself. For example: "I feel insecure," or "I'm worn out and overstressed," or "I don't want to put myself into this woman or this relationship," or "I'm afraid of taking this man into my body or my life."

Many sexual problems are rooted in past trauma. In traditional Chinese medicine, trauma is considered an energetic force with short- and long-term repercussions. Whether its origin is primarily physical (from an injury or disease) or emotional (from a disturbing event), trauma seeps into the body like a burn, affecting deeper and deeper levels of the self. Like a scar, an energetic residue of the trauma may remain long after the obvious wounds have healed, stored as body memories. I have, for example, treated middle-aged people for symptoms related to forgotten high-school athletic injuries. The tissue may have healed twenty-five years earlier, but the trauma moved deeper into the body and eventually led to arthritis or some other chronic disorder.

The same holds true of sexual traumas. A woman who was raped or sexually abused may have been treated for her physical injuries and counseled for psychological wounds, but her body might retain a memory of the event, inhibiting her enjoyment of the sex act in the present. The same might be true of a man who was sexually molested as a boy. Even lesser traumas, such as the abandonment, rejection and humiliation most of us have experienced in romance, can leave a silent residue that haunts a person's bedroom later in life.

Part of the body's response to trauma is to stop the movement of chi. This is a protective device that shields us from new, and possibly painful, information when we are already overwhelmed by the effort to cope. Since sexual activity generates chi and invigorates its flow within the body, this natural defense mechanism can shut down our sexual desire. That's why we seldom feel like making love when we've been traumatized. In some cases, the process leaves a lasting mark, resulting in future symptoms like the ones we are about to discuss.

Since so much has been written about this subject, our discussion is limited to key points you might not find elsewhere. Depending on the severity and urgency of your problem, I encourage you to consider treatment from a qualified practitioner of Chinese medicine. Acupuncture, Chinese herbs and individualized lifestyle recommendations have helped millions of people overcome sexual obstacles and dysfunctions (see Appendix). I urge you to seek out reliable information and assistance from psychologists and medical doctors as well.

LOW SEX DRIVE

The clinical terms for it are hyposexuality and inhibited sexual desire (ISD). In traditional Chinese medicine, it is usually a sign of a chi deficiency in the genitals, kidneys or pelvic bowl.

As explained earlier, the brain and genitals derive their chi from the same source. Mental strain and debilitating habits can deplete sexual chi or draw it away from the genitals for other purposes. The bottom-line treatment is to increase kidney chi and ensure that it moves properly to where it is needed to fuel healthy desire. In addition to acupuncture and herbs, lifestyle adjustments are crucial: couples have more sex when they are less stressed and hassled because there are fewer demands on their minds. Chi naturally returns to their genitals, from where it was drawn to support workaday responsibilities.

In addition to the recommendations in chapter 9 for strengthening the kidneys, make sure to get sufficient exercise. Moderate workouts can boost one's sex drive because muscular movement stimulates chi in the meridians and helps release overall stagnation. Don't overdo it, however, or your body will be forced to use sexual chi to support the needs of your muscles.

Also, make time for love play even if you don't feel particularly desirous. It's the best way to get chi moving into the pelvic area. Remember to devote plenty of time and attention to the foreplay principles in chapter 4, the sexual massage in particular. Your engine not only needs fuel, it also needs time to warm up.

LACK OF RESPONSIVENESS

Some individuals just can't get aroused at all. Others respond adequately up to a point but then begin to feel less sensation. Some (women for the most part) are capable of sexual arousal but can't have an orgasm. From a traditional Chinese medicine point of view, these are different expressions of the same basic problem: a deficiency of sexual chi in the pelvic region. Either the entire body's chi is not abundant enough, or the liver meridian (and possibly other channels as well) is so congested that the chi cannot get to where it is needed, or the body has to divert the chi for use elsewhere. We all experience diminished sensation at times—when we suffer an illness or injury, for example—because the body is using its chi to heal.

Lack of feeling can also be caused by a *fear* of feeling. Fear is the negative kidney emotion and, as we've seen, the kidney governs sexuality. Many people in our culture have been conditioned to believe that it's wrong or dangerous to awaken their sexual power; when that power begins to stir, a woman may subconsciously pull her chi away from the pelvis. A man whose sexual chi is moving up to his heart may get frightened by his sudden vulnerability and unintentionally pull his chi away from his penis. This instantly lowers the intensity of sensation and possibly his erection as well.

Intense feelings can also shut down sexual responsiveness. When the liver is preoccupied with expressing and regulating emotion, it may not perform its other functions as well. These include regulating female hormones and directing chi to the genitals through the liver meridian.

As with other dysfunctions, if lack of responsiveness or the inability to have an orgasm is a chronic problem, see your doctor or consult with a therapist. Please also consider acupuncture treatments that increase the flow of chi to the genitals.

If you're a woman and this problem has been a constant feature of your sexual history, you might benefit from a change of perspective. If your initial sexual experiences did not measure up to your dreams and hopes, you might have thought, "What's the matter with me? Why am I not seeing fireworks like the women in romance novels? Why am I not having dynamite orgasms like my friends?" Such self-deprecating thoughts leave an imprint of fear—fear of failing, fear of in-adequacy, or fear of experiencing more frustration—and because of its association with the kidneys, fear can douse the fire of passion like a rainstorm.

One of the chief causes of unresponsiveness in women is early en-counters with unskilled men. If your first lovers were bumbling adoles-cents or marauders who didn't care about your satisfaction, you may have convinced yourself that *you* were the problem. After all, *they* got turned on! *They* had orgasms! The conviction that there is something wrong with you can turn into a self-fulfilling prophecy. The solution may be twofold: (1) Get it out of your head that you're unable to respond by learning more about your own sexuality, and (2) find a skillful man who is willing to take his time with you—or help your current lover become such a man. Many a frustrated woman has discovered her sexual power through the knowing, gentle touch of the right man.

You can also spend more time with yourself sexually. Thinking of yourself as unresponsive may have damaged your sexual self-image or caused you to feel contemptuous of your sexual organs. Follow the ad-vice in the section titled "Appreciate Your Womanhood" in chapter 6 to regain respect for the power and beauty of your sexuality. Masturbation can also be a helpful part of this process; it can show you that you are, in-deed, capable of deep and pleasurable sensations. You might also want to find ways to bring your sexual fears out into the open and disperse them. Talking it out with your partner or a trusted therapist can help a great deal.

Another way to enhance responsiveness for both sexes is to use breathing and visualization to bring chi to the genital area:

1. Sit or lie in a comfortable position that does not put you to sleep.

2. Close your eyes and take ten or twenty seconds to relax. Let your attention rest easily on the genitals. Then take a deep breath. Imagine the air moving through a tube from your nose to your testes or vagina.

3. At the same time, visualize the incoming breath as a beautiful stream of light. The light can be whatever color comes to mind, and the color can change as your feelings change.

4. Let the warm glow of light remain in your genitals as you continue to inhale and exhale. The more attention you bring to the area, the more chi gathers and the more sensation is possible.

SEXUAL INHIBITION

Some people are uncomfortable expressing themselves in bed. The inhibition can stem from a past trauma, as discussed earlier in the chapter, or from social values and family upbringing. Many women, for example, were taught that female sexual abandon is dangerous at best, evil at worst. In their teenage years, most girls who are sexually expressive are shunned and scorned as sluts, whereas precocious boys are considered rascals or esteemed as future studs or ladies' men.

Not that boys escape inhibition entirely. The pressure to perform in bed—exacerbated by macho media images and the tall tales they hear from their peers—exerts a restraining influence on many young men. So too does the male sense of honor: many boys are taught that it is not right to be sexual with a "good girl" unless they are prepared to make a commitment. Hence, as they mature, they are able to let loose with one-night stands and prostitutes but are inhibited with girls they care about.

Don't be surprised if inhibitions arise seemingly out of the blue, after you've already had satisfying sex with someone. Therapists say that couples sometimes become shy with each other when the stage of infatuation gives way to deeper intimacy. The very seriousness of the relationship and the closeness of the emotional bond can make one feel constrained.

In traditional Chinese medicine, sexual inhibition is a chi stagnation condition. The body gets the message that you're uncomfortable expressing your sexuality, and it complies by putting up an energetic roadblock. Stagnation serves you well as long as your psychological discomfort exists. But if that changes, because you meet someone with whom it's safe and acceptable to make love for example, the blockage becomes a problem, and it may take a concerted effort to remove it.

It often takes a long time to overcome inhibition, because energetic congestion is slow to dissipate. Exposing yourself to sex in a way that feels comfortable can help move the process along. Letting your sexiness come out in safe contexts—e.g., dancing, innocent flirting or watching sexy movies—can set the stage for letting it out in more intimate contexts. In bed, you and your lover should devote lots of time to sensual foreplay. Massage and other forms of touching can help a great deal. Also, pay close attention to the healing exercise at the end of this chapter.

It's also important to take an honest look at your feelings, perhaps with the help of a psychotherapist. Examine the possible roots of your inhibition in your childhood, the precepts of your religion, the values of your elders and social influences in general. Also, consider that your inhibition may be the result of a sexual trauma—or a series of traumas—whose influence is still with you on a subconscious level. You may be reluctant to examine these disturbing feelings, but if they are denying you the pleasure you deserve, it may be wise to force yourself to come to terms with them; the nature of stagnation is such that one must diligently push through it.

CONFLICTING SEX DRIVES

"My love life is like a fox hunt," Nina told me. "I'm the fox and Greg is the hound. Sometimes he literally chases me around the house. It would be fun if I were interested, but I'm really running away."

Nina was worried about the future of her marriage because her husband, Greg, wanted to make love much more often than she did. "I hate to disappoint him or make him feel rejected," she said, "but I don't know how much longer I can go through the motions and pretend I'm enjoying it."

In situations like this, my first objective is to see if either partner has an energetic condition that is causing the disparity in desire. The possibilities include:

1. Constitutionally, one person has stronger kidney chi and will naturally have a higher sex drive throughout life.

2. One person has an overall chi deficiency due to illness or overwork, which has lowered her or his sex drive.

3. One person has a kidney-related deficiency that manifests itself as a hyperactive sex drive.

4. Or, the other person has a kidney-related deficiency that manifests itself as little or no sex drive.

Nina and Greg had no such problem. They were simply not always in sync when it came to desire. Such disparities can usually be managed with simple changes in attitude and behavior.

As I told Nina, if your partner wants to make love and your body is telling you *not* to, you should not feel obligated to participate. Lovers are not entertainers or athletes, who have to perform regardless of how tired or uninspired they are. You may wish to satisfy your lover's needs, but that does not mean you have to have intercourse whenever he or she wants to. The best way to get people to hate sex is to push it on them when their body doesn't want it. You may love chocolate cake, but if it's shoved into your mouth too often you'll not only lose your taste for it, you'll also develop an aversion to it. Having sex when you don't want to sends mixed signals to the body, creating chi stagnation by moving energy and halting it at the same time.

At the very least, you can decline the invitation to have sex in the spirit of love and offer the promise of future bliss. But here's a more interesting alternative:

I asked Nina what would happen if Greg came home late from work very hungry. "Would you feel obliged to have supper with him if you had already eaten?" "Of course not," she replied. "But you might keep him company while he ate, wouldn't you? And maybe nibble a bit or sip some wine yourself?" She concurred. "Why not treat sex the same way?" I suggested. Nina realized that her obligation to Greg could be lovingly fulfilled in more creative ways than throwing open her legs and counting the cracks on the ceiling until he was finished. She could, so to speak, give him the pleasure of her company while he satisfied his hunger.

If your lover is hungry for sex and you are not, you can hold him in your arms or caress him while he masturbates. You can stroke his skin, nibble his ear or kiss him. You can whisper sexy words in his ear or tell him erotic stories. You can also participate orally or manually to whatever degree you wish. In this way, he doesn't feel rejected and you don't resent him.

Although the man is usually the more ardent one, the typical roles are sometimes reversed. A man whose woman wants sex when he's too pooped to rise to the occasion does not have to say no and leave her feeling unwanted and abandoned. He can let her feel the warmth of his love while she pleasures herself.

The bottom line is, there are many ways to love and help your partner express her or his sexuality. Even if your actual physical involvement is limited, a genuine, sincere presence can produce greater intimacy than reluctant intercourse, and it spares your lover the pain of rejection.

There is another potential benefit as well: witnessing the beauty of your lover's sexuality, and feeling the power of his or her sexual energy, may very well inspire your own. Remember, yin sexual energy is hidden, sometimes even from its owner. Making love may be far from your mind, but deep within, your body may be quite interested indeed. The desire simply has to be coaxed from its hiding place. Once it appears, the magnificent beauty of that desire can be expressed with passion, drama and exuberance.

This point can't be emphasized enough. In many instances, when couples complain that the man's sex drive is stronger than the woman's, the real problem is a failure to appreciate the subtlety of yin. This is one reason why it's so important to master the arts of seduction and foreplay.

When Sex Is a Drain

Another reason for different interest levels is that one partner is using sex to draw energy from the other. Most often, this occurs when one body becomes yin or yang deficient and tries to balance itself by siphoning energy from the partner during intercourse. After a while, the body from which energy is being drawn protects itself by losing interest in having sex with the taker. Unless the deficient partner finds other ways to nourish his or her chi, neediness will eventually make the lover hostile and resentful.

If a yin-deficient woman becomes hypersexual in an attempt to draw the needed energy from her man, her assertive lust might excite her partner. But if the woman is draining his sexual strength, his body will feel fatigued after making love and he will eventually pull away.

How can you tell if someone's desire is rooted in a yin deficiency? These are the most common clues:

1. When they get tired, their sexual desire increases.
2. They get more ardent as they age.
3. One partner has a dramatic increase of desire in a short period of time (often misinterpreted to mean the *other* partner has *lost* desire).

Here are some do's and don'ts that will help ameliorate the chi deficiency:

DO:

* Take in plenty of warm and room-temperature fluids.
* Avoid cold food and drink.
* Do the exercises in chapter 6 for circulating chi.
* Get enough rest to reduce the effects of stress in your body.
* Adopt the lifestyle practices described in chapter 9.
* If your partner is turning away from you sexually, don't take it personally. Listen to the explanation and respect his or her feelings. It may be an energy issue, not a personal rejection.
* If you're not monogamous, limit your number of sex partners or stop having sex for a while.

DON'T:

* Use sex just as a stress release valve.
* Have sex when under the influence of alcohol or drugs.
* Routinely have ejaculatory sex when tired.
* Make love on a full stomach.
* Have sex with multiple partners.

VAGINISMUS

An involuntary contraction of the muscles near the entrance to the vagina, vaginismus can make intercourse uncomfortable, painful and, in severe cases, impossible. Depending on whether it is considered psychological or physical in origin, conventional treatments include psychotherapy and the use of a vaginal dilator, a painless procedure that gradually loosens the muscular contraction. From the perspective of traditional Chinese medicine, vaginismus is a sign of chi stagnation in the vaginal area. The stagnation can be the actual cause of the problem or the result of a physical disorder (overdeveloped vaginal muscles, for example), a physical trauma such as an injury, or a psychological history that caused the person to believe that penetration by a penis would be painful. The bottom line is, the individual is energetically closed off from receiving.

In addition to seeking appropriate medical help, it is important to clarify certain issues. Ask yourself:

* Do you truly want to receive the man you are with (or anyone else, for that matter)?
* Why would being receptive be dangerous in some way?
* What is your man bringing to you sexually that could be making you afraid?
* What did you experience in the past that may have traumatized you?
* What ideas or attitudes have made you feel it was unwise to let a penis inside you?

Remember, the yang aspect of yin is discerning. Determine what is appropriate for you to receive, and from whom. If you face these issues clearly and honestly, you may find that you feel safe enough to release your vaginal muscles from the need to protect you.

If your lover is compassionate and patient, you can work on the energetic aspect of the problem together. You need to get chi moving in your pelvic area. One way is to devote lots of time to loving foreplay and then use specific exercises to enhance your capacity to receive. For example, sit on his lap or between his legs while facing him, without having intercourse. Press your genitals against his and perform the Golden Circle exercise together several times. The energetic exchange will facilitate the movement of chi.

Also, have your man use his finger—with lubrication if necessary—to open your vagina, slowly and gently. This should come after at least fifteen minutes of other foreplay activity, and only when you are sure you're ready. You might find it easier to open up if your lover simultaneously touches your clitoris so you feel aroused. Trust in this case is as vital as patience. Agree with your lover beforehand that you are not to be pushed farther than you can comfortably go in any session, and under no circumstances is intercourse to be forced.

VAGINAL DRYNESS

Occasional dryness can be handled with a water-based lubricant such as KY jelly. For persistent dryness—which can be caused by anything from the soap you're using to menopause—see your gynecologist to rule out physical causes. In addition, consider the following possibilities.

Your body may be telling you it does not want to be penetrated by the man you're with. When a woman does not want to receive, her vagina will get the message and respond with dryness or tightness. Another possibility is that you may be receiving insufficient stimulation. You and your lover should study the foreplay techniques in chapter 4 and make sure you give your yin plenty of time to get aroused. Wetness is yin; the more yin, the more wet. You should both respect the speed at which you respond, and make appropriate adjustments if your response pattern has changed since you began making love together. Remember, once yang finds a way to get to the goal, it will repeat that successful pattern over and over; yin benefits from a variety of approaches.

Your dryness may also be the result of a yin deficiency. You're prone to this if you work too hard and too fast, if you think too hard and too fast, if you don't know how to slow down, or if you give more than you receive. See chapter 9 for advice on how to overcome a yin deficiency.

Dryness can also be hormone related. Because estrogen is the yin sex hormone, when it decreases—whether through menopause or hormonal changes at any stage of life—the woman has proportionally less yin strength and more yang strength. Naturally, if you are experiencing menopause, you should seek proper medical advice. Also, bear in mind that a large number of women have been able to enter menopause more comfortably by using acupuncture and Chinese herbal remedies.

PREMATURE EJACULATION

Charles Darwin would probably laugh if he knew that humans now consider the rapid expulsion of sperm a problem. Speedy ejaculation would seem to have evolutionary advantages: primitive males who could have sex with a large number of women in a short period of time had a better chance of fathering offspring. Call it survival of the quickest. Now, rapid ejaculators are at a disadvantage: they're less likely to keep desirable mates satisfied.

Looking at premature ejaculation from this Darwinian perspective offers more than irony. It can help men—and the women in their lives—understand that nature did not design the male body to be a long time coming. In addition to millions of years of evolution, culture, too, encourages speed; when young men masturbate in the bathroom, or sneak their girlfriends into the bushes or the backseat of a car, they learn to hurry up and finish before someone intrudes. It's only when they mate with women who value their own sexual needs that men have to reverse evolution and long-standing habits. Slowing down is a new skill, and in many ways as unnatural to the human body as sitting in a chair all day.

Thinking of quick ejaculation as a disease to cure instead of a natural habit to unlearn can have the unfortunate effect of making the situation worse. A man is never inadequate because he needs to learn new skills; he's merely untrained. And he is not a failure if he doesn't learn the new skills overnight.

Chinese medicine can supply vital help by addressing energetic weaknesses. If you can't slow the ejaculation process down even with good training in the appropriate skills, the problem is most likely rooted in a yin deficiency in the kidney organ system. Yin serves as a container for yang energy. If yin is weak, it can't hold yang in the body, and the man completes the sexual process very rapidly. My colleagues and I have helped countless men overcome premature ejaculation with acupuncture and Chinese herbs. Treatment with Chinese medicine gives the body the necessary strength to implement ejaculatory control skills. However, as with all yin phenomena, training the body to sustain an erection and delay ejaculation takes time.

One way to get used to being inside a woman without ejaculating is to simply be there, limp or hard, without any movement. Take the pressure off yourself to maintain an erection. Don't strive to have an orgasm or provide your lover with one.

The techniques in chapter 6 will help you cultivate the ability to postpone ejaculation. If you give them a fair try and do not find any improvement, you might want to see a trained counselor or sex therapist to help you understand any emotional issues that may be contributing to the situation—or have resulted from it.

SEXUAL DYSFUNCTION

As with other sexual dysfunctions, difficulty achieving or maintaining an erection is regarded as either psychological or physical in origin. If the problem is consistent—and especially if it has come upon you suddenly—it's important to have a urologist rule out medical causes.

From the point of view of traditional Chinese medicine, impotence has three possible energetic roots: (1) a yang chi deficiency, which prevents the penis from rising and getting hot, (2) chi stagnation, resulting from either a deficiency or intense emotions, (3) an overall chi deficiency in the pelvic area, which diminishes the ability to feel sensation. The nerves need chi to do their job of transmitting messages, so a man with insufficient chi requires more stimulation for a longer period of time before he can adequately respond.

Take Richard, for example, a man who had a history of losing his erection before he ejaculated. Invariably, he would panic and think there was something physically wrong with his "plumbing" or that he was beset by deep psychological demons. Either of which might be true in some cases, but in Richard's the cause was strictly energetic: a yang deficiency in the kidney organ. He was dealing with emotional issues all right, but they were the *result* of his energetic problem, not the cause. In other words, the kidney deficiency produced erection problems, which, in turn, led to fear, anxiety and depression. Richard's problem was successfully treated with acupuncture, Chinese herbs and the following behavioral adjustments, which I would recommend to anyone wrestling with erectile problems:

1. When making love, give yourself enough time to warm up. Often, what seems to be impotence is actually a predictable consequence of aging or fatigue, both of which dissipate yang chi. It simply takes longer to get erect than it used to. Time allows yin chi to get involved, and it's yin that holds yang—and that quintessential yang expression, an erection—in place.

If your man is having difficulty maintaining an erection, try making the process of arousal more holistic for him by touching and caressing him all over—but not on the genitals. This will inspire yin, and since yin attracts yang, an indirect route can be the best way to get to your destination: a firm, excited penis. You can emphasize nongenital stimulation during the early stages of love play or even devote entire sessions to it, agreeing in advance not to attempt intercourse.

2. Don't force your body to have sex when it is tired. Any man who is experiencing symptoms of sexual weakness has to be doubly care-

ful to conserve his yang chi. Pushing yourself when yang is already depleted will magnify the problem. As mentioned earlier, sexual yearning can be a symptom of a worn-out body; if this is a common pattern for you, pay particular attention to this advice.

3. Express your emotions. If the liver meridian is busy processing powerful emotions, it can't transport sufficient chi to the genitals. Letting the feelings out can help open the channel, freeing your body to respond more efficiently. Express yourself to your lover, or a friend, minister, counselor or private journal.

4. Practice the energy cultivation exercises and the semen retention techniques in this book. They will help you draw chi into the genitals without expelling it.

5. Don't panic. Because their sense of manhood is at stake, men often overreact to erection problems. Like sleep and love, erections have to come naturally, not through strenuous effort. Don't worry. Unless you have a serious medical condition, you'll live to see your penis rise again.

6. Keep having sex. Studies have shown that if a man begins to lose his erectile ability, the most therapeutic approach is for him to be *more* sexually active, not less so. Making love increases the flow of oxygen into the penile tissue, allowing for firmer erections. Most men get so frightened at the first sign of flagging virility that they avoid sex. That only makes the problem worse.

HOW DEPRESSING

One of the hallmark symptoms of clinical depression is inhibited sexual desire. Unfortunately, the disorder has you coming and going: a side effect of many of the drugs used to treat depression is reduced sexual performance.

Depression is the result of stagnant emotional chi in the liver organ and possibly also the liver meridian, which runs through the genitals. As a result, emotions do not move in and out of the system in a healthful manner and chi does not circulate well in the pelvic area, where the fires of passion ignite.

A good way to get chi into the pelvis is to move your body. External movement promotes the internal movement of chi. So get your heart rate up: stomp around, dance, play sports, do aerobic exercise.

One of the best things you can do to get chi moving into the genitals again is to make love. It may be the last thing you feel like doing, but do it anyway. It may feel strange at first, since when you're depressed you may not enjoy the things you usually find exciting. You may want to stop, thinking it's a waste of time and that you'll never get turned on. But, if you take the time you need to build up arousal, you can invigorate the chi in the liver channel and help break up the stagnant chi that causes depression. Remember, the problem is emotional or energetic, not sexual; deal with the core issue without getting further depressed over the symptom.

For depressed patients I often recommend frequent lovemaking sessions of relatively short duration, in which there are no goals other than to get chi moving. This tends to be more effective than attempting an orgasmic marathon every once in a while. One caveat: Making love should not be regarded as a substitute for the treatment of depression; don't use sex as a way to avoid dealing with emotional issues.

People with chronic depression should see a psychologist or an M.D. I recommend that you also see a doctor of Chinese medicine. Acupuncture, Chinese herbal remedies and lifestyle advice geared to the individual's Energetic Profile can be very helpful in treating depression. Bear in mind, however, that if the depression has been caused or exacerbated by serious problems in your relationship, you may need the aid of a marital counselor.

NO BABY, NO SEX

Infertility can ruin your sex life. Not because it stops you from having sex but because you start having sex only to conceive. The pressure to get pregnant can stifle the spontaneity of lovemaking. Plus, doing it when you don't really want to sends mixed signals, causing chi to stagnate instead of flowing to the genitals to support lovemaking. In addition, the built-up frustration of not having conceived in the past affects the liver, as does the toxic effect of chemicals if you're taking fertility drugs. These factors, too, will impede the natural flow of sexual chi.

There are essentially two things you should know about infertility:

(1) You have options. High-tech medicine has performed miracles for many infertile couples. However, the success rate is painfully low, the cost is excessive and the emotional toll can be high. From the perspective of traditional Chinese medicine, the problem can have many possible causes: The man may have a low sperm count due to a yin deficiency in the kidney organ system; his sperm may move sluggishly due to a yang deficiency; his seminal fluid may be too viscous due to a yin deficiency. From the woman's side, because of a fast-paced lifestyle or emotional strain, the yin in her body might not be strong enough for her egg to receive sperm (this becomes more common as women get older). Alternatively, her yang energy might not be keeping her uterus warm enough to hold the fetus in her womb; this can lead to miscarriages. By uncovering and correcting the underlying energetic conditions, traditional Chinese medicine has often been successful treating infertility—and the side effects of mainstream fertility drugs—while at the same time empowering the couple's sexuality.

(2) You should work hard to protect your sex life. While trying to conceive, it's important to separate lovemaking and procreation. If sex becomes only a means of conceiving a child, it can come to be associated with pain and frustration, stifling romance completely. One solution is to set aside times when you make love for love's sake, with no intention of becoming pregnant. Nonejaculatory intercourse and sexual play *without* intercourse are perfect because they provide closeness and pleasure without the possibility of conception.

PREGNANT WITH PASSION

Sometimes a woman's interest in sex will dissipate during pregnancy. The body may say no because it is trying to preserve its kidney energy, which is needed to support the pregnancy and can be depleted by ordinary sex practices. It's important to pay attention to those signals. On the other hand, she may feel very amorous. So much chi is involved in creating a new life that her body tries to replenish it by taking some in from her sexual partner. Or her kidneys are calling on their reserve chi to support the pregnancy, and the abundance of energy can make her more desirous.

The best way to know if a change in your sex drive is a symptom of energy loss is to examine your daily schedule. Are you always on the go? Do you give yourself time to rest? Do you feel hyped-up much of the time? If you see that the rest of your system is on overdrive, your sex drive may be as well. If this is the case, you need to rest more (afternoon naps are great), drink more fluid (preferably without ice), and eat warm, easily digested food. Keep your body cool with wet cloths on the back of your neck. Take vitamin and mineral supplements. And consider acupuncture treatment and Chinese herbal remedies; they are quite effective in keeping the pregnant body strong and symptom free while facilitating easier childbirth.

Pregnancy is actually a great time to make love. Women are even more beautiful then, because their storehouse of kidney chi is being used to support the pregnancy, giving them that familiar glow. Also, many pregnant women tend to be proud of their bodies, and this brings greater confidence and feminine strength to lovemaking. It's also a time when couples put more care and awareness into their loving, because they have to protect the mother and fetus. So, unless your doctor has suggested a medical reason for abstaining (high blood pressure, for example), you can assume that if your body is healthy enough to carry a baby to term, it is strong enough to enjoy sex without harming the pregnancy.

One great advantage to having sex during pregnancy—aside from not having to worry about getting pregnant, of course—is that it encourages creativity. It forces men and women to find new ways to give each other pleasure and try new positions.

Rear-entry positions, with the woman on her hands and knees or lying on her side with pillows between her legs, have worked for many couples throughout the entire pregnancy. One recommended position for the second trimester is to have the woman lie on her back with the man standing at the foot of the bed; this keeps him from collapsing his weight on her. In the third trimester, side positions are great. She can lie on her side with her upper leg raised, her partner lying behind her, entering from the rear; or she can lie on her side and pull her legs up at a right angle to her torso while he enters from a kneeling position, perpendicular to her. He can lift her upper leg and either hold it in place or lean it against his chest.

A TIME TO HEAL

Every couple—even those with none of the problems in this chapter—can energize their bedroom by setting aside time for sexual healing. To one degree or another, we all have scars from past pain or frustration in the sexual arena, and they can affect our sexuality without our knowledge. The body stores much of that pain in its muscles. That's why past traumas can be recalled when we are touched.

The yin and yang aspects of our sexuality experience pain differently. Because it is the initiating force, yang energy is vulnerable to rejection. When a sexual overture is turned down or a romantic expectation is dashed, yang chi is injured. Yin energy, the receptive force, is susceptible to injuries of abandonment. If one partner walks out of the relationship or is insensitive to the other's sexual needs, the result is injury to yin chi.

Yin and yang injuries can affect either gender, but we are more likely to be injured in our primary trait. Since men are predominately yang and are usually the aggressors in the mating game, they tend to encounter more yang injuries. Injuries to yin chi are more likely to affect women, especially if their partners are selfish, unsupportive or sexually hasty. The result in either case is interference in the flow of the injured chi. This makes less yin or yang available, and the deficiency shows up in behavior, both in and out of bed. If the injury is not healed, or continues to be aggravated by rejection or abandonment, physical symptoms related to stagnation arise. They begin in the pelvis, with, for example, prostate swelling in men and fibroid tumors or menstrual cramps in women. The stagnation might later rise, causing problems ranging from digestive disorders to neck and shoulder pain to dry eyes to headaches, mood swings and depression.

One way to heal yin and yang injuries is to talk about them. Expression helps to break up stagnation. Allow each other to open up about past sexual and romantic pain—both major and minor hurts from previous relationships and your own. If done with love and trust, the process can bring you closer than ever and open the door to more powerful lovemaking in the future. I recommend taking turns and limiting each partner to ten minutes at a time. Be sure not to accuse or blame; simply express your pain.

Another way to heal past injuries is to set aside time periods of twenty to thirty minutes, during which one partner is given exactly what he or she wants. This may include anything from loving compliments, to massage, to a shoulder to cry on, to specific sexual favors. The giver should devote his or her complete attention to the partner's desires and satisfy them with generosity and patience.

To heal deeper wounds I recommend a physical process. The following exercise will:

1. Facilitate the movement of chi into the genitals.
2. Help remove the physical memory of past trauma.
3. Help relax the muscles in the pelvic region.
4. Increase trust and intimacy between partners.

Remember, the aim is sexual healing, not sexual arousal. Set aside at least an hour when you and your partner can be alone, undisturbed and unhassled by outer concerns. During that time, one of you will be the receiver and the other the giver. These roles should be total and exclusive for that session; next time, you will change places.

Create a peaceful, attractive, comfortable atmosphere. You might want to play soft, relaxing music, burn a scented candle and place flowers near the bed. Set the lighting dim but not too dim, as you want to be able to see each other clearly and look into each other's eyes. The temperature should be neither too hot nor too cold. Both of you may wish to bathe or shower before getting started.

The receiver should adopt an attitude of trust and surrender. Whether you're male or female, this is the time to let your yin take over and be totally receptive. If you have trouble trusting your partner, the issue should be discussed openly and honestly before you begin.

The giver should adopt an attitude of generosity and strength. Let the best of your yang nature shine: give creatively and abundantly, while paying close attention to your partner and learning from his or her reactions how to give more effectively.

The receiver lies down in bed, nude. Have a sheet or something silky at hand to cover your body should you become chilled or embarrassed.

The giver massages the beloved's body gently and lovingly, perhaps using a nicely scented massage lotion or oil. Beginning with the feet, move slowly up each leg, relaxing the muscles and moving blood and chi toward the pelvis. Don't touch the genitals.

Next, massage the hands and arms, then the face, chest, belly and abdomen, moving slowly toward the genitals. (See chapter 4 for more massage tips.)

The receiver should use words, sighs or gestures to let the partner know when something is painful or some area needs special attention. Remember to breathe deeply and allow yourself to emote—make whatever sounds you feel like letting out.

Once you've relaxed into the process, the giver should focus on the pelvic region, from the lower abdomen to the upper thighs. Massage as firmly as you can without causing pain. Increasingly, put most of your attention on these areas:

- the tissue just above and just below the pubic bone
- the inner thighs
- the groin, where the legs meet the pelvis
- the perineum (the area between the genitals and anus)

Most of us have a great deal of tension stored in those areas, and many emotions from past experiences are locked in as body memories. The idea is to release the tension and remove the energetic stagnation that blocks complete, healthy sexual expression.

While many couples find the process pleasant and relaxing, be aware that it may liberate stored-up feelings from past pain or hurt. Anything and everything can come up—anger, fear, pain, guilt, shame, etc. Some of the feelings, good or bad, might be directed at the giver. If this happens, remember that something positive is taking place. Releasing emotions stored in the body can be an important aspect of healing. However, while the receiver should not hold back from expressing any feelings that come up, it is important not to be accusatory. Use phrases like "I feel angry (or hurt)" rather than "You're the problem."

The giver must not do anything to discourage or repress the partner's expression. This is the time to be magnanimous. Encourage your beloved to let it all out by whispering phrases like "It's okay, I understand" and "I'm here for you." Don't argue, don't correct, don't analyze, don't ask questions, don't defend yourself. Above all, don't take anything personally, no matter how personal it gets. If the emotions get very intense, stop massaging and hold your partner in your arms.

When the emotions subside, resume the healing massage. Begin by gently soothing the areas that may have triggered the emotional outburst.

I recommend doing the entire process for half an hour to an hour. If at any time the receiver insists on stopping, the giver should comply immediately. When you stop, embrace and lie together calmly and lovingly for a while.

As soon as it's appropriate, make a date for the next session, in which the giver and receiver will reverse roles. Make the process an ongoing part of your life together. Even if your sex life is great, there is always healing to be done.

While I don't recommend this the first time you do the exercise, at a later date you may want to include the genitals in the process—again, with healing in mind, not sexual stimulation as such. You should agree beforehand that no matter how turned on you get, you will stay in your giver and receiver roles for the entire exercise.

Feel free to *follow* the process with the customary give and take of sexual play. Lovemaking can be especially wonderful following such an intimate exercise. But it should be done only if both partners really want to and feel comfortable making the transition.

Chapter 8

A SINGLE BOAT
UPON THE RIVER
Life Between Relationships

Male and female created he them.
—GENESIS 1:27

Feminists may wear T-shirts saying "A woman without a man is like a fish without a bicycle," and macho guys may joke about treating women like snakes (slip a loop around their necks so they can't get away or come too close), but in truth most of us feel discontented when we're not partnered. Never more so than on the heels of an intimate relationship. When you're used to the companionship of a lover, being alone again can feel like withdrawing from an addictive substance: you crave another's presence, your skin aches to be touched, your loins practically groan because your sexual chi is all dressed up with nowhere to go. Some people find loneliness so agonizing that they do everything in their power to avoid it.

When he and his wife ended their fifteen-year marriage, Blake immediately asked friends to set him up on dates. He placed ads in personals columns even before he found a place to live. Within a week he met a new woman, slept with her and spent virtually every night for the next four months watching the gleam in her eye. The classic rebound relationship ended when Blake's girlfriend dumped him for another man.

His response was to place ads in three newspapers, enroll in a dating service and make another round of calls asking friends if they knew any single women.

Two weeks later he was in my office. He wondered why so-and-so wouldn't go to bed with him. After all, they'd had a great time on their first three dates.

"Blake, why are you doing this?" I asked.

"Doing what?"

I told him frankly that his frenzied dating was a way to avoid the pain of being alone, and that his constant hunt for pleasure would end up hurting both his health and his heart.

"Nah, I'm fine," he said, "I'd just rather be with someone than be alone."

"There are times when you *need* to be alone," I replied, "and if you become successful at that, the coupling part will work a lot better."

Of course, there are many happy exceptions, but most single people eventually feel a longing for intimacy. No matter how we alter our behavior, thoughts or attitudes, our bodies remain predominately yin or yang, and they need the opposite energy to feel complete. For the most part, it takes the spiritual discipline of a monk or nun to find contentment and wholeness in long-term celibacy. Yet, even Pope John Paul II has commented on how difficult it is for a celibate to uphold that vow.

Nevertheless, while it may not feel heavenly, it doesn't have to be hell either. Solitude can be a golden opportunity for healing and growth, an opportunity to learn to love and respect yourself so you can better love and respect another. Going within is a yin act. If you do it well, you will be better equipped to turn your attention outward, in the yang direction, to focus on a beloved and create a whole that is greater than the sum of your individual parts. You can know another person only as well as you know yourself, and you can penetrate another heart only as deeply as you've peered into your own.

In a nutshell, the job of a single person is threefold: to recover from the pain of the past, to create a satisfying existence in the present and to prepare for a more fulfilling relationship in the future.

HEALING
AFTER THE SPLIT

*I never found the companion that was
so companionable as solitude.*

—HENRY DAVID THOREAU

After the loss of a love, it's essential to allow yourself the opportunity to recover mentally, emotionally, physically and sexually.

Mending the Mind

As noted earlier, we are often attracted to people whose energetic strengths complement our own weaknesses. With that in mind, one important exercise is to list the qualities that you admired, enjoyed and needed in your ex. Ask yourself these questions:

- What qualities attracted you to your former lover in the first place?
- What held your interest over the course of the relationship?
- What about him or her inspired you?
- What do you miss the most?

The purpose of the exercise is to identify qualities you might be able to develop in *yourself*. By filling in the gaps in your own personality, you will be able to give yourself some of what you now think you need from another person. This will not only make you more comfortable while alone; it will also make you a more desirable mate for someone else—someone stronger and more complete than those you've attracted in the past.

Healing the Heart

As odd as it may sound, one of the fastest ways to get over the loss of a love is to feel the pain of that loss. Psychological experiments have found that people who are told *not* to think about a specific topic for a period of time will later think about it far more, and with greater intensity, than those who devote that time to purposely thinking about the topic. If feelings are denied or suppressed they become stuck and exaggerated, leading to obsession with the very thing you are trying to avoid. In Chinese medicine good health entails feeling every appropriate emotion. When emotions are expressed, the chi that comprised it can be used for other purposes.

You may not be able to cry or scream out in rage—or laugh, for that matter—any old time emotions happen to crop up. But if you schedule a time when you are free to focus on feelings that have to be subdued during your regular routine, heartbreak can be remedied more effectively.

You may run through an entire cycle of emotions many times before you feel completely healed. Sadness, relief, fear, anger, anxiety and exhilaration can become sadness, relief, fear, anger, anxiety and exhilaration once again, and several times more. If disturbing moods crop up at unpredictable times, don't take it to mean you're getting worse, or backsliding. It's all part of the mourning and recovery process.

Protecting Your Body

The body is very vulnerable at times of emotional chaos because its protective chi (immunity) is being used to facilitate coping. The body also takes longer to heal than the mind or feelings. So, don't push yourself at work, for example, as a way to avoid your pain. Be kind to yourself. Treat yourself the way you would treat your best friends if they were in your situation.

It's especially important to protect your respiratory system. Remember the song "Adelaide's Lament" from the musical *Guys and Dolls*? From waiting and waiting for her lover to propose, the lyric states, "a person could develop a cold." The ditty contains great wisdom from the perspective of Chinese medicine, which notes that sadness can weaken the lungs, causing anything from colds to allergies to asthma.

Be aware that you may experience cravings during this period—for chocolate, for example. Chocolate is considered a bitter herb and a heart yang tonic. It warms the heart, taking the place of the lover who once provided that service. While a small amount may actually be helpful to the heart, as shown by recent medical studies, too much has a sedating influence. You might also crave coffee, alcohol or drugs; they affect the liver, which regulates the flow of emotions. People sometimes turn to these substances to reduce the intensity of their pain. The liver has to work so hard to cope with their toxic qualities that its ability to process emotions becomes sluggish. This results in temporary relief from pain, but long-term damage to the organ and a prolonged mourning period.

The best policy is moderation in all things, including moderation. While you're healing, there is no reason to deny yourself the occasional indulgence; have a rich meal or a thick piece of chocolate cake now and then if it makes you feel better. But don't overindulge. And look for healthy options to help you cope. Instead of smoking, find someone to hug. Instead of getting high, get some exercise. In fact, exercise should be given a prominent role as it helps the body circulate chi.

In addition to the general lifestyle advice in chapter 9, here are some suggestions for keeping your body together while healing your heart and soul after a breakup:

- Make sure to get enough sleep. How much is enough? What you feel you need, not what you think you should need. Go to bed a little earlier to ensure that you get enough rest, and don't hesitate to take naps if you need them. You may find that you tire easily because your body is coping with your loss.
- Eat properly. Follow commonsense dietary guidelines. If you lose your appetite, eat small amounts anyway—no fewer than two meals a day. If you don't nourish yourself now, you may find yourself feeling ravenous later, and that can lead to weight gain.
- Stay warm. It's especially important to keep your chest, neck and upper back warm. Many acute respiratory illnesses invade the body

in those areas, and sadness makes us more vulnerable to lung problems. If it's chilly, wear a hat and scarf. Err on the side of overdressing.

• Take long, hot, luxurious baths or showers to relax your muscles and calm your nerves. Find other ways to spend time around water as well (swim, sail, walk beside a lake, etc.); water exerts a calming yin influence.

• Get massages and hugs. Being touched helps the body make the transition from being coupled to being single. If you have never had a professional massage, try one. If you like it, go back once a month, or more often if you can. And give a hug at least once a day.

• Try exercises that relax the body and coordinate breath and movement, such as yoga, tai chi, rowing, speed walking and jogging.

• Take time regularly to turn inward in prayer or meditation.

• Spend time in nature. Bask in the sun; its warmth nourishes the yang energy in your body. And in the moonlight; it nourishes yin.

• Sit with your back to a fire; warming the back strengthens the kidneys.

• Take up a new hobby or develop a new interest. When the mind is content, the body's chi flows better. Intellectual pursuits pull chi out of the pelvis and into the head.

Sexual Healing

Regardless of the cause of your breakup, you will probably benefit from sexual healing. As mentioned earlier, sexual wounds—whether from a major trauma like rape or molestation or an emotional injury such as rejection or humiliation—leave an energetic scar in the body.

Chapter 6 offered an exercise for regaining appreciation for one's womanhood (see page 156). I strongly recommend that single women practice this, especially if their sexual self-esteem has been diminished by rejection or abandonment. Get to know and love the focal point of your sexuality. Appreciating the beauty in this part of yourself will make it easier to share that beauty unabashedly with the next man in your life.

A man's self-esteem is also linked to the way he perceives his genitals. A man who thinks of his penis as too small usually feels small about himself as a person; a man who sees his penis as undependable or uncontrollable tends to lack confidence in general. Get to know your penis. Examine it in a mirror. Explore its folds and crevices, the road map of its veins, the topology of its terrain. Touch it respectfully. See it as you would want the next woman in your life to see it. The more you respect your genitals and the more comfortable you are with them, the safer you will feel when a woman gets close to you, and the more you will be able to give to her sexually.

SUCCESSFUL ABSTINENCE

Involuntary celibacy can feel like torture, but it doesn't have to. With the right attitude and the right practices, a period of abstinence can be an opportunity for rejuvenation and self-discovery.

People who find themselves suddenly single tend to react in one of two ways: some, like Blake at the beginning of this chapter, can't wait to have sex and will do it with almost anyone; others can't imagine making love for quite some time. Both reactions are perfectly understandable. Because the lungs are the parent organ to the kidneys in the Nourishing Cycle, sad people seldom feel sexy. Their lungs are expending so much chi to cope with sadness there is not enough available to nurture the kidneys, resulting in a lowered sex drive. The other extreme—the urge to jump into bed immediately after a breakup—is not unlike a strong craving for chocolate or alcohol. It's a symptom of mourning, the body's way of compensating for a loss. As with other cravings, it can be self-defeating to overindulge.

According to Chinese medical theory, it would seem prudent to wait a while before getting sexually involved again. There are several reasons for this. When you have sex too soon, judgment and discernment diminish and your sense of reality becomes distorted. This effect is magnified on the heels of a broken relationship, often resulting in the familiar rebound phenomenon, in which you find yourself ga-ga over someone who is totally wrong for you. The comedian Robin Williams once said that God gave man a brain and a penis, but only enough blood to run one at a time. If you apply this idea to women as well as men, and substitute "chi" for "blood," you'd have a pretty accurate statement of why Chinese medical theory would recommend a period of abstinence between intimate liaisons.

Another reason to avoid premature intimacy is that exchanging sexual chi with someone exposes you to that person's Energetic Profile. When your chi is being used to cope with strong emotions—as is usually the case after a breakup—you are even more vulnerable to the influence of your sex partner's imbalances. The physical closeness may feel exquisite, but if the match isn't healthy, energetically speaking, it can create confusion and a sense of instability during this time of transition. This is especially true if you had relied on your former partner to balance your own energetic weakness.

A third reason to proceed slowly on the path to intimacy is that jumping into bed with someone can make you feel worse. Physical contact may soothe your pain temporarily, but if your body is not truly ready to receive from another person, making love causes chi stagnation, producing a numb, hollow feeling, leading to more intense emotional anguish. Sexual touch can bring up body memories of past loving, which can exacerbate the mourning process.

A period of abstinence not only gives you time to heal your wounds, it also helps you regain your equilibrium and allow your own energetic dynamic to settle into a new independent pathway. How much time should pass before it's healthy to make love again? It depends on the duration of your previous relationship, the depth of your loss and how actively you engage in the healing process. Generally speaking, the more intense the pain, anger, fear and confusion, the longer it takes to readjust.

During this period it can be very beneficial to spend time with members of the opposite sex. Relatives, co-workers and platonic friends can supply some of the yin or yang energy you used to receive from your lover. They can also provide insights that your same-sex acquaintances might not have. After a while, you may want to explore relatively safe ways of putting your attention on sex—and on being sexy. If you feel ready, the following activities can reacquaint you with your sexiness even before you feel ready to date:

- Watch erotic or X-rated movies.
- Read romantic or erotic novels or poetry.
- Flirt innocently, in situations that you know won't go anywhere.
- Go to parties or clubs and simply observe—and note how it feels to *be* observed.
- Get dressed in your sexiest outfit and go where no one of the opposite sex will see you.
- Then wear the same outfit someplace else and watch how the opposite sex reacts to you.
- Write a list of the qualities you consider sexy about yourself.

Not a Walk in the Park

Having said all that, we must acknowledge that prolonged abstinence is not natural and certainly not easy. The sages of antiquity recognized that abstention can severely diminish sexual energy and even lead to mental instability, distorting one's sense of reality because of its effect on the heart through the Discipline Cycle.

Certainly, many religions have ancient and honorable traditions of celibacy for monastics. Chinese Taoism itself has such a heritage. For the most part, only adepts who have mastered the art of transmuting sexual energy into fuel for spiritual growth are able to manage celibacy with grace. Others either succumb to temptation or struggle in torment. But temporary abstinence has none of the dangers of long-term celibacy. In fact, it allows the body to build up a natural concentration of sexual energy, which can increase vigor and sensitivity when you return to lovemaking.

To ease the discomfort and help you make constructive use of a period of abstinence, here are some tips:

1. *Move the energy.* As we saw earlier, a variety of physical and mental ailments can result when sexual chi is allowed to stagnate. Moving the energy around not only helps prevent illness but also alleviates some of the frustration of going without sex.

Vigorous physical exercise is one way to move energy. Work with your doctor or a qualified trainer to develop a moderate workout routine that includes aerobics and muscle strengthening. The gentle Chinese martial art *tai chi chuan* is an excellent practice because it generates chi and circulates it through the body in a gentle and balanced way. I also recommend the stretching routines of yoga as a way to alleviate tension and move energy. Pay special attention to postures that stretch the muscles of the lower trunk, thighs and hips.

Above all, practice the breathing and visualization exercises in this book, which are designed to cultivate and manipulate sexual chi. They have been used to great benefit by both laypeople and monastic celibates for centuries. Here's some special advice if you're heartbroken over a concluded love affair: When doing the Golden Circle exercise, pull the chi up during the in-breath and hold it in your heart while retaining your breath. As you exhale and the chi moves back down, imagine the pain leaving your heart. This helps release some of the energy that has congested in the heart and allows healing chi to nourish the organ.

2. Protect your liver.   During periods of abstinence, it's best to avoid stimulating the liver; irritation will further congest sexual energy in the pelvis and intensify emotions. Avoid, or at least cut back on, liver-stimulants like coffee, alcohol and recreational drugs, even if you crave them. Also, do not take medication unless it's prescribed by a doctor and is absolutely necessary; the liver uses a great deal of energy to metabolize drugs.

3. Reach out and touch.   Draw closer to your friends and family. Instead of talking on the phone, meet in person. This allows you to touch and be touched, both emotionally and physically. We don't always realize it, but our bodies can miss being touched more than they miss sexual release. If you have the opportunity to hold someone's hand, put your arm around a shoulder or get hugged, take full advantage of it. If you feel an aversion to being touched, understand that this often occurs when someone is used to sexual closeness and is suddenly without it. It's important to be aware of this tendency and to work through it; denial will deprive you of the healing power of touch.

Flying Solo

> *Hey, don't knock masturbation.*
> *It's sex with someone I love.*

—WOODY ALLEN IN *ANNIE HALL*

In truth, the ancient Chinese view of masturbation was less like Woody Allen's than D. H. Lawrence's. "In masturbation there is nothing but loss," wrote the author of *Women in Love* and other novels. "There is no reciprocity. There is merely the spending away of a certain force, and no return." Because they considered the exchange of male and female energy to be of paramount importance, the Chinese advised men to ejaculate only inside a woman's body. Of course, the men for whom the sages recorded their advice had so many women at their beck and call it would have been absurd for them to masturbate.

Since women have a greater abundance of sexual chi, female masturbation was viewed more positively. A woman would have to have several orgasms a day for years to upset her balance of yin and yang dramatically and weaken her sexual chi. In fact, the women at court were advised to use masturbation to strengthen the muscles and skills that contribute to sexual artistry. Many ancient sex toys were invented to ensure that during masturbation women would stimulate all parts of their vaginas and vulvas.

When practiced in accord with the precepts of Chinese medicine, self-pleasuring can reacquaint both genders with the beauty of their own sexuality, enhancing confidence, skill and control. Learning more about your sexual self will also help you teach your next lover to satisfy your needs. Here are some guidelines:

1. *Take your time.* Most people, especially men, treat masturbation as a rush to the finish line. This is because they view masturbation

solely as a way to relieve sexual tension, and sometimes because they feel foolish or guilty for doing it. Hurrying prevents you from fully enjoying the grandeur of your sexuality and learning more from the experience. It's far healthier to proceed slowly and comfortably. Languishing in sensory pleasure enables your body's yin energy to become involved and all stages of arousal (as described in chapter 4) to come into play. I recommend setting aside a minimum of fifteen minutes, even though you can get the job done faster.

2. *Don't force it.* Don't *try* to have an orgasm. Generally speaking, when you find yourself straining to come, you are either in too much of a hurry or your genitals lack sexual energy, forcing you to use your muscles to push chi into the pelvis. Straining creates tension and drains chi from other parts of the body. It is not only healthier to be patient, it's ultimately more pleasurable.

3. *Experiment.* Instead of just doing the familiar things that bring you to orgasm, use masturbation as an opportunity to explore new methods of sensation and arousal. Move your pelvis in different ways. Mimic the thrusts and positions in chapter 5. Touch yourself—and not just your genitals—in new and different ways. This will make you a more skillful and versatile lover in the future.

4. *Practice moderation.* As discussed in chapter 6, too much ejaculation can deplete a man's sexual energy, and too little can disturb his spirit and distort his sense of reality. You can tell that you're masturbating too frequently if you begin to get tired in the late afternoon or your orgasms are not as strong as they used to be. In addition, a woman might feel coldness or weakness in her lower belly or back, and a man might notice that his testicles or lower back feel cold or achy. I recommend that men use periods of solitary sexuality to practice withholding ejaculation and circulating sexual energy, as per the instructions in chapter 6.

5. *Touch all of you.* Be sure to stimulate all parts of your genitals. Women tend to focus exclusively on the clitoris, and men pay inordinate attention to the head of the penis in order to hasten or-

gasm. Because of the connections between genital reflexology points and the organs, balanced stimulation is best for your body as a whole.

6. *Protect your energy.* Once you become sexually stimulated, it is important to move your sexual energy; allowing it to stagnate in the pelvic area can lead to feelings of frustration and a variety of health problems. Use the Golden Circle exercise along with deep breathing to circulate the aroused chi, either as you climax or instead of moving on to a conventional orgasm.

Holding your genitals as you climax helps keep the chi within the body so it can be recycled. Women can cup their left hand (the yin hand) over their vulvas and place the right hand on their throat, heart, solar plexus or lower belly. Men can use both hands to cover the penis (especially the head) and the scrotum. Also, it's important for men to treat semen with respect. After it leaves your body, the vital fluid remains alive for some time. Don't wipe it away contemptuously, as if it were a waste product. In ancient China, it was not unheard of for a man to consume his own semen as an elixir, either by drinking it mixed with an herbal tonic or by having oral sex with a woman in whom he ejaculated. You may not want to go that far, but you might try this: Ejaculate into your hand and rub the semen into the skin of your lower belly while imagining that you feel its potent chi soaking into you.

Immediately following orgasm, whether you're a man or a woman, focus all your attention on the crown of your head. This naturally draws chi upward to that area so that less is expelled from the genitals. When you've done that for about three minutes, rub your hands together until they're warm and place them on your lower abdomen, letting the heat radiate into your pelvic bowl.

CULTIVATE YOUR
INHERENT STRENGTH

Perhaps the most important task for a single person who wants to prepare for future romance is to develop his or her primary energetic trait. Functioning in a manner that is congruent with the dominant energy of your body, as exemplified in the propagation model, is strengthening and balancing. If you are in harmony with the basic masculine or feminine dynamic of your physiology, you are more likely to attract and choose an appropriate lover and bring out the best in both of you.

Being single is an excellent time to foster behavior appropriate to your primary energetic trait since you're not working on a relationship at the same time. For a man, that means cultivating the yang ability to give, wait for feedback and use the feedback to give more appropriately. For a woman, it means cultivating the yin ability to receive with discernment and transform what you receive into what you want and need. (Some couples part because of secondary trait problems. Look over both the yin and the yang sections and determine which areas would best prepare you for your next love affair.)

Cultivating the Feminine Dynamic

When Janice ended her nine-year marriage, she felt a strange combination of loss and relief. The relief came from the fact that she would no longer be energetically depleted by her demanding ex. "I'm all gived out," she said. "I gave to him heart and soul, but no matter how much I gave, he never became a happier person, with me or with himself."

Another patient, Randi, also felt depleted when she broke up with her man, but for different reasons. A beautiful model, she had been whisked off to a magnificent estate on a tropical island by Douglas, a wealthy older man. But her handsome, powerful prince turned out to be a control-aholic. He was not outwardly abusive, but he subtly and slowly took over Randi's life. After three years in her picture-perfect environment, she finally began to realize she was in pain. Cut off from her family, friends and promising career, she felt empty inside. She had luxury, beauty and creature comforts beyond her wildest dreams, but at the cost of her autonomy and self-esteem.

It would have been easy for Janice and Randi to blame the men in their lives and feel victimized by bad choices. But that would have been simplistic. In truth, they did not bring to their relationships the full power of their primary trait. Janice's orientation was to give. That is not yin's job. On an energetic level, a woman's primary task is to receive what her partner and her circumstances offer, evaluate it, determine whether it's what is best for her, and then transform it accordingly. Perpetual givers like Janice neglect themselves. To cite a dramatic example, Mother Teresa is said to be so driven to give that doctors practically have to beg her to eat.

As for Randi, she allowed herself to receive, but she was weakened by what she received. She lacked the ability to discriminate between what was appropriate to receive and what was not. Yin is self-oriented; when it's strong it looks out for itself properly.

Lacking true receptivity, some women become controllers. Since they can't work with what is given to them, they figure out what they need in advance and go after it, often demanding what they want from others manipulating them into giving it. Others become rigid; without the ability to receive new information, they hold on tightly, often obsessively, to old patterns—exactly the behavior that women have long, and accurately, accused men of.

Some women become martyrs. Unable to discriminate between that which is healthy and that which is destructive, they take in primarily the latter. The resulting pain reinforces the notion that it's not safe to receive, so they keep on giving and giving, even though it destroys them and their relationships.

A woman who lacks yin skills might also be uncomfortable receiving a compliment or a gift. She might insist that her man return a present on the grounds that he can't really afford it, or reject an offer to be taken out to dinner and cook a meal herself even though she's tired after a long day.

I recommend evaluating your yin abilities in all aspects of your life. Ask yourself:

- What am I giving in various situations and what am I receiving?
- Am I giving more than I'm getting?
- Am I receiving what I want and need?
- Are my desires fair and reasonable?
- If I'm not getting exactly what I want and need, am I doing what I can to transform the situation?
- Am I letting others know my needs and wants, and do they understand me?
- Am I taking in sufficient information and using it to determine if my needs will be met?
- Do I feel needy?
- Am I allowing others to support and help me?

You may also want to evaluate your most recent love affair, asking yourself the same questions in the past tense: e.g., Did I let my ex-lover know my needs and wants, and did he understand me? This can help you understand why things went wrong and prevent a recurrence in the future.

Here are some ways to practice appropriate receiving when not in a relationship:

- Accept the generosity of others.
- Let women friends and platonic male friends take you places.
- Pay attention to how nice it feels to have your male friends compliment you, admire you, touch you or give you a friendly hug.
- Let others pick up the check if they offer to.
- Accept compliments (if you don't really believe them, pretend they're true).
- Listen closely to what people say to you; don't let it go in one ear and out the other.
- Try to feel deeply the concerns of others and the unspoken feelings behind their words.
- Pay close attention to how good it feels when you are offered the love of friends and family.
- Notice the consideration and courtesies extended to you by co-workers and service people.

- Try to feel grateful for small gestures of kindness; don't take them for granted.
- Return the smiles of strangers.

Cultivating the Masculine Dynamic

Kevin's wife of twenty-two years walked out on him. Understandably, he felt angry and betrayed. But he was not entirely blameless. His rigidity and inability to give appropriately had set him up for a fall. His wife, Emily, had been extremely unhappy the last several years of their marriage. When their son went off to college, she tried to revive her romance with her husband. She wanted to go on old-fashioned dates, take moonlight strolls and escape for weekend getaways together. She wanted intimate, stimulating conversations. In earlier years, she and Kevin had had all that, but Kevin lost interest. A dutiful husband, he was happy to work hard to provide for his family. He enjoyed the pleasure Emily received from their lovely home, the garden he planted and the patio he built. He believed he had been taking good care of his wife and giving her what she wanted. This was convenient thinking; he wasn't really paying attention to what she told him. Over the years Emily had said repeatedly that while she was grateful for all he had done, she would rather he earned less money and spent more time with her.

Kevin was a giver, but he gave what he wanted to give, or what he assumed it was proper to give. He did not have the yang skill of giving what his woman really wanted and needed. He was not an able listener (the yin within yang) and did not know how to respond creatively to Emily's feedback or requests. He is hardly alone. In two-thirds of all divorces it is the woman who leaves. Their men are often flabbergasted to learn after the fact that they had not been giving appropriately.

Look back at your last relationship and ask yourself these questions:

- What were the things my woman most wanted from me?
- Which of those did I fulfill?
- Which did I not fulfill?
- Did she feel she was having her needs met?

- Were her wishes fair and reasonable?
- Was *I* being fair and reasonable?
- When she told me what she wanted, how did I respond?
- When she said she was unhappy, how well did I pay attention?
- Did I try to see things from her point of view?
- Could I have been more creative or energetic in changing the situation?

Now, ask yourself the same questions about your present life: e.g., Do I try to see things from the other person's point of view?

Here are some ways to practice your yang skills while you are single:

- Evaluate each area of your life and ask yourself if you are giving appropriately.
- Pay close attention to how others respond to what you contribute; don't automatically assume that what you're giving is what they need or want.
- Pick up the check when it's not expected of you, even with male friends and co-workers.
- Do volunteer work with the needy and helpless, expecting nothing in return.
- Contribute to charities.
- Get involved in your community.
- Spend time with female friends and coworkers, and treat them as generously and politely as you would a date.
- Encourage others to express themselves to you, and listen closely to their thoughts and feelings.
- If you're a father, spend as much time with your kids as possible, and pay close attention to their emotional needs, not just their financial needs.
- Spend time with nieces and nephews or the children of friends.
- At the end of each day, ask yourself, "What have I learned because I paid closer attention to what was said to me?"
- When you wake up each morning, ask yourself, "What can I do for others today?"

If you follow the advice in this chapter, you will be able to adapt to the single life with greater ease, comfort and contentment. You will also be better equipped to attract a suitable partner and to make your next love affair more fulfilling than the last one. It is my hope that you and your future lover will share what the next chapter promises: a lifetime of passion.

Chapter 9

UNTIL THE SUN SETS
Living a Life of Passion

Pleasure is the beginning and the end of living happily.

—EPICURUS

Life without love and passion is a life not worth having lived.

—RUMI

We tend to think of sexual passion as something that is either there or not there, like sunshine. We assume it comes and goes independently of what we do, like fluctuating interest rates. In fact, passion can be created, encouraged, enriched and strengthened. Like other areas of life, it can grow and thrive or wither and die, depending on how much attention, energy and skill you devote to it.

RECIPES FOR ROMANCE

Jobs. Parenting. Housekeeping duties. Errands. You barely have enough time for a good-night kiss, let alone prolonged lovemaking. The solution? Scheduling. It may sound unromantic and unspontaneous, but if you want lifelong passion, you have to make time for it, or else a million less important items will constantly get in the way.

I recommend making dates for the purpose of romance and intimacy—and keeping them. Make whatever arrangements are necessary—

baby-sitters, hours off from work, etc.—to ensure that you have enough time for passion.

The Perfect Date

A loaf of bread, a jug of wine and . . . *zzzzzzzzz.*

I don't know who invented the romantic ideal of wining and dining followed by passionate lovemaking, but whoever it was did not understand the human body and probably had mediocre sex. To make love well, your body needs certain conditions, just as it does if you're competing in an athletic event or taking an exam. No matter how sublime the meal or elegant the setting, or how thrilling the show and romantic the moonlit stroll, or how sparkling the champagne and the jewelry, if you're stuffed, fatigued and tipsy, your lovemaking won't match the standards set by the rest of the evening. Your bodies will simply not respond with their maximum potential.

As we've seen, the basic requirement for sexual activity is to have plenty of blood and chi in the pelvic area. Without it, firm erections and moist vaginas are not likely to be found, and stamina, sensitivity and loving awareness are, at the very least, compromised. Gazing into each other's eyes over a candlelit dinner will certainly put you in the mood, but asking your body to digest a rich meal and make love at the same time is like trying to fill a tub with the plug out. The system can't supply the needed amounts of blood and chi to two different parts of the abdomen at the same time without shortchanging both. It's hard enough to think straight after a big meal, let alone perform vigorous physical activity. If you've ever tried to jog or play ball after eating, you know how true this is.

If you're planning a romantic evening of relaxed companionship and passionate lovemaking, keep the following in mind:

1. The shared pleasure of a sumptuous meal is a lovely way to unite two loving souls. But if you also want to unite sexually, give your body plenty of time to digest. Dine at the beginning of your date and allow at least two hours between the last bite of food and the first nibble of your lover's lips. This means getting started early.

Also, eat foods that are low in fat and animal protein, as they take less time to digest. Limit or eliminate your meat portion. If you're eating Italian, try pasta primavera or a marinara sauce; if you're eating Asian food, favor noodle or rice dishes with vegetables.

2. Try having an early dinner before you go out, and make your date a dessert date. A light dessert—as opposed to something large and sinfully rich—is a fun way to enjoy each other's company and share something sensuous and delicious without overtaxing your system or using up a big portion of the evening. It leaves plenty of time for a long, relaxing chat or stroll as you digest your food before making love.

If you know you're going to have a rich dessert, make sure you eat some protein at dinner; it will make your strength more stable for lovemaking by keeping your blood sugar on a more even keel.

3. Or, make love *before* dinner. Instead of using the intimacy of a meal to bring you together, why not work up an appetite with a delicious intimate encounter? Extend the warmth and closeness generated by your time in bed with a later meal. Eating a frozen dinner in the kitchen can feel like a gourmet feast in Paris when you gaze at each other with satisfied eyes.

4. If you consume alcohol on your date, keep it moderate. Since it lowers inhibition, alcohol can be a sexual asset if one of you is nervous or shy. By congesting the liver channel, it increases sexual interest because the stuck chi gives the illusion that the channel is full. But drinking ultimately inhibits sexual function by sedating the nervous system, making you less responsive and less sensitive. Also, because the kidney has to support the liver in the Nourishing Cycle, dealing with alcohol can overtax it, and we've seen the effect depleted kidney function has on sex. For some people, a small drink shortly before sex provides the relaxing benefits of alcohol without as many detriments. For others, even that will backfire.

5. Be careful about your after-dinner coffee. If you feel you need caffeine in order to have enough energy to make love, you probably shouldn't make love. The energy you appear to get from caffeine is false chi. If you can't make love without it, take a nap first.

6. The room you make love in should be cozy and warm. If your skin is cold, your body has to use up energy to warm it, making less chi available for sex. Pay special attention to your feet. The kidney and liver meridians begin down there. If your tootsies are chilled, the cold energy will move up these channels into your genitals and more energy will be needed to get you sexually hot. Try socks.

7. If you've been looking forward to a wild night of passionate abandon, but you're exhausted or stressed-out when you get to the bedroom, don't push it. Don't make your date about getting to or-gasm come hell or high water. Be honest about your fatigue, and take the pressure off yourselves. Use the sexual energy you do have to enjoy a calmer, gentler intimacy. Or, get some sleep and restore your strength for a passionate morning.

8. Drink something hot after making love. Because of the vigorous nature of the activity, sex uses yang chi. Taking in warmth puts some back into your system. Herb or green tea or hot cider are ideal. Cof-fee, black tea and cocoa are not the best choices, since it's best not to stimulate the body with caffeine after making love. Hard liquor should be avoided; because the body perceives it as a toxin and works to get rid of it, alcohol can further deplete the chi you've used during sex.

A Romantic Vacation at Home

Here's a way to plan a passionate weekend without sacrificing your fam-ily responsibilities (if you don't have children, modify this accordingly):

1. Spend Friday night at home with the entire family.

2. Around 10:00 on Saturday morning, send your children to visit friends or relatives, with the understanding that they'll return Sun-day afternoon around four.

3. You and your sweetheart can do whatever work you need to do around the house or in your offices, but agree to stop by 1:00 P.M.

4. At 1:00, turn off phones, pagers, fax machines and every other form of outside communication, except for an established way for the kids to reach you in case of an emergency.

5. When the final chores are done, relax. Go out and do something easy and enjoyable together based on your shared interests: play tennis or golf; go bowling; toss a Frisbee; visit a museum or art gallery; go to a nursery and buy plants; take an adult-education class; have a picnic and a walk in nature; take a nap. Have fun together in a way that conserves, or even strengthens, your energy for lovemaking.

6. That evening, go out on a special date. Do something that elicits happy memories or something you've both looked forward to doing. Make the evening romantic and seductive, but do not make love. Allow a tantalizing sense of anticipation to build and give your yin sexual chi plenty of time to warm up. This can be exceedingly romantic for couples who have been together a long time. During your date, avoid discussing the kids or family-related business, and don't socialize with friends. Instead, share things about your lives you usually don't have time to discuss.

7. Get a good night's sleep.

8. On Sunday morning, sleep in.

No, it's still not time to make love. Have a small, cozy breakfast—in bed, if possible—then cuddle awhile. Give yourselves an hour or so to digest breakfast. Eating before you make love gives you the strength to continue for longer without having to take a break. It is easier to forget about the rest of the world if your belly isn't reminding you that you haven't had breakfast.

9. Then go to it. Devote the rest of the time before your children return to long, luxurious lovemaking.

The schedule ensures that you will be rested and ready when you make love. When your kids come home they will find two glowing, contented parents who are better equipped to love them and each other.

Men sometimes see this routine as a woman's dream, but frustrating from the male point of view. I say, try it, fellas. You'll like what happens when the yin in both your bodies has plenty of time to warm up. On other weekends, you can give full reign to your yang aggressiveness and jump into bed the instant the kids leave.

I recommend giving yourselves these weekends at least four times a year. Plan around them and make them a high priority. Vary the formula to suit your needs, but remember the Three R's: Rest first, Romance second, Romp third.

ABSENCE MAKES THE HEART GROW FONDER

Life maintains balance through the fluctuation of opposites. Just as night can't exist without day, or heat without cold, or yin without yang, there cannot be closeness without distance. Time apart is absolutely imperative for maintaining passion.

Over the course of a lifetime, intimate partners move through emotional cycles of togetherness and separation. There are times when you can't stand being apart and times when you have to get away from each other. These cycles are a natural expression of paradoxical human needs: for autonomy and independence on the one hand and partnership and intimacy on the other. Too much separateness threatens the union at its core. But if you try too hard for perpetual closeness, you run the risk of smothering each other and destroying your individuality.

Everyone's need for time alone is different, of course, but we all have it. We need occasions to reconnect with ourselves, to retain our sense of who we are and solidify our unique identities. So, if you want her to be nuts about you, give her your blessing to take weekend trips with her friends. If you want him to rejoice in your arms, welcome his nights out with the boys.

WHEN NOT TO DO IT

As Hamlet said, "The readiness is all." There's no use putting a love-making scenario into motion if your timing is off. That would be an invitation to failure, and failure, according to traditional Chinese medicine, dissipates the body's life force.

Although their basic rule was, essentially, "More is better," the ancient seers had remarkably precise ideas about when to have sex and when not to. Intercourse opens the body's energetic system. This is wonderful for intimacy but not for protection, either physically or emotionally. Therefore, it's good to avoid sex when you are vulnerable to illness or emotional upset.

One of those vulnerable times, according to the ancients, is during a period of natural instability. Because intercourse merges yin and yang, it was thought best to abstain when the interaction of the two forces in nature was chaotic or turbulent. Some of the conditions they singled out were storms, eclipses, the night before a new moon, solstices, equinoxes and New Year's Day.

Like most modern Westerners, you will probably take those admonitions with several grains of salt. However, the following circumstances were also regarded as times to protect the body by refraining from sex:

- When you're healing from an illness
- When you're drunk or under the influence of drugs
- When you've just eaten
- When you're fatigued
- When you're very hot or very cold
- When your body is dirty
- When you're highly emotional

From both the medical and romantic points of view, this list makes sense. When the body is engaged in survival activities such as digesting food, nourishing tired tissue or eliminating toxic substances, blood and energy flow mainly to areas outside the pelvis. You are not in a position to function at maximum strength sexually, or to receive all the pleasures and health benefits that sex has to offer. Asking your body to perform both functions at once would be like expecting your car to take you on a joy ride while it's being serviced.

With respect to the last item on the list, the body needs a great deal of energy to cope with intense emotional states, whether negative feelings like anger and grief or positive ones like exuberance and joy. The emotions have to settle down before sexual passion can take center stage. It's okay to begin the seduction process while you're emotional, but if the intensity of feeling persists, it's best to stop the sexual play and deal with the feelings. When they subside, lovemaking can resume on a stable platform.

GROWING THROUGH CONFLICT

Conflict can be a passion killer, but it doesn't have to be. It is both inevitable and necessary for the success of your marriage. The ever-shifting nature of yin and yang guarantees that masculine and feminine energies will clash. In the natural world, the interaction of yin and yang destroys the old to give rise to the new. In the forest, for example, a destructive fire (yang) also opens the husks of seeds so they can give birth to new life with the next rain (yin). In relationships, too, an episode that appears to be destructive can be a catalyst for a new phase of growth. Accepting conflict and resolving it properly can foster harmony and passion in the long run.

Mismanaging Conflict

Couples mishandle conflict by reacting with either extreme yin or extreme yang behavior. An inappropriate yin reaction would be to give in to control or domination (i.e., just to take it). Another would be to stuff down feelings instead of expressing them. Suppression on the outside leads to inappropriate expression on the inside. It heats up the organs, making it harder to calm down and causing a buildup of emotional and energetic irritation. This can destroy health and eat away like acid at a sexual relationship.

Even more dangerous are extreme yang responses: arguments, ferocious battles, verbal or physical abuse. If receptive yin becomes overwhelmed by the yang of two aggressive combatants, neither party will be able to listen or learn, and no understanding will be reached. Rage triggers the adrenaline rush of the fight-flight reaction, giving us access to speed, strength and instinct at the expense of intelligence. We end up saying or doing things that are violent, vengeful or downright stupid. This cuts deeply, penetrating to the inner, yin level of the self, where we are more vulnerable and wounds heal more slowly. The searing pain of yang hitting yin can stifle love and passion for years.

A patient of mine named Joanne had injured her hand quite severely in a cycling accident. Because her husband, Martin, had been so loving and helpful during the crisis, she wanted to do something special for him. During her recuperation, she crocheted a blanket for his birthday, even though her injuries allowed her to work on it for only short periods of time. After months of effort she presented him with her labor of love. Martin seemed pleased. But a few weeks later, during an argument, he criticized her craftsmanship and hinted that he would rather have received a new set of golf clubs. Afterward, he apologized. But, three years later, when I was treating Joanne, she brought up the blanket incident as if it had happened the day before. Even though her marriage was basically sound, part of her had been on guard ever since. In bed she was not as spontaneous and passionate as she once had been; often, as soon as she started to get aroused, the hurt from that trauma would surface. (While this example features a woman in pain, men too can be wounded when their yin is penetrated.)

A Balanced Response to Conflict

To resolve conflict effectively and avoid extreme reactions, utilize the qualities of both yin and yang. If you or your partner overreacts to a conflict with excessive yin behavior, suppressing feelings or withdrawing entirely, correct it by adding some yang: find creative solutions; blow off steam with physical activity; express your feelings to each other or, if that's not appropriate, write them down, talk to a friend or go to some isolated place and scream at the top of your lungs.

To keep the fire of an excessive yang reaction from consuming the situation, draw on yin abilities. Sit together in silence, or separate until one or both of you are ready to listen and a rational discussion can begin. Postpone the dialogue if necessary. If you are both unwilling to be receptive, accept that you need some time before you attempt to resolve the conflict. And be patient. Remember, yin builds slowly; it can't be rushed, so don't try to force receptivity into existence.

Keeping passion alive through the inevitable ups and downs depends more on yin abilities than yang ones. In traditional Chinese medicine, death occurs when the body's yin and yang energies separate. Love dies the same way—when the masculine and feminine break apart irreversibly. Some relationships explode in a burst of yang, with violence, abuse or desertion. Most die from the slow decay of yin. It's analogous to what happens to the body: If we don't get air (yang), we die quickly; if we don't get enough food (yin), we die slowly. When yin deteriorates, partners become unwilling or unable to receive. And no matter how generous one person is, the giving is wasted if the other is not receptive. To reverse the Beatles' lyric, the love you make is equal to the love you take in.

In most conflict situations, following the behavior patterns of the propagation model on page 25—give-wait-receive and receive-transform-contribute—brings new life to a couple, just as it creates new life in the womb. Partner A initiates the resolution process by expressing feelings and sharing information. Partner B receives the input, processes it and transforms it, perhaps by adding fresh ideas, a new perspective or a measure of compassion. One way to do this involves the use of mirroring: after one partner expresses herself, the other articulates the gist of it. This tells the first person that she has been heard and allows her to determine whether or not she has made her point. When Partner B offers this contribution to Partner A, the latter receives it and continues the process. Remember, if yang takes over and tempers start to boil, resort to yin behavior: pause, or even separate for a while, to give yourselves time to cool down.

THE PASSIONATE
LIFESTYLE

By now, it should come as no surprise that Chinese medicine considers physical health the foundation of a vigorous, enduring and fulfilling sex life. Artful techniques and romantic intentions are worth little if your body is tired or ailing, or if energetic imbalances prevent sexual chi from getting where it needs to go. The suggestions that follow are based on fundamental Western and Chinese concepts and selected for their ability to keep sexual energy strong. The ancients believed that a woman who followed these guidelines would have a blush on her cheek like the sunrise, and a man who did so would wield a strong sword forever.

Eat Well, Love Well

A proper diet is a crucial element in the prevention and treatment of disease, and absolutely vital in maintaining sexual vitality over the course of a lifetime. If we do not eat well, our bodies have to draw on reserve sexual chi to supply nourishment.

Here are some basic dietary tenets:

1. *Sit and relax.* When you eat with your attention on something else, gulp down food while standing or moving about, swallow when you are wound up or tense, blood and chi are diverted from digestion to other parts of the body. If you sit calmly, dine slowly, chew thoroughly (at least ten chews per bite) and put your attention on the eating process itself, more energy is available for digestion, allowing it to do a more thorough job. Also, Chinese medicine suggests that we eat only until we are 70 percent full. This prevents postmeal fatigue, a common phenomenon when we fill ourselves to capacity.

2. *Emphasize warm food.* Eat food that is warm or at room temperature and avoid iced drinks. For proper digestion, once cold food is consumed, the body has to bring the food's temperature up to

ninety-six degrees. In the long run, the vitality used to heat up food deprives other bodily functions, including sexuality.

3. *Fewer calories, more nutrients.*   To maintain metabolic efficiency, antiaging researchers suggest eating fewer calories, as long as the calories you consume are nutrient rich. To do this, cut down on fat, sugar and refined flour; their high calorie counts are not justified by their scant nutritional value. Favor nutrient-rich foods such as whole grains, fresh fruits and vegetables, legumes, fish, low-fat meats and nonfat dairy products. Deep-fried foods, sweets and products made from white flour are nutritionally poor.

4. *Eat lots of fiber.*   Take in 25 grams of fiber a day. Good sources include bran cereals, whole grains, brown rice, whole-wheat breads, legumes and fruits and vegetables that are lightly cooked or raw. Aside from the familiar benefits of taking in fiber, it should be noted that constipation can intensify unpleasant genital odors.

5. *Maximize vegetables.*   The Chinese tradition is not vegetarian, but it considers vegetables indispensable at every meal, while meat is seen as a side dish. A typical Chinese meal contains mostly vegetables, with about four ounces of meat, a formula supported by antiaging experts in the West.

6. *Drink plenty of fluid.*   Western doctors recommend eight glasses a day (coffee, black tea and caffeinated sodas don't count, since they are diuretics and actually deplete the body of more fluid than they add). Chinese medicine agrees with the importance of fluid intake but advocates moderation: four to eight glasses a day, preferably of good, pure water. The kidneys filter the fluids we take in, but overdrinking requires too much work without compensatory gain, weakening the organs' ability to support sexual vigor. Doctors of traditional Chinese medicine also advocate minimal drinking before, during and after meals. Too much liquid dilutes the concentration of digestive juices. If you need to drink during meals, sip small amounts of warm or hot liquid.

7. *Eat less as the day progresses.*   As the saying goes, eat breakfast like royalty, lunch like a merchant and supper like a pauper. Data on weight loss and overall health consistently show that the first meal is

the most important of the day. Avoid sugars for breakfast; favor complex carbohydrates (e,g., toast or cereal) and protein. This helps stabilize your energy level so you don't need to call upon reserve kidney chi to compensate for slumps. To ensure that you have a hearty appetite in the morning—and to enhance sleep and digestion—eat lightly in the evening and take your last meal several hours before going to sleep.

8. *Eat all five flavors.* The Chinese group foods into flavor categories, each of which serves as a tonic for a specific organ: salty (kidney), bitter (heart), pungent (lung), sweet (spleen) and sour (liver). A well-designed meal includes most, if not all, of the flavors.

9. *Eat organic foods.* When you have the option, buy fresh, organically grown produce, grains, legumes and meats. Studies have shown conclusively that pesticide residues from commercial processing have deleterious effects on health, especially the health of children, because they include toxic substances and destroy many of the body's disease-fighting bacteria.

10. *Cool the coffee.* If, when your body says, "I'm worn out," you reply, "Have a cup of coffee," you deprive your body of the rest it needs and force it to cope with the effects of a stimulant. The long-term result can be, among other things, fatigue and diminished sexual function. I tell my patients to do the following when they feel tired and are tempted to compensate with caffeine:

* Set aside three to five minutes to allow yourself to feel really tired.
* Sit down where you won't be disturbed.
* Rest your feet flat on the floor, close your eyes, let your shoulders flop and your hands hang limp.
* Let yourself feel as exhausted as you actually are. The more fatigued you let yourself feel, the less tired you will be when you return to activity.
* When the time is up, stretch or walk around briefly to get your blood moving before returning to work. You will feel much better.

You may need to do the exercise two or three times a day for a while if you're extremely worn out.

11. If it feels bad, don't do it. Obey your body's signals. If you don't like something, don't eat it—no matter how good it's supposed to be for you.

Nourish Your Kidneys

Aphrodisiacs have a long history in traditional Chinese medicine. However, anything taken into the body to excite the genitals quickly is regarded as an artificial stimulant and unhealthful. Doctors of traditional Chinese medicine prefer long-term results to quick fixes and the false or illusory energy produced by stimulants. You can strengthen sexual energy and improve performance with sexual tonic herbs and acupuncture treatments (see Appendix). These work to balance the system as a whole, tonifying weakened areas so the body can respond with its own natural vigor. This takes time, but the results are infinitely healthier and more enduring than the quick fix of an aphrodisiac.

Keeping your kidney organ strong will ensure that your sex drive and sexual strength remain vital. In addition to caring for your overall health, I recommend including in your regular diet—although not necessarily every day—foods that are known to be kidney tonics. This will gradually strengthen your sexual energy and help maintain it in the long run. If your sexual energy is now low, eat more of these foods, but in small amounts only. If you consume too much of a tonic, you can actually weaken what you are trying to strengthen. Kidney substances include:

- foods with a salty flavor (this does not mean added table salt, but foods with a naturally salty taste such as celery, seaweed and fish)
- black, gray and dark blue foods (e.g., black beans, blue corn, blueberries, miso, olives, dark mushrooms)
- fish (freshwater is helpful, but ocean fish is better)
- lamb
- beef
- seafood (shrimp, crayfish, lobster, oysters, sea urchins, mussels, abalone, sea cucumber, etc.)

- eggs
- tofu (well cooked)
- bone marrow (use this to make soups)
- deer meat
- organ meats (especially kidneys)
- quail and quail eggs
- walnuts
- molasses (a teaspoon in a cup of hot water is a nice kidney and spleen tonic and tastes great on cold days)

In addition to diet, these practices will help strengthen a weakened kidney organ:

- Make sure to get adequate rest when tired, especially between 3:00 and 7:00 P.M.
- Keep your feet warm.
- Keep your lower back protected and warm.
- Drink at least four glasses of room-temperature water a day.
- Avoid loud noise and music.
- Practice the sexual strengthening exercises in this book.

Tonify Energetic Deficiencies

At various times in this book, the notion of yin or yang deficiencies has been mentioned. To maintain sexual interest and skill, it's important to redress energetic imbalances by strengthening the appropriate quality. If you have several of the following symptoms, you might have a deficiency (some can signify a serious medical condition; bring all symptoms to your doctor's attention).

SIGNS OF YANG DEFICIENCY

- pale complexion
- tendency to feel cold
- cold hands and feet

- low energy
- sleeps excessively
- drinks few fluids
- lack of appetite
- slightly overweight
- recurrent abdominal bloating or heartburn
- soft or weak voice
- dizziness
- water retention
- lack of aggressiveness
- laziness or lack of motivation
- understated emotional expression
- overly self-focused
- neglects appearance
- poor listener
- fed up with being rejected romantically
- loss of sexual desire
- (if a man) decline in ability to get erections

SIGNS OF YIN DEFICIENCY

- sweats easily
- tendency to feel warm
- dry skin
- loss of head hair
- excessive thirst or no thirst at all
- frequently hungry
- constipation
- often appears to have high energy
- tension in the muscles
- slightly underweight
- appears puffy
- domineering personality
- overly aggressive
- tendency to speak loudly
- emotionally expressive

- frequently irritable
- insomnia
- not interested in making love
- prefers quick, intense sex with little foreplay
- feels abandoned by lover in bed or daily life
- gives too much and neglects own needs
- doesn't get enough rest
- uncomfortable receiving compliments or gifts
- commitmentphobia
- unsociable or loner, or extremely sociable, with superficial relationships
- (if a woman) either very quick to orgasm or nonorgasmic, or would rather give an orgasm than have one
- (if a woman) vagina doesn't lubricate well
- (if a man) does not maintain erection
- (if a man) ejaculates within a few minutes of sexual stimulation

How to Strengthen Yin and Yang

One way to strengthen a deficient energetic aspect is to be treated by a doctor of Chinese medicine. Acupuncture and herbs have been used for millennia for this purpose. You might be tempted to use commercial herbal products marketed as chi, yin or yang tonics at a pharmacy or health food store. I have to caution against their use: herbs are potent medicines and should not be used without a professional diagnosis to determine which ones, in which combinations, at which dosages are appropriate for you.

One thing you can certainly do on your own: Increase your consumption of foods that tonify yin or yang, depending on which you need. However, don't overdo it. A small amount of a yin or yang tonic will strengthen that aspect, but too much will further sedate it. So, increase your consumption slightly (up to 20 percent of your total caloric intake) for an extended period of time, or eat a lot of those foods (as much as a third of your caloric intake) for a couple of days and then cut back.

If you need to strengthen yang energy, cut back on raw and cold-temperature foods, and increase your consumption of:

- black beans
- green leafy vegetables
- chili peppers
- green onions
- cinnamon
- garlic
- ginger
- pepper (Cayenne is superior to black.)
- curried foods
- wild game
- beef
- poultry
- lamb

If you already eat a lot of red meat (i.e., more than once a day or more than four ounces per serving), you may need to cut back to tonify yang chi. It may seem paradoxical, but the typical Western diet can cause yang deficiencies because the body needs to use its yang chi to digest all that meat.

Activities that tonify yang are those you find stimulating and exciting, plus any involving sunshine, daylight, heat and fire. For example:

- spending time in the sun
- outdoor athletics
- sitting in saunas and steam rooms
- sitting in front of fires

To tonify yin energy, avoid spicy foods and the yang tonics listed above, and increase your consumption of:

- freshwater fish
- shellfish
- celery
- cooked root vegetables

- algae (spirulina, etc.)
- fresh fruits and juices
- green vegetables
- mushrooms
- uncooked oils
- sprouts
- sugar and honey (small amounts only)
- lean cuts of pork
- dairy products

If you do not digest any of these foods well, you may want to ask a nutritionist, doctor or acupuncturist to recommend enzymes or other remedies that strengthen digestion.

Activities that tonify yin are those you find calming, plus any that involve water, earth, nighttime and moonlight. For example:

- swimming
- bathing
- fishing
- walking on a beach or riverbank
- being in nature
- gardening
- sitting outdoors in the dark at night
- moonlit walks
- listening to waterfalls and wind

Monitor Your Stress Level

Over time, a system besieged by chronic stress becomes vulnerable to weakness and illness—including a depressed sex drive and diminished sexual function. This is in part because the adrenal glands, which are part of the kidney organ system that governs sexuality, become overworked.

It would be superfluous to discuss the many stress-reduction techniques in the marketplace. As I advise my patients, find a combination of exercise, proper diet, relaxation, prayer or meditation, nutritional supplements, psychotherapy and other procedures that works for you. Remember, erotic love is both rejuvenating and calming to the spirit and body.

Early to Bed

Lack of sleep depletes yin energy and shunts chi from the genital area to keep the rest of the body functioning. The Chinese say that one hour of sleep before midnight is equal to three after midnight. Sleep is a quintessential yin function, dark, quiet and still. As such, it is most effective when the yin aspect of Earth is strongest. Yin energy increases from noon on, as the earth moves into darkness. Yang increases after midnight, as sunrise draws closer.

If you have trouble falling asleep, remember that while sleeping pills may address the symptom—i.e., you'll sleep better that night—they do not cure insomnia. Unfortunately, they can create dependency and actually interfere with the natural sleep cycle. There are many natural alternatives, including proper exercise, relaxation techniques, hypnotherapy, nutritional support and Chinese medicine. I've found that acupuncture, Chinese herbs and appropriate lifestyle practices are extremely effective in helping patients sleep longer and deeper.

Get Physical

To maintain sexual vitality your body needs to keep its blood and chi flowing smoothly. This way the genitals can be properly supplied when need arises. Exercise facilitates that. Scientists say that aerobic fitness ensures that blood will move to the genitals, arms and legs during sex without compromising the rest of the body. Research indicates that it also enhances vaginal lubrication and improves the distribution of sex hormones. In one study, 40 percent of women who began a regular exercise program reported increased arousal during sex; 31 percent said they had sex more frequently.

A good workout routine should include:

1. Aerobic exercise to maintain good circulation, keep blood pressure down and lower cholesterol.

2. Strengthening exercises to sustain physical strength, muscle mass and bone density.

3. Stretching exercises to keep muscles and joints flexible and reduce tension.

Make sure your routine matches your ability level and overall condition, so you don't overdo it or injure yourself.

FIRE IN THE BELLY

The area of the body that extends from about an inch above the pubic bone (which sits just above the genitals) to about an inch and a half below the navel is called the *tan tien* (pronounced "don teeyen"). It is considered the stove that generates the fire that drives all our metabolic functions. When the energy in the tan tien is strong and moves efficiently, all the organs function well and disease is less likely to occur.

It is from the tan tien that we draw our energy for all life's activities, and it is *to* the tan tien that the body naturally sends the energy generated by sex. When, because of aging, energy imbalance or illness, the tan tien is deficient in chi, the area becomes cold and it takes longer for the person to become sexually aroused. The following exercise will increase your awareness of this key part of the body and stoke the fire of the kidney organ and thus strengthen sexual energy.

1. Practice the exercise in either of three positions: standing with feet apart and legs slightly bent at the knees; sitting with your back straight (men should sit at the edge of the chair so that their genitals can hang free); lying on your side with lower leg extended and upper leg bent at the knee.

2. Keep the lower belly bare or loosely covered, so you can easily reach it with your hand.

3. Rub your hands together until they feel hot.

4. With your left hand, stroke the tan tien in a clockwise motion, creating a circle from just below the navel to just above the pubic bone. Do this for nine complete orbits.

5. Again, rub your hands until hot.

6. With your right hand, rub the tan tien counterclockwise for nine orbits.

7. Increase the number of circles in increments of nine—to eighteen, twenty-seven, thirty-six and so forth, up to a maximum of eighty-one. Always rub an equal number of times in each direction.

Rubbing your hands together generates energy in the form of heat. When absorbed into the tan tien, the heat energy adds to your storehouse of sexual chi, making more of it available for lovemaking and healing. Anyone who wants to increase sexual sensation, achieve stronger orgasms and enhance overall health will benefit from the practice. It also helps relieve sexual frustration, since it can be used to draw excess chi out of the genitals.

To magnify the effect of the exercise, place the hand that is *not* rubbing on another body part. This brings heat energy to that area. Women might want to cup their vulva with the spare hand or rest it on their heart or breast. Men are encouraged to hold their scrotum, perhaps gently massaging the testicles, as though they were pearls in a velvet bag. Many Taoist teachers use this procedure to elevate kidney yin, which increases sperm count and rejuvenates flagging sexual energy. Holding the penis is also recommended, but not if it is erect.

If you would rather just let the hand rest in your lap, place the tips of your thumb and index finger together. Used throughout Asia for thousands of years, this position allows the heat energy in your hand to recirculate into the body.

BREATH OF FIRE

This exercise increases sexual vitality by bringing chi taken in from the air directly into the genitals. If practiced daily, the exercise should produce noticeable benefit in about two weeks.

For Men

1. Wear boxer shorts, loose trousers or nothing from the waist down.
2. Either stand in a comfortably relaxed position with your feet apart or sit on the edge of a chair so your genitals hang free.
3. Inhale a large gulp of air through your nose and imagine swallowing it as if it were a liquid. Feel a ball of air move down your throat and into your chest.
4. When the ball of air is in your solar plexus, contract your stomach muscles and push it down into your pelvis.
5. Press downward as if you were moving your bowels, forcing the pressure into your scrotum. At the same time, visualize the air filling your testicles.
6. Hold your breath as long as you can. Eventually, you can work your way up to as much as a minute.
7. Exhale and relax completely, taking a few deep breaths if you need to.
8. Repeat the exercise as many as nine times. Eventually, do up to six sets of nine, taking calm deep breaths between sets.

For Women

1. Wear loose clothing and remove any constrictions of the waist and abdomen.
2. Sit comfortably, with your back straight and your feet flat on the floor.
3. Inhale through your nose, swallowing the air as if it were a ball moving down your throat to your chest.
4. Let the ball of air roll down to your solar plexus, then contract your stomach muscles and push the air into your pelvis.
5. Apply pressure downward so your vagina feels as if it were expanding from the inside, like a balloon.
6. Tighten your vaginal muscles and hold your breath for as long as you can without undue strain.

7. Exhale and relax completely. Take some deep breaths if you feel the need.

8. Repeat the practice up to nine times. Eventually, you may do up to six sets of nine, taking relaxed deep breaths between sets.

Breathe Life into What Ails You

You can use breath to move chi into any part of the body that needs healing energy. Disease is caused by either too much or too little appropriate chi or an invasion of inappropriate chi. By opening the flow of chi into and out of an organ, you give the body an opportunity to restore the proper energy balance.

The lungs convert the air you breathe into a form of chi. If you feel pain or know that a particular organ is weak or diseased, breathe directly into it:

- Close your eyes and put your attention on the needy area.
- Imagine the breath moving directly to its target, bringing with it health-enhancing chi.
- Hold your breath, keeping your attention on the part of the body you wish to heal.
- Visualize the energy in the area filling with light.
- Exhale through your mouth.
- As you expel the air, imagine the pathology departing the unhealthy organ or body part, leaving it filled with vibrant health and light.

GETTING THE MOST
OUT OF MONOGAMY

Sex is the one thing that you can't get elsewhere. Lots of people other than your spouse can help raise your kids, cook your food or build your house. Plenty of others can invest your money, plan your vacations, listen to you when you feel down or help you solve problems. Someone else can help you do just about anything in life. But, if you're in a monogamous relationship, only one special person can have sex with you. That singular soul alone is empowered to ignite your passion and unleash its power to heal and uplift.

I suggest you take the time to clarify—both in your own mind and with your partner—exactly what monogamy means to you. Generally, monogamy is a negative commitment. It's defined by what you will not do: you will not have sex with anyone other than the partner to whom you made the vow. Shouldn't there be a positive aspect to it? Something over and above staying faithful? Shouldn't spouses agree to fulfill each other sexually, just as they promise to provide each other with food, shelter, companionship and child care?

Sadly, a great deal of pain and dissatisfaction result when partners don't realize that they have different ideas about their sexual commitment. With a positive, proactive approach to monogamy, they know exactly what their beloved is committed to doing and not doing. Ideally, they agree to satisfy each other sexually within the limits of their physical and emotional capacity.

The Sexual Discussion

You and your partner can take a major step toward lifelong passion if you clarify your commitment to monogamy. If you can pledge yourselves to a positive commitment while being honest and realistic about your limits, you are off to a very good start in building a joyous romantic future. If you are in a brand-new relationship, it might be too soon for this process; use your judgment as to when it would be appropriate. If you are not in a relationship at all, I suggest asking yourself what you would answer if you were involved with someone you cared deeply about. This will help prepare you for your next love affair.

Here are some recommended questions for discussion:

- Aside from procreation, what do you think is the purpose of your sex life?
- Which sexual activities do you feel must be part of your ongoing love affair?

- Ideally, how often would you want to have sex? What variables might alter your answer?
- If you and your partner disagree on the previous questions, what might reasonable compromises be?
- What should be done when one of you wants to have sex and the other does not?
- Are you interested in exploring new sexual activities and skills? If not, are you willing to explore them for your partner's enjoyment?
- Do you think it's a good idea to share your fantasies, or should they be kept private?
- Do you both have permission to speak out when the other does something in bed that you don't like?
- What should be done if one of you wants to engage in a practice that the other finds objectionable?

If you've been together a long time, you may be surprised at what you learn from this process. If you're just starting out, you have no idea how much frustration you will be spared—and how much more pleasure is in store for you.

Discussion Guidelines

Expressing your feelings about something this intimate requires delicacy and trust. I suggest that you follow these guidelines:

1. Remember, there are no right or wrong answers to these questions. Nor is it necessary for you and your partner to agree on your responses. What *is* vital is that you be fully aware of each other's attitudes and willing to accommodate your differences. It's far better to be aware of your differences than to let them undermine your relationship insidiously. In my experience, motivated couples are usually able to negotiate a loving compromise. If that becomes difficult, you might consider working with a therapist or counselor.

2. Intense emotions should be expressed only with the explicit permission of the other partner. The goal of this exercise is not to ex-

press anger, resentment or frustration, but to share personal information and preferences.

3. The words "You should" are not to be used. Keep the discussion focused on what each of you believes, likes and needs.

4. Phrases like "I feel," "I want" and "I like" are to be encouraged.

5. Give yourselves a time limit. I suggest at least ten minutes and no more than forty for each session, with a maximum of ten minutes for each question. If, at any time, one of you feels too uncomfortable to continue, stop and set a time to pick up where you left off. I recommend using an alarm to time each segment. This allows you to concentrate on each other without having to glance at the clock.

6. Each partner should state his or her answer completely before the other responds. I suggest taking turns going first.

7. When the discussion ends, put your attention on something else. You need time to let the content of the discussion sink in slowly, especially if discrepancies have surfaced. Do something enjoyable and distracting together. Or, if one of you needs some time alone, honor the feeling.

8. If the exercise seems intimidating to either of you, try writing your answers separately and exchanging them a day or two in advance. Or, discuss them with a friend, therapist or religious adviser before going over them together. You can even have your discussion in the company of a therapist or member of the clergy.

9. Reevaluate your positions at agreed-upon intervals (for example, once a year).

Options for Monogamy Agreements

Some couples like putting their agreement in writing. These sample passages from agreements written by my patients might give you some ideas of what to include in yours.

- I am commited to making our sex life a consistent and joyous part of our marriage. I will make time for physical intimacy at least three times a week and explore new ways to love and please you.
- I agree to make our sex life enjoyable for you, although I am not willing to bend my schedule to meet your sexual needs. When I am interested in making love, I will do whatever is necessary to make your experience thoroughly satisying.
- Our sex life is a high priority and I promise to do everything I can to give you pleasure. However, it is your responsibility to let me know what you need and want.
- I have no explicit sexual obligations to you. But I do stand by our marital vow and will remain monogamous no matter how challenging that may be.

CONTINUING EDUCATION

Doctors of Chinese medicine are advised to read every book they can get their hands on and refer to them dutifully for twenty years of medical practice, at which point they're to put the books away and allow the knowledge to flow from their minds intuitively. I suggest that you do the same with sexual knowledge, but without the twenty-year stipulation. All great artists continually deepen their technical understanding, refine their skills and expand their repertoires. Sexual artists should be no exception.

Make erotic love a lifelong study. Reread this book from time to time. Try techniques you hadn't attempted earlier because you didn't feel ready. Read other books. Take seminars and workshops. Try a few sessions with a sex therapist—not because something is wrong, but simply to learn more. Watch videotapes. Pick up pointers from magazine articles. At each step, bring the knowledge you acquire to your bedroom and mix it liberally with creativity and imagination.

A VISION
OF THE POSSIBLE

In closing, I would like to share a poem that I wrote to exemplify the majesty and sacredness of erotic love between two adoring partners. I hope it mirrors the glory you and your beloved find in each other's arms.

OUR DREAMS REALIZED

HIS DREAM
My love, so sweet
Drifting downstream now
Eyes closed
Hair awry upon the pillow like Ophelia

You let me touch you tonight
My fingers melting into all those warm, soft places
Heroes my fingers
Once again you have let them save you from the silence of sexlessness

And I
Humbled by your pleasure
Having heard your cry
The fire beneath your skin
Waking me to the truth of my own life

Ah . . .
To be a man whose woman is sated
Is there a greater bliss?
A mightier identity?

I give you my heart for your vulnerability
And breathe deeply
Knowing my rightful place in life by your unencumbered sigh
A dragon slayer, a magician, the starlight in your eye, father of your children
Your cheek will forever be soft to me
And I always the grandest of men

Damp with perspiration
Intoxicated by your scent
I am sleepy my love
Let us dream together

HER DREAM
Candlelight and sunshine illuminate your face the morning after
I didn't notice the candles burning ere we slept
I didn't notice anything

But all the years paid off last night in a delightful carousel ride
Our history playing like music in the background

What wouldn't I give you now that you have held me so near
And made being you about giving to me
Like full moon diamonds on a churning ocean
I shine brighter when you love me
No matter the day or week or decade

Starry-eyed and giggly
Wiggling around like an eight-year-old beside you
All my naughtiness
Last seen who knows when
Gushed out as I teased you awake again and again

You grumbled, rolled over and reached for me grinning
Only to pull me close and love me some more
You beast
I just adore that game

Now as you sleep I think about our future yet unknown
There will come a time, my love, when we must leave this place, this life
And will say our final good-bye

So I want you to know right now and always
That by your love
I have deeply lived
And through your touch
I have already known heaven

APPENDIX

FOR FURTHER INFORMATION

If you would like information about Dr. Dunas's newsletter, or a catalogue of health and sexual aids, including Chinese herbal and nutritional tonics, you may contact Dr. Dunas directly. You may also wish to be added to her mailing list for future seminars, books, tapes and other resources.

To reach Dr. Dunas:

E-mail:	fdunas@ix.netcom.com
Internet:	www.passionplaypage.com
Mail:	Felice Dunas, Ph.D.
	P.O. Box 328
	Topanga, CA 90290 USA
Toll-free telephone:	(888) 488-HEAL [-4325]

The following organizations can help you locate a qualified practitioner of Chinese medicine:

American Association of Oriental Medicine, (610) 266-1433, E-mail: aaom1@aol.com. This professional organization of licensed acupuncturists will give you up to three phone numbers of practitioners in your area at no charge, or complete lists of members in as many as three states for a five-dollar fee.

National Acupuncture and Oriental Medicine Alliance, (253) 851-6896. Another professional organization that will refer you to members in your area.

National Commission for the Certification of Acupuncturists, (703) 548-9004, Web site: www.nccaom.org. This organization sets the training requirements for the U.S. and administers the national licensing exam. It will refer you to practitioners licensed by the organization. Send three dollars per state to P.O. Box 97075, Washington, D.C., 20090-7075.

Accreditation Commission for Schools and Colleges of Acupuncture and Oriental Medicine, (301) 608-9680. It will provide a list of all accredited institutions in the U.S. You may be able to obtain from a local school a list of faculty and graduates who practice in your area. Many schools also operate clinics where professional treatment may be obtained inexpensively.

National Acupuncture Foundation, (202) 882-4650. This organization has information regarding the many colleges and universities around the country that specialize in Traditional Oriental Medical training. Many of these colleges have clinics through which quality but inexpensive treatment can be obtained.

In addition, many states have licensing boards and statewide membership organizations for qualified practitioners. Any of the national groups can give you information about the status of acupuncture and Oriental medicine in your state. The largest state organization is: California Association of Acupuncture and Oriental Medicine, (800) 477-4564. Other referral sources include health practitioners (chiropractors, massage therapists, physical therapists and openminded M.D.'s) whose opinions you can trust.

When choosing an acupuncturist, keep the following points in mind:

1. Acupuncture requires extensive training. Unfortunately, because this sophisticated practice is not yet regulated in all states, poorly trained people can present themselves as qualified. Make sure you select a practitioner who is properly educated; ask for complete information about his or her training and licensing status. No less than a two-year training program for nonphysician acupuncturists is acceptable. The current requirement in most training institutions is three to four years.

2. Make sure your acupuncturist is licensed by the National Commission for the Certification of Acupuncturists (NCCA) or by the appropriate governing board in your state.

3. Poorly trained practitioners may include medical doctors, chiropractors and physical therapists. Short-term programs (200–300 hours) have been set up to teach medical practitioners about acupuncture and Oriental medicine. These courses offer abbreviated knowledge at best. While many who have participated in these programs are able to help patients with simple problems, their training is limited. If you are considering being treated by such a practitioner, ask about his or her experience in treating the kind of health issues that concern you.

4. Acupuncture is only a small part of the traditional Chinese medical system. A practitioner who is trained also in herbal and nutritional medicine, exercise and other treatment modalities might be able to address your condition more holistically.